From Revival to Evangelism

or

The Effects of Spiritual Renewal

by

Charles W. Carter

ISBN 0-88019-205-4

Schmul Publishing Co., Inc.
Wesleyan Book Club 1986 Salem, Ohio

Charles W. Carter

Printed by
Old Paths Tract Society, Inc.
Shoals, Indiana 47581

This book is affectionately dedicated to Elizabeth, my beloved companion and prayer support, whose consistent Christian life exemplifies the grace that I preach, and to our two beloved sons who have given us just cause for pride in their respective achievements, Professor Donald W. Carter and the Rev. Norman L. Carter.

Table of Contents

Introduction

The Psalmist's earnest plea to God, "Wilt thou not Thyself revive us again, that Thy people may rejoice in Thee?" (Ps. 85:6), is the agonizing heart-cry of vast numbers of God's people all over the world. The failure of modern materialism and religious secularism to satisfy the spiritual thirst of humanity has wrung from the hearts and lips of many within the church the cry of the prophet, "O Lord, revive Thy work in the midst of the years, in the midst of the years make it known; in wrath remember mercy" (Hab. 3:2b). Many modern prophets, both religious and political, are telling us that our civilization is doomed unless we have moral and spiritual reform. Such reform will come only with spiritual revival.

Much confusion exists relative to the relationships and distinctions between revival and evangelism. Indeed, for the most part the two terms are used interchangeably and synonymously. However, they do not convey the same meaning when properly understood and used. James Hastings (*Dictionary of the Bible*) says that "to revive is literally to come to life again." Webster defines revival as "to restore or return to consciousness or life; to raise from languor, depression or discouragement; to render or become active, operative, or flourishing again." *The Random House Dictionary of the English Language* defines revival as "to quicken or renew in the mind . . . to return to life, consciousness, vigor, strength, or a flourishing condition."

Revival is for the church, the people of God. Evangelism is for the unconverted—the non-Christian. Revival is the renewal of life in the church. Revival is the Spirit of God speaking to the church. Evangelism is the impartation of life to men who are dead in trespasses and sins. Evangelism is the church speaking to unconverted men. Revival must oft come to the church and the individual Christian. Evangelism is an initial work directed toward the conversion of the sinner. Revival begins from within the church. Evangelism extends without to the unconverted. Without spiritual revival the church will die. Without evangelism men will remain in sin and progressive degeneracy.

Initially, revival restores lost or languishing spiritual consciousness in the life of the Christian. To the Christian believers in the church at Ephesus (as perhaps other churches of Western Asia Minor) Paul wrote, "Awake, sleeper, and arise from the dead, and Christ will shine on you" (Eph. 5:14). At yet a later period Christ directed a message to this same people, who had been born in dynamic evangelism, but had lapsed, in which he said, "I have this against you, that you have left your first love" (Rev. 2:4). With the loss of relationship with Christ always goes fear of the consequences and ultimate unconcern, indifference, and eventually, worldly conformity. Under the impact of the Spirit of God in genuine revival there comes an awakening, a consciousness of what has been lost, sorrow for the loss, and diligent effort toward recovery.

Again, spiritual revival restores lost relationships. The Psalmist spoke as a follower of God when he said, "He restores my soul." Sin and backsliding impair man's relationship with God and complicate the whole course of life. Revival restores grace to the soul of truly repentant man and brings him again into the joyful favor of God. Sin and backsliding disrupt the peace and fellowship of the church. They divide fellow-Christians and families, setting them at variance. Sin separates; grace unites. Sin beclouds; grace clarifies. Sin deadens; grace enlivens. While lost spiritual ground or grace does not necessarily mean lost relationship, it may—and will—eventuate in such if the condition is not corrected by revival and return to God. Lost relationship with God, however, always means lost grace. Esau sought in vain for his father's blessing in the absence of the birthright (see Heb. 12:16, 17).

Broken and mutilated fellowships may be repaired and restored by spiritual revival. It was to Christians that James wrote, "Confess your sins to one another, and pray for one another, so that you may be healed [that the breaches in your fellowship may be healed]" (Jas. 5:16). Broken fellowships preclude divine acceptance. Said Jesus, "If therefore you are presenting your offering at the altar, and there remember that your brother has something against you, leave your offering there before the altar, and go your way, first be reconciled to your brother, and then come and present your offering'' (Matt. 5:23, 24).

Beclouded, distorted, and perverted spiritual perspectives will be corrected when the church experiences true revival. The Psalmist suffered from such a faulty perspective of life and religion, and had actually become envious of the wicked, almost to the point of renouncing his faith in God, "until," he says, "I came into the sanctuary of God; then I perceived . . ." (Ps. 73:17). In the year of Uzziah's death the situation was depressingly dismal and discouraging, even to the soul of the prophet, until he experienced a renewed revelation of God, as expressed in his own words, "I saw *also* the Lord," and then exclaimed, "The whole earth is full of His glory" (Isa. 6:1, 3, KJV).

Revival will restore the vitality of God's people. When his prayer of penitence had reached the point of saving faith, and he realized that spiritual restoration had become a gracious reality in his life, the Psalmist exultantly exclaimed, "He put a new song in my mouth, a song of praise to our God; many will see and fear" (Ps. 40:3). To the Christians at Rome Paul wrote, "If the Spirit of Him who raised Jesus from the dead dwells in you, He who raised Jesus Christ from the dead will also give life to your mortal bodies through His Spirit who indwells you" (Rom. 8:11).

The restoration of spiritual victory in the life of the Christian is a most gracious and welcome fruit of revival. Little wonder that the unconverted see so little of attractiveness in the lives of God's people when they are as powerless before the pressures and enticements of the world as was Samson in the lap of Delilah with his locks shorn. While professed Christians are slaves of sin, they have nothing to offer unsaved people that will liberate them from their bondage to Satan.

Spiritual revival inevitably restores spiritual zeal and activity to the people of God. The Psalmist confidently predicted that when his forgiveness and deliverance should come from God, "Many will see and fear, and will trust in the Lord" (Ps. 40:1-3). When David came to the climax of his quest for restoration from his fallen state, he rested his case with the Great Judge, in confidence of forgiveness, and cried out, "Then I will teach transgressors Thy ways, and sinners will be converted to Thee" (Ps. 51:13). The unconverted world will feel the impact of the witness of the church when the church experiences revival. Spiritual powerlessness becomes spiritual powerfulness under the energy of God's Spirit restored to the hearts of God's people.

It has been the author's constant conviction throughout the years that genuine revival and vital evangelism are born of the faithful preaching of the Word of God accompanied by prevailing intercessory prayer. Early in his Christian ministry he developed the art of expository evangelistic preaching. From this course he has not deviated, believing that real revivals are born of faith in God who reveals Himself by His Spirit in and through His Word.

For about eighteen years the author was a missionary to Sierra Leone, West Africa where, in addition to educational and administrative responsibilities, he engaged in extensive revival and evangelistic activities. During these years he was privileged to witness the renewal of the African church which had lapsed into discouragement and spiritual apathy, and had become largely devoid of evangelistic efforts. With the renewal of the church there followed intensive and extensive evangelistic activities that carried the message of salvation into new pagan communities where the message of salvation had not previously gone. Individual and community conversions occurred over a wide area of northern Sierra Leone. Miraculous spiritual and moral transformations of sorcerers, witch doctors, and sin-benighted communities were wrought under the Spirit's power. New churches came into being in villages and towns over a wide area of the jungle land. From these churches the light of the gospel has shown forth across the subsequent years.

Though the author has engaged in extensive educational activities, both in America and more than a dozen other countries abroad, revival and evangelism have been the chief motivating factors of his life's service throughout the years. These services have included camp meetings and church revivals, preaching throughout most of America, Eastern Canada, Africa, Mexico, the Caribbean Islands, the Bahamas, South America, Japan, the Philippines, India, Korea, Taiwan, and Australia. While teaching in colleges and seminaries in many of these countries, revival and evangelism have always held the chief place in the author's interest and activities. Even while teaching in colleges and universities in America on a full-time schedule for many years, the writer preacher regularly in church revivals and camps over weekends and during vacations; often traveling great distances for these meetings.

That America and the modern world are overdue a spiritual awakening is obvious to vast numbers of concerned people today. An era of situation ethics and secular theology with the accompanying breakdown of faith in God and His Word, and the corruption of civilization itself, has brought America to the brink of moral destruction. The alternatives appear to many to be spiritual revival or national ruin.

People who scoffed at revivals forty to fifty years ago are frankly admitting today that the hope of modern man is not to be found in material progress or gain, and that if we are to save this generation and ourselves, it must be a salvation of the spirit. Philosophical materialism is rapidly becoming an outmoded system that failed to fulfill its promises. The appeal for hope today is to the spiritual and moral nature of man.

When such great minds as Elton Trueblood, Albert Schweitzer of Africa, Arnold Toynbee, the noted British historian, and P. A. Soroken, the world-renowned sociologist of Harvard University, have recognized the decay and degeneracy of society and insisted that a spiritual and ethical remedy is imperative if our civilization is to be saved, certainly it is important that the church accept the challenge and set forth on a new mission of spiritual revival and world evangelism.

The messages of this book consist of expositions of the appeals of God through His Word to the spiritual nature and needs of men today. *It is not a book of revival or evangelistic methods, but rather of the "Biblical message" of revival and evangelism.* Methods have changed and will change again with people, times, and conditions under which the message is delivered. The divine message itself is as unchangeable as the character of God and the spiritual needs of men. The messages of this book are not speculative, nor are they the idealistic theories of an inexperienced dreamer. They have been delivered to congregations in revival campaigns over a great deal of the world during many years of revival and evangelistic ministry, and have proven their effectiveness under the blessings and power of God's Spirit in the impact they have made upon the lives of multitudes of people. While preparing his "expositions" for *The Acts of the Apostles*; reprinted by Schmul Publishers, and co-authored with Dr. Ralph Earle, the author's convictions were greatly deepened by the evidence discovered in the Book of Acts that the New Testament Christian pattern is one of spiritual revival and consequent evangelism wrought by God's Spirit in and through the church. That conviction is reflected in these messages.

The messages of this book are not written for the scholar. They are designed, rather, to awaken and stimulate interest and activity in spiritual revival and evangelism among ministers of the gospel and Christian laymen. This is a book for ministers and Christians interested in and concerned about spiritual revival and vital evangelism today.

In addition to the messages appearing previously in the author's work, *Road to Revival* (1959), published by the now non-existent Higley Publishing Company of Butler, Indiana (a book many years now out of print), ten significant new additional chapters have been added. The original chapters have, for the most part, been extensively revised and updated.

Unless otherwise indicated, most of the Scriptures quoted in this volume are taken from the *New American Standard Bible* (La Habra, California: The Lockman Foundation, 1960, 1962, 1963, 1968, 1971). For permission to use the text of the NASB, gratitude is hereby expressed to the Lockman Foundation. Such works cited or quoted in this volume, which are presently under copyright, as also such as are not, are duly acknowledged in the documentations.

This book is sent forth with the earnest prayer that it may be used of God to help create an interest in and concern for true spiritual revival in the hearts of God's people wherever it is read; and that it will produce a conviction of the necessity of revival within the church, as also of the church's responsibility to evangelize the unconverted world of this and every subsequent generation until Jesus returns.

Chapter I

The Wages of Sin Versus the Gift of God

"For the wages of sin is death, but the free gift of God is eternal life in Christ Jesus our Lord" (Rom. 6:23).

Webster defines wages as "a stipulated payment for service performed." Every activity of human life has as its objective some reward. Nor is it necessarily a selfish motive that prompts man to aim at compensation in life. Responsible parents can be satisfied with no less a reward than children brought successfully to maturity and sent forth into society to live honorable and useful lives and make worthy contributions to their generation. Teachers in the classrooms expect as their reward, in part at least, the mental and cultural development of the students under their instruction. The businessman expects success and a reasonable profit in his business enterprise. The manual laborer or office worker anticipates the receipt of his paycheck with which he may be able to pay his rent and grocery bill, and meet the other necessities of life for his family.

The Wages of Sin is Man's Earned Reward

Three facts may be definitely stated with reference to wages. *First,* wages are paid by the one for whom the work is done; *second,* wages are paid to the one who does the work; *third,* wages are paid in proportion to the amount and quality of work done. In the light of these generally recognized principles, is it not strange that so many should labor faithfully and diligently throughout life in the service of sin and Satan and expect at the termination of life to present themselves before God, against whose interests they have diligently labored, for the reward of eternal life!

The wages of sin is physical death. Physical death culminates at the departure of the spirit or personality, the ego, from its temporal dwelling, the body. What physical man should have been in the absence of sin scientists and philosophers have been unable to determine; what he is to be when saved, purified and transplanted does "not yet appear" (1 John 3:2 KJV). But that physical suffering, disease, and decay are traceable to sin, not necessarily directly, although in some instances a direct connection is undeniable, sound reasoning leads man to conclude. Sin, as the violation of the laws that govern physical life, laws established by God, merits and procures for the transgressor the sentence of death. Execution may be delayed, but it is only a matter of time. The duly earned wage of sin against physical law is physical death.

The wages of sin is mental death. All sin originates (observe that it is not stated that sin exists in or is confined to, but *originates*) in the mind of man. Evil conceived and nurtured in the mind usually finds expression in a life of unrighteousness. Sin thus conceived and nurtured will be duly rewarded in the payment of death to the mother of its conception. Human experience and observation bear unmistakable testimony to the existence of beautiful, living, well-formed and healthy bodies indwelt by minds that are dead to all of life's highest ideals and values, minds in which decomposition and decay have done their deadly work. Nor are these unfortunate persons to be found only in the hospitals for the mentally ill or violently insane. Mental stagnation or perversion occasioned by disobedience to natural and divine law ultimately eventuates in mental degeneracy and death.

The wages of sin is death to moral and spiritual values. Persistent, willful sin against God eventually severs man's spiritual relationship with God. The soul deprived of the presence of the Divine is rendered incapable of self-preservation, and rapidly falls into a state of moral death and decay. Man deprived of spiritual relationship with God becomes morally irresponsible and may lose natural affection for his home and family and neglect their interests, murder his neighbor, illegally possess himself of the property of others, turn traitor to society and civilization, and thus merit the wages of death—exclusion from society and God. The chief character in Edgar Allan Poe's masterpiece of horror, *The Black Cat,* exemplifies well the possibility of 'conscience crucifixion' with its resultant moral and spiritual death.

The wages of sin is everlasting death. Everlasting death is permanent separation from God, with all of its attendant horrors. There is a teaching of modern psychology to the effect that all that is known to man is known by comparison or contrast. If this is true, as some hold, then death, in consideration of the existence of sin, is the natural antithesis of life, and everlasting destruction is but the logical antithesis of final preservation and glory. Hell, in view of the Fall and the consequent existence of sin, is the logical antithesis of heaven.

The infidels and skeptics of a few generations ago were not altogether amiss when they objected to the doctrine of everlasting destruction on the grounds of God's goodness and mercy for His creatures. Where they so seriously erred was in failing to comprehend that man's soul is not lost in eternity through the lack of divine mercy, but rather as consequent upon the life he has lived, or the course he has pursued. Man chooses his own destiny. Everlasting separation from God and consequent destruction are the natural results of the life he has lived. Death or separation, for such is death in its final analysis, is the due reward rendered for the service of sin. The attitude of sinful persons and the deeds of sinful lives, from their very nature automatically and everlastingly separate those persons from God, whose very nature is holiness, righteousness, and justice. Anything less than such a separation would be a gross reflection on the character of God. "The wages of sin is death."

The Gift of Eternal Life is by God's Grace

"A gift is the voluntary transfer of real or personal property, without any consideration" (Webster). A fourfold proposition may be stated with regard to God's gift of life to humanity.

God's gift of life to humanity is gratuitous. God was under no obligation to fallen humanity, morally or otherwise, to bestow life upon them while they were dead in trespasses and sins. Man procured the penalty of death through willful disobedience to the known will and law of God. Man has no claim upon God for restoration of life. God, out of the superabundance of His love for the human race, offered the gift of life through His Son Jesus Christ. "God so loved the world, that He gave His only begotten Son, that whoever believes in Him should not perish, but have eternal life" (John 3:16).

God's gift of life to humanity is unmerited. In the words of the great commentator, Adam Clarke, "A man may merit hell, but he cannot merit heaven—a sinner goes to hell because he deserves it; a righteous man goes to heaven because Christ died for him." Were it not that God's love and mercy transcend His justice, all men would stand everlastingly condemned before Him. Man may not hope for salvation on his own merit, but in the transcendent love and mercy of God in Christ. A sinner dare not plead for God's justice. He must ask for mercy if he is to hope for eternal life.

God's gift of life to humanity cannot be earned. The aggregate wealth of humanity could not purchase from God a moment of life. A dying queen is reported to have exclaimed, "Millions of money for a minute of time." Money may help to prolong physical life, but it will not purchase a moment of either physical or spiritual life when death appears. The blood that flows in royal veins, the power wielded by the dictators of earth, or the wealth of oil rich nations cannot move God from the course of justice. The most logical and convincing arguments produced by the brain trust of society will not cause God to deviate from the course of justice. The most righteous and devoted labors of man cannot procure from God the bestowment of life. How, then, cries sinful man in desperation and near despair, can man be saved—"what must I do to be saved?" (Acts 16:30). The answer is found in the words of sacred writ: "Believe in the Lord Jesus, and you shall be saved" (Acts 16:31).

God's gift of life to humanity is through Jesus Christ. "He who has the Son has the life; he who does not have the Son of God does not have the life" (1 John 5:12). "In Him [Christ] was life" (John 1:4). This is a proposition which will bear careful analysis. The doctrine of spontaneous generation in natural science has been sufficiently disproved to merit little if any further consideration. With Henry Drummond we would observe that in order that the inanimate may become possessed of life, life must be transmuted from the animate to the inanimate kingdom. The inanimate will forever remain inanimate unless the animate world reaches down and transmutes life to it, and thus transforms and transplants it into the higher realm of the living. Man through sin is rendered spiritually inanimate. Life is non-resident in him. Spiritual spontaneous generation is non-existent. Man must forever remain in the realms of death, unless life is transmuted to him from a higher source. God is that one and only source of higher life. This need of transmuted life for mankind is met in the person and redemptive work of Jesus Christ the Son of God. In conversation with the Jewish Ruler, Nicodemus, Jesus said, "Unless one is born again, he cannot see the kingdom of God" (John 3:3). "You must be born again" (John 3:7). God in Christ reaches down into the spiritually inanimate kingdom and touches lost humanity with His life, thus transforming and transplanting man into the kingdom of His life—"the kingdom of His beloved Son" (Col. 1:13). "For the wages of sin is death, but the free gift of God is eternal life in Christ Jesus our Lord" (Rom. 6:23).

Man is hopelessly self-imprisoned in the inescapable jail of his own sin until he is freed by the only Victor over sin and its consequences, that Man Jesus Christ. No one has comprehended and expressed more eloquently man's hopelessness without God than the French existential thinker, Jean Paul Sartre, in his master-work *No Exit!* Christ who said "I am the door" is the only way out, the only Exit. Sartre and his followers had not found that Door! For them there was *No Exit!* But for the penitent believer, Christ Jesus, the Savior of men, is man's spiritual exit from the bondage of sin and spiritual death into the spiritual liberty of the sons of God.

Chapter II

The Future State of the Lost*

"And in Hades [hell—A.V.] *he lifted up his eyes, being in torment"* (Luke 16:23a).

Nowhere in the Bible is clearer light thrown on the future plight of the lost than in the solemn and serious record of Christ's words given to us in the Gospel according to Luke, chapter sixteen and verses nineteen through thirty-one. That account reads as follows:

> There was a rich man who was dressed in purple and fine linen and lived in luxury every day. At his gate was laid a beggar named Lazarus, covered with sores and longing to eat what fell from the rich man's table. Even the dogs came and licked his sores. The time came when the beggar died and the angels carried him to Abraham's side. The rich man also died and was buried. In hell, where he was in torment, he looked up and saw Abraham far away, with Lazarus by his side. So he called to him, Father Abraham, have pity on me and send Lazarus to dip the tip of his finger in water and cool my tongue, because I am in agony in this fire. But Abraham replied, Son, remember that in your lifetime you received your good things, while Lazarus received bad things, but now he is comforted here and you are in agony. And besides all this, between us and you a great chasm has been fixed, so that those who want to go from here to you cannot, nor can anyone cross over from there to us. He answered, Then I beg you, father, send Lazarus to my father's house, for I have five brothers. Let him warn them, so that they will not

---

*This chapter was published in part previously in the *Preacher's Magazine* (June, July, August, 1982) by the Nazarene Publishing House, Kansas City, Mo.).

also come to this place of torment. Abraham replied, They have Moses and the Prophets; let them listen to them. No, Father Abraham, he said, but if someone from the dead goes to them, they will repent. He said to him, If they do not listen to Moses and the Prophets, they will not be convinced even if someone rises from the dead (NASB).

We shall here note the importance of considering the future state of the lost. It is not the purpose of this message to argue the etymological meaning of "hell," as the term appears in the King James Version, or *hades* as in the American Revised and certain other versions. However this may be with its varied interpretations, the real significance of this record is that for a man to die without saving faith in God is to experience a state of lostness beyond the present life where inexpressible suffering will characterize him forever.

If it should be allowed, as some doubtfully contend, that the Greek word *haides* (*Hades*), or the Hebrew word *Sheol,* always and only mean the place of departed spirits, or the grave, yet this admission would in no sense change the condition of the state of the lost, as described by Christ in Luke 16:19-31. Such hopelessness would be quite as unbearable in the grave, if consciousness existed, as if it were in some other state or remote part of the universe. Furthermore, it is, in reality, the spiritual personality, rather than the physical body, that suffers in the realm of ultimate lostness.

The real significance of Christ's teaching here concerns the state of those ultimately lost, rather than the particular place or location in which they suffer the agony of their lostness. The only possible evasion of the real significance of the everlasting state of the doomed person, as depicted here by Christ, would be to deny the genuineness of this passage, something critics have failed to do, or deny the validity of Christ's teachings, which would be tantamount to denying His divinity. To do this would be to completely wreck faith in the whole New Testament and the Christian religion. The teaching of Christ must be reliable here as elsewhere. It is absurd to credit the genuine teachings of Christ on one subject while denying His teachings on another point.

The reality of everlasting lostness is validated by other New Testament writers, including Paul in Galatians 6:7, 8 and Second Thessalonians 1:7-9; by Peter in Second Peter 3:9, 10; and by John in Revelation 21:8. Many of the world's greatest theologians have believed in and taught the scriptural doctrine of the everlasting lostness of the souls of those who depart this world without the saving grace of God. And many of the world's greatest literary artists have reflected their belief in the everlasting lostness of men without God in the future life. Such is true of Dante in his *Divine Comedy,* of Shakespeare, of Goethe, of Milton's *Paradise Lost*; and it is true of Jean Paul Sartre, however unwittingly, in his play *NO EXIT!*, notwithstanding his boastful claims to atheism.

Some have argued that this record in Luke is only a parable. Others with equal force have held that it is history. Whether history or parable, the spiritual meaning of this account in Luke 16:19-31 is the same—if history, it is a record of what has happened; if a parable, it is a teaching of what may happen. If it be allowed, with Edersheim and others, that it was not Christ's primary purpose to set forth the doctrine of the future life of the lost in this record, yet it would have to be admitted that incidentally, if not primarily, He did so. It is sometimes objected that the doctrine of hell is not found in the Mosaic revelation; yet it must be admitted that the doctrine gradually developed in Jewish thought and was clearly and firmly established in Jewish theology by the time of Christ. Further, it is evident that Christ, the Son of God, accepted, taught, and thus divinely validated this doctrine; otherwise He should have been guilty of propagating a falsehood.

For nearly a half century the doctrine of hell has been exceedingly unpopular in the pulpits of the Christian Church. Nor has this unpopularity been limited to the liberal branch of Christianity. A large percentage of the pulpits in various branches of the evangelical churches have evaded anything more than a casual mention or reference to hell as the final state of the lost. It may even be questioned whether many still believe in hell as depicted in Luke 16. A sort of "modified universalism" characterizes the thinking of a great many Christians, both in the pulpit and in the congregation.

The noted Scottish Bible scholar and author, William Barclay, who is read widely by evangelicals, declares himself to be a committed Universalist. He pointedly states:

> In one thing I would go beyond strict orthodoxy. I am a convinced universalist. I believe that in the end all men will be gathered into the love of God . . . If one man remains outside the love of God at the end of time, it means that that one man has defeated the love of God—and that is impossible."

Here Barclay fails to recognize human moral freedom to shut one's self out of God's mercy.

With Origen, Barclay believes in Hell as a punitive correction for unbelievers, from which they will be won through divine love to ultimate salvation—a sort of unorthodox Protestant purgatory. This position he supports with a series of exceedingly plausible arguments.[1]

The doctrine of the future life is one of the most seriously neglected teachings of Bible truth in the pulpit today. Seldom is there a sermon on the fate of the doomed; seldom do we read in a religious periodical a sermon on hell. It is a tragically neglected theme. Many of the ills that afflict the Church of Jesus Christ, and the world in which the Church of Jesus Christ ministers today, are traceable to the neglect of the doctrine of the future life, both of the blessed, and of the doomed.

This neglect has given rise to a number of deplorable conditions within and outside of the Christian community. Dr. Jan Karel Van Baalen, in his book *The Chaos of Cults*, has said that "the modern cults represent the unpaid bills of the Christian Church."[2] Russellism (Jehovah's Witnesses) and the Seventh-Day Adventist movements, with their emphasis on "no-hellism" and "annihilationism," are largely due to the fact that the Christian Church has failed to duly emphasize the doctrine of the future life—to teach clearly the revelation of the Scriptures on this tragic reality. The Spiritualist

---

[1] *William Barclay: A Spiritual Autobiography* (Grand Rapids: Wm. B. Eerdmans, 1975), pp. 59-61.

[2] Jan Karel Van Baalen, *The Chaos of Cults* (Grand Rapids: Wm. B. Eerdmans, 1955), p. 15.

cult, which is disposed to pry into the mysteries of the unknown, is flourishing today in very large measure because the Christian ministry has been entirely too silent on what the Bible has to say about the state of the righteous, and the state of the unrighteous, in the after-life. In the absence of clear teaching on the future life, Spiritualism and other cults of like nature have attempted to find out what has not been clearly taught in the pulpit, by means that are not legitimate. Thus, Russellism, Spiritualism, Seventh-Day Adventism, and others of the modern cults are, as Van Baalen has said, representations of the unpaid debts of the Christian Church.

Outside the religious community there are also devastating results of the neglect of the doctrine of the future life, including moral relativity, or no ultimate truth (ethical situationism), and, consequently, no final responsibility of man to God. As a result, man may set up for himself a standard of truth by which he may measure his life in the present, without regard to God or the future. Hence, we have an ever-changing standard of truth, and we have, as the ancient Greek Sophists put it, "every man his own measure of truth." Fearlessness to do wrong is evident on every hand. The daily newspapers are replete with reports of crime, and such accounts of crime are flashed on thousands of television screens throughout the land every evening. Because people have ceased to fear the future, they are living only in the light of the present, without any sense of responsibility to God or the life beyond. They act as they are motivated, and, consequently, we are reaping an awful harvest of crime and immorality largely because there has not been a due emphasis on the doctrine of the future life and humanity's moral responsibility to God.

The shocking increase in suicides may be resultant in considerable measure from man's lost sense of the future life, and thus any responsibility to God or the future. Said the Apostle Paul: "If we have only hope in Christ in this life, we are of all men most to be pitied" (1 Cor. 15:19). If there is no future life, no consequence of sin, no reward for the righteous, then in the unspeakable desperation of man's mind and soul he may seem quite logical in taking his own life, for he sees it as the easiest way out, since death ends all.

Many have thus reasoned and have attempted to put an end to the miseries of life by suicide. A black custodian in a building in New York was heard to say, as he stood on the street with a gathered crowd of spectators and watched a desperate man leap to his death from a fifteenth story window, "If a man has no God, nothing is left but to jump."

This neglect resolves itself into a form of humanism and goes directly hand in hand with destructive higher criticism and unbridled liberalism in theology. Destructive criticism and humanistic irresponsible liberalism would not exist had a proper emphasis been kept on man's responsibility to God, for the future as well as the present, and had there been kept in view a clear sense of the awful consequences of evil. Important as the present life is, it can only be lived and evaluated properly as it is lived in the light of, and in relation to, future responsibility before God. Heaven is not only the reward of the righteous, it is also a condition making possible the everlasting, unimpeded progress and development of redeemed personalities. Hell is, on the other hand, both God's most merciful provision for the unrepentant sinner, and the natural consequence of the sinner's willful course in the present life.

The charge so often made that a God of love and mercy is too good to cast His children into hell is rendered invalid by the fact that unconverted people are not the children of God by redemption, and that God does not cast these unconverted people into hell. The doomed man has rejected the only means of salvation, offered in the person of Jesus Christ, and has procured for himself the reward of his own choosing; he has taken himself beyond the reach of God's mercy. Sinners experience hell of their own free choice. Hell is the destination at the end of the road that willful sinners follow. They procure it against God's will. Adam Clarke has significantly remarked: "A Christian goes to heaven because Christ died for him; a sinners goes to hell because he deserves to go there."

Further, the idea of God in hell punishing the doomed for their sins committed while they were on earth, is totally unworthy of the Biblical revelation of God's person, purpose, and character. John declares that the Christian God is *love*, and that He is *light* (1 John 4:8; 1:5; cf. John 1:4-90). The Bible represents sin as the works of darkness, and the final consequence of sin as *outer darkness* (Matt. 8:12; Eph. 5:11; 6:12; Col. 1:12; 2 Pet. 2:4, 17; Jude 6, 13; Rev. 16:10, 11). Scripturally and logically hell is where God is not present. It is outer darkness where the light of God never penetrates. It is the ultimate destiny of the person who leaves the present life with his back toward God. Thus, the total responsibility for ultimate lostness rests with the person who rejects Jesus Christ and all that He has done to save that person.

If our spiritual personalities are not in danger of being everlastingly lost without the saving mercies of Christ, then the death of Christ has lost its redemptive significance. Paul would have then been entirely amiss when he wrote to the Thessalonians, "You turned . . . to wait for His Son from heaven, whom He raised from the dead, that is Jesus, who delivers us from the wrath to come" (1 Thess. 1:9, 10).

The Scriptures are clear and consistent in their teachings on sin, hell, salvation, and heaven. The Gospel has significance only as it becomes clear that it is the good news of salvation from sin and its awful and ultimate consequences —hell. Many people never lift up their eyes to heaven until they do so out of the hopelessness of hell. Many never lift up their eyes toward heaven to pray until their prayers are ineffectual, until it is too late for their prayers to be answered.

Somewhere in his writings, Dr. John Paul tells a most interesting story concerning a farmer and a pig. It seems that one bright starry night a farmer discovered that his pig had gotten out of the pen. He succeeded in apprehending it, but in the struggle that ensued the pig was thrown over on its back. It struggled and squealed in an effort to free itself from its captor, and then suddenly, says the story, the pig ceased to struggle and squeal. The farmer carefully observed the animal, and then discovered that it evidently had its eyes focused on something out yonder in the heavens. Then it occurred to the farmer that the pig's eyes were so set in its head that while it stood on its four feet, it had never seen anything but the earth beneath it, but now, when thrown over on its back, for the first time in its life, it had caught a vision of the majestic starry heavens, and was so enraptured with that vision that it forgot it was being held captive.

The foregoing is only a story, but sincerely, many people have never seen heaven with its incomparable bliss until they have viewed it out of the hopelessness of their doomed state. What a tragedy that so many do not look up until it is too late to attain that glorious vision—heaven!

Dr. G. L. Robinson, formerly Old Testament professor at McCormick Theological Seminary, once told the story of an incident which he declared was the most convincing argument for the existence of hell that he had ever encountered. One dark night as he stepped from his cab in front of his hotel in London, there staggered up to him a half-drunken street-woman. Addressing herself to him, she said, in the street language of a London underworldling, "Meester, ye are a meenester, ain't ye?" Dr. Robinson replied that he was, and then asked her how she knew he was a minister. The woman replied: "I knowed ye was when I seed ye." Then she continued: "Meester, when ye go back to yeer people, ye tell them that there is a hell and ye tell them that I said there is a hell; and ye tell them that I know there is a hell, because I have got it right inside here," pointing to her bosom. Then she staggered away and lost herself in the darkness of London's underworld. Said Dr. Robinson: "As I went to my hotel that night I did so more deeply convinced of the reality of hell than I had ever been in all of my life."

Likewise, many people do not require an extended argument for the existence of hell. Many, like the street-woman of London, could testify that they have already felt the pains of hell in their own bosoms. The hell that lies beyond is an intensified continuation of the hell that many experience in the present world. The Psalmist once exclaimed, "The pains of hell got hold upon me" (Ps. 116:3 KJV). This text, *in hell he lifted up his eyes,* immediately raises the question in the mind of the serious reader: What did this doomed man see when he lifted up his eyes in hell? That question is answered in Christ's own words in Luke chapter 16.

In rapid succession it dawned upon the doomed man in hell that he had lost his final opportunity for everlasting life; "In hell he lifted up his eyes"; that there was no mercy in hell; that he was now utterly hopeless and helpless; that he was possessed of insatiable desires; that memory of lost opportunities plagued his consciousness; that he was incarcerated in a prison of everlasting doom with *NO EXIT*; that his earthly life's influence upon others had been misspent;

and that at last he was personally morally responsible for the truth he had known on earth and neglected to his awful peril.

The real significance of hell is the soul's awful consciousness of its lostness—its total loss of contact with God. That there are degrees of lostness in the present life is evident, but that there is also the possibility of an ultimate total loss of God from the spiritual consciousness of man, is equally real. Such a condition is hell! It is a hell that many have initially experienced in the present life, some even to the dethronement of reason. But it is a hell that will haunt the mind of man who is ultimately lost through endless millennia in the world to come. Then lost man will be utterly alone with no voice to be heard except the echo of his own wail of woe, and no familiar landmark to establish his sense of personal identity or give him direction. Whatever the biblical figures employed to describe the horrors of hell may be, the real meaning is utter lostness, expressed by Christ as "outer darkness" (Matt. 25:30).

Again, the meaning of hell is ultimate and utter hopelessness. The soul that is lost in hell will be so by reason of the willful rejection of God's provision of salvation in Christ Jesus. Thus man in hell will have terminated there against God's will and at the expense of having taken himself beyond God's reach. Hell is "outer darkness." "God is light and in Him there is no darkness at all" (1 John 1:5). Therefore hell is outside of and beyond the presence and reach of God. Thus if man would, he could not save himself, nor can God save him from the hell that is beyond this life and outside of God, for the finally impenitent. If man *will not* be saved in this life, he *could not* be saved in the life to come. One has significantly queried, concerning the effects of hell on character: "Like the photographer's bath, may its effects not be to develop and fix existing character, rather than to change it."[3] With the Apostle Paul, in faith we "wait for His Son from heaven, whom He raised from the dead, that is Jesus, who delivers us from the wrath to come" (1 Thess. 1:10).

---

[3]James Orr, *International Standard Bible Encyclopedia,* 4:2503.

It is as much the moral responsibility of the Christian minister to declare the awful and solemn truth of the scriptural doctrine of hell, from which Christ died to deliver man, as it is his moral duty to declare the glorious truth of God's love and mercy expressed in Christ's redemptive work on the Cross. Redemption takes its meaning from its power to deliver man from the ultimate consequence of sin, the awful ultimate state of the lost, which is hell!

The prophet Ezekiel saw this responsibility placed upon the servant of God and said,

> Now as for you, son of man, I have appointed you a watchman for the house of Israel; so you will hear a message from My mouth, and give them warning from Me. When I say to the wicked, "O wicked man, you shall surely die," and you do not speak to warn the wicked from his way, that wicked man shall die in his iniquity, but his blood I will require from your hand. But if you on your part warn a wicked man to turn from his way, and he does not turn from his way, he will die in his iniquity; but you have delivered your life (Ezek. 33:7-9; cf. 3:17-21).

However, it should be noted that the ideas of immortality, or everlasting life, and of everlasting existence, are to be sharply distinguished one from the other. Immortality belongs to the redeemed only, as it consists of the life of God (*zoe*) imparted to the believer at the moment of his conversion to Christ. Jesus said: "I give eternal life to them" (John 10:28; cf. Rom. 6:23). And Paul wrote to Timothy that Christ "alone possesses immortality" (1 Tim. 6:16). Certainly the lost will have everlasting existence in the future state, but they will not have immortality, for that belongs to God and those to whom He imparts it in their salvation.

Men may have their way; they may deny God's will for their lives; they may realize their godless ambitions; but they must remember that just beyond this life without God is hell. "And in hell he lifted up his eyes being in torments."

Such need not be the doom of any soul. God has provided a way of salvation—of escape from sin and hell for every man and woman. *Hear those gracious words of hope for all!*

"For God so loved the world, that He gave His only begotten son, that whoever believes in Him should not perish, but have eternal life" (John 3:16).

Hear those gracious words of invitation from the lips of the divine Son of God!

"Come to Me, all who are weary and heavy laden, and I will given you rest. Take My yoke upon you, and learn from Me, for I am gentle and humble in heart; and you shall find rest for your souls" (Matt. 11:28, 29).

Hear those gracious words of promise! "The one who comes to Me I will certainly not cast out" (John 6:37).

Hear those words of divine urgency! "Today if you hear His voice, do not harden your hearts" (Heb. 4:7b).

But finally, hear that solemn question directed by the Spirit of God! "How shall we escape if we neglect so great a salvation?" (Heb. 2:3).

CHAPTER III

The Tragedy of Spiritual Alienation

*"To the angel of the church in Ephesus write
... You have left your first love ... He who has
an ear, let him hear what the Spirit says to the
churches"* Rev. 2:1, 4, 11).

Verses one through seven of the second chapter of the
Book of Revelation are the record of the Lord's letter to the
church of Ephesus in Western Asia Minor, written sometime
during the fourth quarter of the first Christian century. This
letter, like most of the Book of Revelation, is written in rather
highly figurative language, but figures that convey certain
definite spiritual realities. We shall allow the record to speak
for itself.

To the angel of the church in Ephesus write: The
One who holds the seven stars in His right hand,
the One who walks among the seven golden lampstands, says this: I know your deeds and your toil
and perseverance, and that you cannot endure evil
men, and you put to the test those who call
themselves apostles, and they are not, and you
found them to be false; and you have perseverance
and have endured for My name's sake, and have
not grown weary. But I have this against you, that
you have left your first love. Remember therefore
from where you have fallen, and repent and do the
deeds you did at first; or else I am coming to you,
and will remove your lampstand out of its place—
unless you repent. Yet this you do have, that you
hate the deeds of the Nicolaitans, which I also hate.
He who has an ear, let him hear what the Spirit
says to the churches. To him who overcomes, I will
grant to eat of the tree of life, which is in the
Paradise of God.

The author of this letter is Jesus Christ, the living Son
of God. The transmitter was John the Revelator. The revealer

and interpreter of the message was the Holy Spirit. The letter was probably written primarily to the minister, here called a "star," or an "angel,"—the messenger to the church of Ephesus. While probably addressed primarily to the minister of the Ephesian church, the letter was nevertheless intended ultimately for the members of the church also, which church is represented here under the figure of a "candlestick," or "lampstand." The message is the Word of God, "sharper than any two-edged sword" (Heb. 4:12a). It should be noted that the two-edged sword of God's Word has the special significance of both judgment and mercy, as it has throughout the Scriptures. This is likewise evident in the flaming sword in the hand of the cherubim at the entrance to Eden, which sword turned every direction. One edge was punitive judgment for their disobedience. The other edge was mercy that prevented them from reentering Eden and thus eating of the tree of life and living forever in their sins.

Paul founded the church at Ephesus on his third missionary journey. It was here that the church was first established in the home of Priscilla and Aquila. Here the twelve disciples (sometimes mistakenly referred to as the disciples of John the Baptist) received the Baptism of the Holy Spirit under the ministry of Paul (Acts 19:2-6); here the eloquent Apollos, from Alexandria in Egypt, was led into the deeper spiritual life by Priscilla and Aquila (Acts 18:24); here a great spiritual awakening occurred under the ministry of Paul (Acts 19); and here the great apostle to the Gentiles labored for over two years to establish the Ephesian church and to evangelize western Asia Minor (Acts 20:31). Timothy was the pastor of the Ephesian church when Paul wrote the two pastoral epistles to him; and tradition has it that the apostle John was later pastor of this church, and that he finally died in Ephesus at a very advanced age. Another tradition holds that Jesus' mother, Mary, spent her last days in the church at Ephesus. Thus the Ephesian church, like many churches since, had a rich spiritual heritage. It had a great moral and spiritual responsibility, as great privilege always entails great responsibility. The words of the text of this message indicate that these Christians had, unfortunately, fallen from their original spiritual eminence: They had left their first love.

The Lord's Fourfold Commendation
of the Ephesian Church

In the first instance Christ commends them for their deeds, their toil, and their patient endurance: "I know your deeds and your toil and perseverance" (v. 2). Paul ends his great dissertation on love in the first Corinthian letter with the famous trilogy expressed in his conclusion: "But now abide faith, hope, love, these three; but the greatest of these is love" (1 Cor. 13:13). Again he commends the Thessalonian Church thus: "Constantly bearing in mind your work of faith and labor of love and steadfastness of hope in our Lord Jesus Christ in the presence of our God and Father (1 Thess. 1:3). Now it will be observed that while the Thessalonian Christians had added to their faith, *work,* to their love, *labour,* and to their hope, *steadfast patience,* or *perseverance*, these Ephesian Christians had retained, as but empty shells of profession, their works devoid of faith, their toil devoid of love, and their patience or steadfast endurance, devoid of hope. They maintained their profession of Christianity while having lost the content or reality of the Christian experience.

The Lord commends the Ephesian Christians for their aversion to evil: "I know . . . that you cannot endure evil men" (v. 2); and again, "Yet this you do have that you hate the deeds of the Nicolaitans which I also hate" (v. 6). It appears that the evil men of verse two and the Nicolaitans of verse six are the same. These same evildoers are condemned in the letter to Pergamos (Rev. 2:14-16), and are likely referred to in the letter to Thyatira (Rev. 2:20-22). The Nicolaitans are named specifically but twice in the New Testament (Rev. 2:6, 15). Some suppose these Nicolaitans to have been antinomians, or men who denied that Christians were bound by the moral law, and that sin ceased to be sin for those who had faith in Christ.[1] Ramsey holds that the Nicolaitans were pseudo-Christians who tried to bring about a compromise, first with Graeco-Roman society, which held customs that were both luxurious and idolatrous; and second,

---

[1]John likely used *Nicolaitan* to represent the Hebrew *Balaam* and that which that word connoted (See 1 Cor. 6:13-19; Gal. 5:19-24; 2 Peter 2:1-22; Jude 4:4 19).

to effect a compromise through compliance with the Roman state, and for a show of loyalty through burning incense to the statue of the emperor.[2]

Irenaeus held that these Nicolaitans were the followers of Nicolaus of Antioch who was a proselyte converted at Pentecost and became one of the seven men chosen to serve in the distribution of provisions to the Hellenist Christian widows (see Acts 6:5). Irenaeus held that Nicolaus had forsaken sound Christian doctrine and with his followers lived in unrestrained fleshly indulgence.[3] This position was confirmed by Hippolytus who said the Nicolaitans were indifferent concerning what a man ate or how he lived.[4] Clement of Alexandria said that the followers of Nicolaus misunderstood and perverted his teachings and lived in shameless indulgence.[5] Drumwright sees a possible allusion to the doctrines of Balaam who seduced "the Israelites to immoral and idolatrous unions with the women of Moab" (Num. 25:1-5; 31:16).[6] Refraining from idolatry and fornication were two of the four prohibitions laid upon Gentile converts for membership in the Christian church at the first general church council (Acts 15:28, 29), the other two requirements being abstention from violence ("blood"), and the eating of unbutchered meat ("things strangled"). It would appear from the letter to Pergamum that the teachings and practices of the Nicolaitans were related to, if not identical with, those of Balaam who seduced the Israelites to compromise with evil by eating meat sacrificed to idols and to commit fornication with the Moabitish women (Rev. 2:14, 15; cf. Gal. 5:13). Drumwright says:

> They were a people who used Christian liberty as an occasion for the flesh, against such Paul warned (Gal. 5:13). The enticement to such a course of action was the pagan society in which Christians

---

[2]Ramsay, as cited by J. R. Dummelow, ed., *A Commentary on the Holy Bible* (New York: The Macmillan Co., 1936), p. 1074.

[3]H. L. Drumwright, Jr., *The Zondervan Pictorial Encyclopedia of the Bible*, Merrill C. Tenney, gen. ed. (Grand Rapids: Zondervan Publishing House, 1975), 4:435.

[4]*Ibid.*

[5]*Ibid.*

[6]*Ibid.*

lived where eating meat offered to idols was common. Sex relations outside marriage were completely acceptable in such a society. The Nicolaitans attempted to establish a compromise with the pagan society of the Graeco-Roman world that surrounded them. The people most susceptible to such teachings were, no doubt, the upper classes who stood to lose the most by a separation from the culture to which they had belonged before conversion.[7]

It would appear that the Nicolaitans' doctrine was an insipid form of Gnosticism which held that only the spirit of the believer was the recipient of grace and the body, which was the source of evil, was of little worth, the destruction of which through dissipation would be a benefit in releasing the spirit from its evil bodily prison. Eusebius held that the Nicolaitan doctrines did not last long. This may be true unless it was but a phase of Gnosticism which indeed plagued the early church and bore its fruit in the later ages of the church. Nor is present-day Christianity entirely free from this brand of teaching, as is evident in the so-called Christian situation ethic. In any event, the Ephesian Christians had not compromised their ideals, principles, or practices. For this they are commended of the Lord. And in this they were far superior to much of the contemporary church that has sacrificed its ideals, principles, and practices on the altar of worldly compromise with secular theology, situation ethics, and even sexual immorality as expressed in pre- and extra-marital sex and homosexuality.[8]

Christ commends the church for its strict doctrinal orthodoxy and discernment of falsehood: "... you put to the test those who call themselves apostles, and they are not, and you found them to be false" (v. 2b). There may have been other apostles than the original twelve in the first century, but that there were false pretenders to Christian apostleship among the apostles, Judaizers, or Jewish Christian legalists,

---

[7]*Ibid.*, p. 436.

[8]See Ronald M. Enroth and Gerald E. Jamison, *The Gay Church* (Grand Rapids: Wm. B. Eerdmans, 1974), pp. 44.; 61 ff.; 74 ff.; 117 ff.; 160 ff.

who deceived the Christians and led them astray, is certainly evident. The Ephesian Christians still knew and adhered to sound doctrine, rejecting false teaching; and for this the Lord commends them most heartily. Again, we may ask, has the contemporary church measured up to this standard?

Christ commends them for their patient endurance, or steadfastness. They were under severe Roman persecution at that time for the sake of Christ's name, for which they suffered: "And you have perseverance and have endured for My name's sake, and have not grown weary" (v. 3).

Thus Christ commends the Ephesian Christians for their works, labor, and steadfast patience, their aversion to evil, and their endurance of suffering for His name's sake.

The Lord's Condemnation of the Ephesian Church

This condemnation consists of a single charge, though that charge is an all-important one: "But I have this against you, that you have left your first love" (v. 4). This charge has three implications.

In the first place, the loss of their first love meant the loss of the spiritual content of their Christian experience. John declared in his epistle that "God is love" (1 John 4:8b), and in his gospel he made love the very foundation and fountainhead of salvation: "For God so loved the world, that He gave His only begotten Son, that whoever believes in Him should not perish, but have eternal life" (John 3:16). To lose the first love from Christian experience is to lose the vitality of that experience. To lose God's love is to lose Christ's presence.

The second implication of the charge is that their first love had been supplanted by a second love. Man is so constituted psychologically that one affection, if lost, must be replaced by another. The stronger affection must win in the emotional tug-of-war in the soul of man. Exactly what the second love of these Ephesians may have been we are not told. That their first love for Christ may have been exchanged for a formal profession of religion that supplanted a vital spiritual relationship appears likely.

The third implication of this charge points to their inevitable weakness and ultimate spiritual and moral degeneracy, unless they should experience restoration to their first love.

The story is told of a once-famous old religious campground in the South where many people were richly blessed in other days, but which had long since fallen into a state of disuse and disrepair. It is said that the archway to the entrance had the fitting name of the camp, which evidently had been the name of the founder, the *Has-Been Camp*. Likewise, over the door of the church at Ephesus might have been written the condemnation by the Lord: "You have left your first love"; "Ichabod," the glory has departed, *The Has Been Church.*

The Lord's Exhortation to the Ephesian Church

This is an exhortation to restoration, which implies four clearly outlined steps.

They are first challenged to "remember" their former spiritual benefits and blessings: "Remember therefore from where you have fallen" (v. 5). Spiritual restoration begins with reflection. Not until one makes comparison of the unfavorable present with the favorable past will the desire for lost benefits be reawakened. It was when the Master compassionately looked at Peter and the cock crew, that "Peter remembered the word of the Lord, how He had told him, 'Before a cock crows today, you will deny Me three times,' [and] he went outside and wept bitterly" (Luke 22:61, 62). Remembrance of the former benefits and blessings from Jesus was more than Peter could bear. The discovery or review of old photographs or possessions of earlier days, such as love letters, wedding anniversaries, family reunions and memorial days, all eloquently testify to the power of memory to awaken anew emotions long buried and dormant. It was such a reflection that produced in the prodigal son the disposition and purpose to return to his father's home: "But when he came to his senses, he said, 'How many of my father's hired men have more than enough bread, but I am dying here with hunger! I will get up and go to my father' " (Luke 15:17, 18a).

The second step in return to the lost first love is "repentance." "Repent," said the Lord to the Ephesians. Repentance has been defined as a godly sorrow for sin with a consequent turning therefrom. It involves sorrow for the loss of Christ's favor and presence, by evil attitudes and action against Him, and a purpose to forsake sinful rebellion. But repentance is more than sorrow for sin. It involves a change of mind and a new course of conduct. Repentance is conversion as well as sorrow for sin committed against God. John the Baptist exhorted his hearers:

> Therefore bring forth fruit in keeping with your repentance; and do not suppose that you can say to yourselves, 'We have Abraham for our father'; for I say to you, that God is able from these stones to raise up children to Abraham. And the ax is already laid at the root of the trees; every tree therefore that does not bear good fruit is cut down, and thrown into the fire (Matt. 3:8-10).

This definition of repentance is vividly portrayed in the experience of the prodigal son. As he draws up his resolutions to return home we hear him saying: "Father, I have sinned against heaven, and in your sight; I am no longer worthy to be called your son; make me as one of your hired men. And he got up and came to his father" (Luke 15:18b-20a). To repent means to change one's mind and course of conduct.

The third stage in the return to the first love which they had lost was "reconstruction": "do the deeds you did at first" (v. 5), or when you first came to Christ. Weymouth's translation of this fifth verse is most illuminating: "be mindful, therefore, of the height from which you have fallen. Repent at once and act as you did at first, or else I will surely come and remove your lampstand out of its place—unless you repent" (v. 5). Reconstruction must ever accompany repentance and return to make them valid. This is made evident in the great redemptive work of Christ outlined in Revelation 1:5b-6a, which reads thus: "To Him who loves us, and released us from our sins by His blood and He has made us to be a kingdom, priests to His God and Father." Having "loved us," and "released us" from our sins, he "made us" anew. God's redemptive work is a work of reconstruction, but we also have our part in that spiritual and moral reconstruction. To the Philippians Paul wrote: "So then, my beloved, just as you have always obeyed, not as in my presence only, but now much more in my absence, *work out your salvation* with fear and trembling; for it is God who is at work in you, both to will and to work for His good pleasure" (Phil. 2:12, 13). Sin and departure from God destroy man's ideals and relationship with God, but grace enables the repentant and restored sinner to rebuild the life for God that sin has wasted.

The final stage in the repentant soul's return to God is "reanimation": "To him who overcomes, I will grant to eat of the tree of life, which is in the Paradise of God" (v. 7b). Here appears to be an allusion to the original tree of life in the garden of Eden from which man was barred through sin: "So He drove the man out; and at the east of the garden of Eden He stationed the cherubim, and the flaming sword which turned every direction, to guard the way to the tree of life" (Gen. 3:24). The forsaking of sin and return to God is always a return to spiritual animation. Said Paul, "But if the Spirit of Him who raised Jesus from the dead dwells in you, He who raised Christ Jesus from the dead will also give life to your mortal bodies through His Spirit who indwells you" (Rom. 8:11). There was joy and feasting on the occasion of the prodigal son's return (Luke 15:23-24) as also at the restoration of Lazarus (John 12:1-2), and there was spiritual animation consequent upon the deliverance of the penitent whose return is described in Psalm 40, and at the conversion of the Ethiopian nobleman under the ministry of Philip (Acts 8:39). God is a living God, and restoration to His favor means the impartation of His life here as well as hereafter. Said Jesus: "I came that they might have life, and might have it abundantly" (John 10:10b).

The Lord's Stern Warning to the Ephesian Church Against the Danger of Final Reprobation

Hear His words: "He who has an ear, let him hear what the Spirit says to the churches" (v. 7a); and again: "or else I am coming to you, and will remove your lampstand out of its place—unless you repent" (v. 5b). The church is to God as the lampstand is to the light it reflects. It is the holder and reflector of the light. It matters not how bright, burnished and conspicuous the lampstand may be, if that lampstand is devoid of oil and the light is extinguished, the lampstand is of no further practical value. It may serve for ornamental purposes, but all will be dark when the light has gone out. Such was the case with the Ephesians. They retained the profession of religion in their works, toil, endurance, moral ideals and strict orthodoxy; but they had lost the light of their first love. The lampstand stood there to no use. Said Christ: Either replenish the oil and light it again with divine love, and illumine the church and the world, or "else I am coming to you, and will remove your lampstand out of its place, unless you repent, says the Lord. The writer has often thought, with a sense of mixed amusement and pity, on the misstatement of an old gentleman who avowedly trusted for salvation in his membership in a secret order. Said he, "I am a *candlestick* for heaven," obviously meaning that he was a *"candidate"* for heaven. How sad that so many Christians and church members, who like my old lodge member friend, are no longer anything more than candlesticks or empty lampstands without light.

When the flame of Christian love burns low and finally dies out of the life of the Christian or the church, Christ will eventually, but sadly, remove the lampstand and close the door of the dark and deserted sanctuary. Said Christ: "If anyone does not abide in Me, he is thrown away as a branch, and dries up; and they gather them, and cast them into the fire, and they are burned" (John 15:6).

That the Ephesian church heeded the Master's warning, repented, and found restoration to the favor and fellowship of God is evident from the fact that it flourished for several centuries. So, likewise, may any Christian who has lost this first love heed the admonition and warning of the Lord and repent, return, and be restored to again experience the joy of the Lord, and bear fruit unto righteousness to the glory of God. To the Ephesian church, the Spirit said, even as He is saying to the spiritually alienated church and individual today: "To him who overcomes, I will grant to eat of the tree of life, which is in the Paradise of God" (v. 7b).

The unusual account is given of a couple who had been deeply in love, but whose marriage had unfortunately ended in the divorce court.

Following the divorce, for which the man was responsible, this former lover and husband began to awaken to a sad sense of lonesomeness and longing for reunion with his former wife and lover. Finally, overcome by an intense desire for his lost lover, he decided to pay her a visit at her parents' home, to which she had repaired after the divorce. There he told her of his love and longing for restoration to her companionship.

This lady then presented a most unusual proposition to the man who had been her husband. Said she, "If you really love me as you now profess, you must first apologize for the injury which you have inflicted upon me. Then if you wish me back as you wife, you will have to court, woo and win my love as you did the first time you won me for your bride." The account has it that he accepted her proposition and thus won her again as his lover and wife.

It is such a proposition that the Lord made to the spiritually estranged Ephesian church, and it is such a proposition that He makes to the spiritually estranged individual or church today: "Remember therefore from where you have fallen, and repent and do the deeds you did at first; . . . To him who overcomes, I will grant to eat of the tree of life, which is in the Paradise of God" (Rev. 2:5a, 7b). When the church and spiritually alienated Christians remember from whence they have fallen, repent and do the first works and return to God as at first, there will be a gracious revival of their love relation with the Lord Jesus Christ.

The Lord's Gracious Promise
To Those Who Return to His Loving Favor

"To him who overcomes, I will grant to eat of the tree of life, which is in the Paradise of God" (v. 7b).

What more wonderful promise could man have from a loving Savior? Man began in the Garden of God (Eden), where he had access to the tree of life, but he sinned and thus lost his access to that tree which God had planted on earth in Eden. Through the meritorious work of Christ, God planted another tree of life, this time a spiritual tree "in the Paradise of God," to which He offers access to all repentant and returning sinners. No man need experience the final loss of his soul in eternity. There is a way to overcome sin and return to the favor of God in Christ. That way has been set forth in this message. The alienated church, and the penitent sinner alike, may overcome by repentance and return to God, and again eat of the fruit of the tree of life "in the Paradise of God," and thus have life everlasting. "He who has an ear, let him hear what the Spirit says to the churches" (Rev. 2:7).

Chapter IV

The Penitent's Prayer

"Have mercy upon me, O God" (Ps. 51:1, KJV).

The occasion for this penitential prayer is found in the story of King David's rise to prominence and power from a humble shepherd boy to the sweet singer of Israel, a successful warrior, and an honored and noble king. This story is too familiar to require recounting. His fall from the staggering eminence into the dark slough of adultery, murder, and hypocrisy is equally well-known. The famous parable of Nathan fearlessly delivered to the self-deceived king is now a religious classic. David's capitulation and deep humiliation of heart and consequent repentance, as recorded in the fifty-first division of the Psalms, reveal greater depths of human depravity and a clearer course of the way of repentance and restoration from the fallen state to the favor of God than any known record. We shall allow the penitent monarch to speak for himself.

Be gracious to me, O God, according to Thy lovingkindness; According to the greatness of Thy compassion blot out my transgressions. Wash me thoroughly from my iniquity, and cleanse me from my sin. For I know my transgressions, and my sin is ever before me. Against Thee, Thee only, I have sinned, and done what is evil in Thy sight, so that Thou art justified when Thou dost speak, and blameless when Thou dost judge. Behold, I was brought forth in iniquity, and in sin my mother conceived me. Behold, Thou dost desire truth in the innermost being, and in the hidden part Thou wilt make me know wisdom. Purify me with hyssop, and I shall be clean; Wash me and I shall be whiter than snow. Make me to hear joy and gladness, Let the bones which Thou hast broken rejoice. Hide Thy face from my sins, and blot out all my iniquities.

Create in me a clean heart, O God, and renew a steadfast spirit within me. Do not cast me away from Thy presence, And do not take Thy Holy Spirit from me. Restore to me the joy of Thy salvation, and sustain me with a willing spirit. Then I will teach transgressors Thy ways, and sinners will be converted to Thee. Deliver me from blood-guiltiness, O God, Thou God of my salvation; Then my tongue will joyfully sing of Thy righteousness. O Lord, open my lips, that my mouth may declare Thy praise. For Thou dost not delight in sacrifice, otherwise I would give it; Thou art not pleased with burnt offering. The sacrifices of God are a broken spirit; A broken and a contrite heart, O God, Thou wilt not despise (Ps. 51:1-17).

King David had grievously sinned and the prophet Nathan had just rebuked him with the parable and the words, "Thou art the man." David's immediate response was, "I have sinned." The very personal and frankly honest nature of this prayer is worthy of careful consideration. The personal pronouns *I, me, my* and *mine* are used no less than thirty-four times in these seventeen verses.

The Penitent's Confession

This is a confession of transgression, the breaking or overstepping of the divine law. Says David, the penitent sinner, "I know my transgressions." Thus, he not only identifies his transgression, but he acknowledges full responsibility for it.

This is a very personal confession: "*I* know *my* transgressions." Frequently the prayer, even of would-be penitents, is ineffectual because it is not personal; it is not specific. Not infrequently one is heard to pray, "*We* acknowledge *our* sins, *our* transgressions. Lord, if *we* have done anything amiss, forgive *us*. Lord, if *we* have grown cold or careless in *our* relationship to Thee or in *our* service for Thee, *we* beg Thee to forgive *us*." God does not deal primarily with groups, with people *en masse*. We hear much of the social mind, but the social mind is fictitious. The social mind does not exist, that is as an entity. The so-called social mind is but a temporary association of individual minds. There may be a superior individual who momentarily largely determines the thinking of the group of which he is the leader, but it is only momentarily that the group thinks as one. When the group has disbanded, individuals go their respective ways. Each bears a sense of his personal responsibility for his decisions and actions. Thus, the social mind consists only of the minds of a number of individuals acting collectively, each of which bears his individual responsibility and has taken his initiative in concurring with the majority opinion, or consensus.

So long as we think and confess in the plural, we shall make little progress in our approach to God. It is only when we, as individuals, acknowledge our personal responsibilities toward men and God and assume personal responsibility for our decisions, our deeds, our wrong attitudes, and our sins, that we shall be able to realistically face a personal God. Even in the group God deals with individuals. On the day of Pentecost it is said that

> they were all together in one place. And suddenly there came from heaven a noise like a violent, rushing wind, and it filled the whole house where they were sitting. And there appeared to them tongues as of fire distributing themselves, and they rested on *each one of them* (Acts 2:1-3).

Thus even though the manifestation of God was to the group, and the place where they were sitting was filled with the presence of God, at the same time God singled them out as individuals and manifested Himself to them as such, "tongue as of fire . . . rested on *each one of them*," ministering to the personal needs of each. They were individualized and ministered to accordingly. David's success in his return to God as a penitent sinner consisted primarily in the fact that he, though a representative of the kingdom of Israel, and its ruler, was nevertheless willing to take responsibility for his personal sins. "I know *my* transgressions," said he.

This confession reveals the haunting presence of guilt. Though David had assumed a very bold and brave front as the supreme ruler of the people of God, as the king, as the sovereign, nevertheless there had not been a moment since the commission of his sins of adultery and murder when he had not consciously felt the guilt of his evildoing. It had been present with him when he sat in the court before Israel and judged the people. When he administered justice to the subjects of his kingdom, there was ever that accusing finger of his conscience pointing at the king and saying to him, "You are demanding justice in your kingdom, but in your own life you are perverting justice. You make a pretense of being just and of requiring justice of your subjects, but in your own heart you are exceedingly unjust. Remember your treatment of your fellows in the kingdom!"

When David lay down at night to sleep, beside him on his bed was the presence of his evil conscience which confronted him in his dreams and haunted him. When he arose in the morning to go about the duties of life, beside him arose, and with him walked the shadow of this accusing conscience. His deeds—his evils—were ever present with him. As he sat at the table in the banqueting hall with his friends in the hour of merriment, David's joy was stolen by the ever-present accusing conscience for the wrong that he had done. Indeed he smiled, he made merry together with his friends, he gave the appearance of a free conscience, of self-possession, of tranquility of mind and soul; but underneath there was that sense of insecurity, there was that rottenness at the foundation of his life that was ever threatening the structure that he was building, or had built. The king sat upon the throne, he ruled the kingdom; but he ever feared that the foundation of the throne would crumble and his rule would collapse. Insecurity characterized his life because of the ever-present consciousness that he was not squaring with reality. His sin was with him—*ever before him.*

David's consciousness of sin resembles the purported cruel Roman practice of executing certain criminals. It is said that by this method the Romans chained a human corpse to the living condemned criminal. Wrists were secured to wrists and ankles to ankles, and the wretched criminal was required to carry about with him this decaying mass of human flesh wherever he went. If he lay down to sleep at night, it lay beside him and haunted him in his dreams. Awakening in the morning he was faced by the ghastly spectacle of the sunken eyes and gaping mouth of the corpse staring him in the face. When he sat to eat his food, he was deprived of his appetite by the gagging stench of putrefying flesh. If he would walk about in his cell for exercise he carried with him the killing weight of this "other self," from which there was no hope of liberation until death itself put an end to the unspeakable ordeal. Some think that Paul is alluding to this cruel Roman practice when he cried out in despair for deliverance from the sinful nature, as is recorded in Romans 7:24; "Wretched man that I am! Who will set me free from the body of this death?" Paul's answer to his own question is the only satisfactory answer that has ever been given: "Thanks be to God through Jesus Christ our Lord!" (Rom. 7:25a).

This confession reveals a sense of moral responsibility to God. Says the penitent Psalmist, "Against Thee, Thee only, I have sinned, and done what is evil in Thy sight." We marvel as we read this confession of the king's personal responsibility to God. Had he not been guilty of the sin of adultery? Had he not taken the wife of Uriah and made her his own? Had he not placed Uriah in the forefront of the battle with the specific purpose of having him slain that his deed of adultery might not be found out? Had he not covered all of this with hypocrisy? Was not David guilty before society and before the bar of his own conscience? Most certainly, but it must be noted that David was sovereign—he was amenable to no court upon earth. He could not be brought to justice by his own people. We know not whether the kingdom, or whether anyone within the kingdom, knew the sin and the crime that David had committed. Perhaps it was thought to be that so-called perfect crime, unknown, unsolved. Perhaps David had no fear that anyone in the kingdom knew it. But even had they known it, there was nothing they could do about it short of revolution, or of the assassination of the king. David was supreme, the ruler of his people. He was the supreme judge. There was no court higher than his court. Thus he could have gotten by, and perhaps have gotten by very successfully before society. He could not be indicted for his crime.

Though David was the sovereign ruler of the people of God, though he was the supreme judge of the supreme court, he was wise enough to know that there was a court higher than the court of Israel, and a judge higher than the judge of Israel. There was that court in heaven above, and that

Judge, the Supreme Judge of all the universe, to whom the king was responsible; and in the wisdom of his awakened mind he cried out, "Against Thee, Thee only, I have sinned, and done what is evil in Thy sight." Like Hagar of old, David could say in his mind, Though no human eye has discerned the wickedness of my heart and my deed, "Thou God seest me." The record is in heaven, though it may not be on the books of crime on earth. If people were only aware of this fact, there is much evil that would never be committed at all. Though man can get by with his evil deeds here, and cover them successfully so they may not be known to the members of his family, to his fellow members in the church, to his business associates, to the community in which he lives and of which he has the utmost confidence and respect—they may not be known on earth, yet remember that God knows.

This fact accounts for the disposition of man to atheism —to discredit and dethrone God. If in the life of man there are those evil attitudes and deeds which he is quite unwilling to square with his fellowmen and with God, and he is able to get by before man, he will then in the hypocrisy of his heart attempt to discredit the authority of God, and his personal amenability to the Supreme Judge, by denying the existence of God and the afterlife. Thus he thinks to clear himself, since there is no authority higher than himself, as he thinks. He attempts to dethrone God and make himself supreme that he may not be answerable to any court higher than the court of his own decisions, his own intellectual or rationalizing judgment. He will clear himself through rationalization and attempt to go scot-free. Atheists are not usually found among those who have been discovered in their sins or crimes. The atheists are usually to be found among the people who have as yet not been discovered in the evil of their hearts and lives. Once they have been apprehended and convicted, they are usually humbled. Whether they acknowledge it freely and openly is not the question. In the secret of their minds, they are convinced that they are not supreme. Until they have been caught they may deceive themselves into believing that they are supreme.

David is a truly awakened soul. The finger of God has been pointed at the specific sin of which he is guilty: "Thou art the man!" David had pronounced judgment upon the unjust, the cruel and heartless rich man who had taken the pet lamb of his poor neighbor's children and slain it that a feast might be provided for his friends, while his own flocks remained untouched. There was awakened by this parable, in the soul of David, a sense of righteousness, justice, and indignation against the injustice of such a man. "Such," he says, "shall pay dearly for his crime, for his injustice." And then in that moment of the awakened sense of justice in the soul of the great king, Nathan, inspired of God, utters those words that cut away the last defense of the king. "Yea, king, thou hast pronounced judgment upon thyself. *Thou art the man!*" "Against Thee, Thee only, I have sinned, and done what is evil in Thy sight," cries the king. David rightly recognizes his amenability to a court higher than any earthly tribunal. Though not subject to judgment by his kingdom, he must answer to God.

David's confession reveals the presence of inherited depravity, as corrupting the heart and responsible for the overt act of sin. Says David, "Behold, I was brought forth in iniquity, and in sin my mother conceived me." There is no covering of the cause of the deed of which he has become guilty, and which has brought so much of misery and woe into his life. David now goes to the very source of the problem. He acknowledges that the sin and the crime that he has committed are the fruit of the nature that characterizes him. It is the manifestation of the disposition to evil. David has known the grace of God. He has tasted of the heavenly gift and of the world to come, and in the light of truth as it has been revealed to him, as he has experienced it, he now sees the dismal depths of the polluted disposition of his own heart.

Like Jeremiah of old, David has allowed the divine X-ray technician to focus the penetrating light of truth upon the inner cancer of his moral being to reveal the malignant nature of the disease that had caused this sickness, and threatened him with death. "Behold, I was brought forth in iniquity, and in sin my mother conceived me." David is not now content to simply confess his sin and ask forgiveness for it. He goes to the root of the matter and lays bare the cancerous condition of his soul that God may go beyond the forgiveness of sin and heal the inner source of the disease, destroy the cancer; cleanse the polluted nature.

The Penitent's Request, or Petition

It is a request for divine mercy. Says David, "Be gracious to me, O God." Though he lived in ancient days when the sacrifices of animals and fowls were made for the sins of the people, David looks beyond these types to the *great sacrifice* that was to be made for the sins of the world; and with the penetrating mind of a prophet he beholds the *Lamb of God* slain for the sins of the world, and cries out, "Have mercy upon me, O God." He offers no animal sacrifice. He anticipates the day of grace, the atonement of the Son of God, and pleads for *mercy* offered in the Messiah who is to come.

David was right in his request for mercy, for sinful man's only hope is in the mercy, and not in the justice of God. Mercy is a higher court of appeal than the court of justice. David could not plead for justice, for had justice been administered to him he would have been condemned, separated, and doomed from the presence of God forever. But he bypasses the court of justice and appeals to the higher court—the court of mercy, where he may have forgiveness and not condemnation—"Have mercy upon me, O God!"

The measure of mercy for which he pleads, not according to his deeds, merits, honor, position, wealth, standing—No! No! David might have presented his position as a king, his service as spiritual leader of Israel, as the warrior who defeated Goliath, the defiant leader of the Philistines, and thus saved the kingdom of Israel from defeat at the hands of these pagan enemies. He might have pleaded before God on the basis of the justice of his rule in the kingdom, of the good name that he had among the people; that he might not be humiliated, disgraced, and the peoples of the surrounding nations—the pagan—be given occasion to blaspheme the name of Jehovah because of the conduct of the king, that God would forgive and cover his sins on the basis of these merits. But, no, David had no merits by which to present himself to Jehovah God. Rather he pled for mercy, "according to Thy lovingkindness." The penitent king, the sinner, now awakened by the indicting finger of God directed through the prophet Nathan, pleads on the basis of the lovingkindness of God, for divine mercy.

It is a request for the complete effacement of sin. "Blot out my iniquities." He is asking that God will use the "ink remover" on the record of his crime; not that he may turn a new page and the old record be forgotten for the time being, only to be rediscovered by his successors and exposed to his posterity, or that it remain there sometime to be discovered during his lifetime and exposed. David wants the record cleared. "Blot out my iniquities"—completely efface them from the records of Israel, and from the record of the Book of God in heaven above. David seems to anticipate the promise of God, that he will remove our sins from us as far as the east is from the west, and that he will bury them in the sea of forgetfulness to be remembered against us no more forever. "Hide Thy face from my sins, and blot out all my iniquities . . . Deliver me from blood-guiltiness, O God, Thou God of my salvation." How wise was this brokenhearted penitent sinner, contrite, prostrate before God, in requesting that God forgive, erase, efface, remove from the record his crime, his sin, never to be remembered against him again!

This is a request for soul-cleansing. Hear him pray, "Wash me thoroughly from my iniquity, and cleanse me from my sin . . . Purify me with hyssop, and I shall be clean; Wash me and I shall be whiter than snow." But someone says, Is it possible for a penitent sinner to pray at the same time for forgiveness of sins and the cleansing of his inner nature? We answer that that will depend upon the degree of light which that penitent sinner has. It must be borne in mind that David had known God, possibly even in a soul-cleansing relationship, before his fall and the consequent repollution of his inner nature. David knows the nature of inward pollution. He well knew the source from which his evil deeds sprang. Now under the bright light of illumination focused upon him by God, he is able to see not only the heinous crime that he has committed, but the pollution of his nature, the dark recesses of his soul where insincerity, hypocrisy, and deception lurk. David well knows, in the light of this revelation of God to his soul, that it will be insufficient to have his sins forgiven. God must go deeper than that and remove the source of the overt act of sin, cleanse the nature that is polluted, remove the inner source that will again spring forth and bear fruit in the heinous sins and crimes from which he is now attempting to be free. Thus, he prays for forgiveness of his overt acts of sin and beseeches God to reach deep into his soul and cleanse the nature in which the sin thrives, to purify the culture in which the bacteria of sin grows and rapidly multiplies. "Wash me thoroughly from my iniquity, and cleanse me from my sin . . . Purify me with hyssop, and I shall be clean; Wash me and I shall be whiter than snow."

But David also recognizes the impossibility of living to the glory of God, though forgiven and restored, in his fallen and broken inner moral nature. He recognizes the impossibility of simply repairing that which God has forgiven. Looking into the deep, dark, dismal, polluted, inner recesses of his spiritual nature David cries out, "Create in me a clean heart, O God, and renew a steadfast spirit within me." Thus David recognizes that salvation embraces the necessity and the provision of a divine fiat, *a new creation.* Paul, likewise, saw this and in 2 Corinthians 5:17 says, "Therefore if any man is in Christ, he is a new creature; the old things passed away; behold, new things have come." David had a wrong spirit, a spirit of hypocrisy, a spirit of deception, a spirit that set him a variance with God. He recognized the need of a new spirit and thus prayed, "Create in me a clean heart, O God; and renew a steadfast spirit within me." A clean heart and the renewal of a right spirit should be the prayer of every penitent sinner.

This is a request for soul preservation. "Do not cast me away from Thy presence, and do not take Thy Holy Spirit from me." Are we to understand that David had not lost his sonship, that David is still the redeemed child of God? Is God's Spirit still within him? Nay! God's Spirit still hovers about him. God in His mercy has manifested Himself to him, giving him opportunity for repentance, reconciliation, restoration to the favor of God, but God's Spirit no longer abides in David.

When Jesus responded to the call of his friends at Bethany on the occasion of the sickness and death of Lazarus, he did not arrive until the fourth day. Now there was current among the Jews (indeed no part of the divine revelation but a borrowing from the pagan concepts of the people who had influenced Jewish thinking) a view that after the death of the individual the spirit, the human soul, hovered about the body for as much as four days, hoping for an opportunity to reenter and revive the dead person. This current pagan belief allowed that any time up to the end of the fourth day the spirit might reenter and revive the body, but that by the end of the fourth day, the decomposition and the offensive odor of the decaying body would become such as to drive the spirit away, and once it was gone it would never return. Thus there would be no further hope of revival and restoration to life. When Jesus arrived, the sister of Lazarus said to Him, in effect: "Lord, my brother has been dead four days. Had you come earlier, then we could have believed for a restoration, but now he has been dead four days. By this time he stinketh." The implication is that it is too late now; the spirit is gone; it has taken its departure; there will be no opportunity for his revival; the situation is an utterly hopeless one: you came too late!

So David, not physically, but spiritually dead, has lingered long in the tomb of moral and spiritual putrefaction, so long in fact that there is danger that the Spirit of the living God will be offended by the foul odor of his immorality and hypocrisy and that the sensitive dove of heaven will take his departure, never to return. David well knows that he has lingered too long in this condition, that there is danger of grieving away forever the Spirit of God who had brooded over, hovered about, longing, hoping for reentrance into his heart and life. Now in his awakened condition, in his fearful situation, realizing the enormity of his evil, David prays, "Do not cast me away from Thy presence, and do not take Thy Holy Spirit from me." Lord, be patient, continue to hover about, reenter my heart and life. Erase my sin from my heart and life. Erase my sin from the record. Forgive it, blot out my transgressions, cleanse my nature, purify my heart, restore within me a right spirit; reenter the inner being and take up Your abode again. "Renew a steadfast spirit within me."

This is a request for restoration of divine favor. "Restore to me the joy of Thy salvation, and sustain me with a willing spirit." The king had known the joys of salvation. He had rejoiced in the manifest presence of God. His soul had been quieted by the sacred visitations of the heavenly One. In his musical recitals the inspiration of heaven had caused him to rise to great eminences, ecstasies of joy and of spiritual insight, and to convey those insights and those emotions, breathed upon him from heaven, to his audiences. He had been instrumental in the hands of God in awakening spiritual desires, of inspiring ideals that lifted the morale of his kingdom. This joy is gone; long since it had departed. For long, David has known nothing of the joy that once animated his life, of the presence of the heavenly One. But now awakened, he reflects upon that which he once enjoyed, but which he has lost. Like Peter of old, in his reflection David weeps bitterly. But in confidence his soul rises up with the request, "Restore to me the joy of Thy salvation." That Spirit that once indwelt him, that assisted him, that fortified him, that strengthened him, is gone. He is now weakened; like Samson, he is deprived of his power. He is as weak as any other man. That Spirit that once enabled him to keep his composure in the presence of the jealously insane Saul; that Spirit that once enabled him to keep his composure when the women sang, "Saul has slain his thousands, And David his ten thousands" (1 Sam. 18:7b); that Spirit that once enabled him to preserve the life of King Saul when he was hounded by the jealous king—even though David could easily have taken Saul's life as he slept; that Holy Spirit is gone! David has lost his composure, his self-confidence. Now he prays, "Restore to me the joy of Thy salvation, and sustain me with a willing spirit."

In the absence of God's presence from the life of a person, moral degeneracy and decay will soon set in. David wisely recognizes the impossibility of maintaining moral rectitude in the absence of the indwelling presence of the Spirit of God.

The Penitent's Covenant with God

This is a promise of gratitude in testimony. "O Lord, open my lips, that my mouth may declare Thy praise." If you blot out my transgressions, if you cleanse my heart, if you renew a right spirit within me, if you reenter my heart and uphold me with your free Spirit, David seems to be saying, then: O Lord, in this restored relationship my lips will be opened, "my mouth may declare Thy praise." I will thank you for it; I will praise you for it; I will honor you.

This is a promise of thanksgiving in song. David had been the sweet singer of Israel, but long since his song was silenced. His oratories had been missed in the sacred halls of Israel; his harp was silent. He now promises that if he is restored, forgiven and cleansed, repossessed of God, that his tongue will sing aloud of God's righteousness. Said the Psalmist, as it is recorded in the fortieth division, "He brought me up out of the pit of destruction, out of the miry clay; and He set my feet upon a rock making my footsteps firm. And He put a new song in my mouth, a song of praise to our God" (Ps. 40:2, 3a). Perhaps this is the experience of the same man of whom it is recorded in the fifty-first division of the Psalms. "My tongue will joyfully sing of Thy righteousness," says David.

This is a promise of service for God. "Then I will teach transgressors Thy ways, and sinners will be converted to Thee." David foresees a life of usefulness in soul-winning when he is restored to the grace of God. His life will become an example, and his mouth will speak words of wisdom that will lead sinners to God. He foresees a revival of religion in the kingdom—"Then I will teach transgressors Thy ways, and sinners will be converted to Thee." Said the Psalmist in the first division of that book, "How blessed is the man who does not walk in the counsel of the wicked, Nor stand in the path of sinners, Nor sit in the seat of scoffers!" (Ps. 1:1). David, a man once blessed of God, had walked in the counsel of the ungodly and, though not openly, in his heart he had identified himself with sinners. David did not retrogress to the seat of the scornful. He was restored from his position among sinners. But now he foresees himself an instrument in the hands of God to open the door of mercy to sin-darkened hearts. He has stood in their way. He has prevented them from entering the kingdom of heaven. He has been an obstructionist in the kingdom of God; but now he promises to be an instructor, a director, an evangel, a messenger of God to lead these men into a saving relationship with God. His service as promised here is twofold: to *teach transgressors* and to *convert sinners.*

The Penitent's Confidence in God

Hear him cry, "A broken and a contrite heart, O God, Thou wilt not despise." He has made his confession—a personal, open, frank, full confession. He has acknowledged the depth of depravity in his life. He has prayed for forgiveness and cleansing and the restoration of the Spirit of God to his heart. He has made his request, multifold as it has been. He has made his promise of gratitude in testimony, thanksgiving in song, and service for Jehovah. Now he is ready to believe. He has opened the doors to every avenue of his soul. The spirit of hypocrisy is gone. The masquerade is over; the mask has been torn away. Self-justification is no more. The broken, contrite, prostrate, penitent sinner lies on his face before the Judge of all the world, now ready to believe. "A broken and a contrite heart, O God, Thou wilt not despise."

Faith functions when adjustments are completed, when full confession has been made, when the heart is laid open and bare before God. When every reservation has been relinquished, it is not difficult to believe. The great and holy Colonel Brengle of the Salvation Army once said that there is but one thing in the universe that will prevent man's faith from functioning in God, and that one thing is sin. The obstacles to faith, so frequently experienced by the individual seeking God, will always be found to resolve themselves into some unwillingness, some failure to open and lay bare the heart and life, some withholding, some withdrawing, some reservation. There are no reservations in the life of the truly penitent sinner. His heart and his mind lie bare before God. "Thou God seest me!" Nothing is hidden; all is confessed now and faith functions naturally, as naturally as the lungs breathe in the pure atmosphere that presses in upon them.

"A broken and a contrite heart, O God, Thou wilt not despise." He is restored; he is again a child of God. Out of the dismal depth of sin, degradation, pollution, hypocrisy, the king—the penitent sinner, over the road of bitter repentance, of full confession—returns to the waiting Father, and the Heavenly Father's arms of love are thrown about his neck. A kiss of pardon is placed upon his cheek, the besmirched robes of sin and hypocrisy are removed, and the robe of righteousness reserved for the returning sinner is placed upon him. The feast of joy begins. King David, the fallen sinner, is restored to the favor of God. And so will any penitent sinner find restoration when he follows the course of this penitent.

Spiritual Restoration Produces Effective Witness

The forgiven penitent promises to become an instructor of transgressors in the ways of God: "Then will I teach transgressors Thy ways" (v. 31). Without a knowledge of God's ways, men follow their own natural inclinations which inevitably lead to degeneracy and ultimate ruin. God's ways are right because they are the revelation of His own righteous character. That righteousness can only be known by one who knows God personally. Such personal knowledge inevitably motivates the redeemed to witness to God's righteousness.

The restored penitent expresses his confidence in the effectiveness of his witness: "Sinners will be converted [or turned back] to Thee." Faith for the effectiveness of the evangelistic witness under the influence of God's Spirit will not go unrewarded. Faith for the salvation of others flows naturally from the person who has exercised faith in God for his own salvation.

His tongue is now loosed in joyful songs of praise to God: "Then my tongue will joyfully sing of Thy righteousness." There is no more effective witness to God than the tongue that is employed in joyful songs of praise to God. It has been well said that if Christians praised God more, unsaved men would doubt Him less. Much of the effectiveness of the early Methodist witness has been credited to their joyful singing. It was said of these early Methodists that they resembled a nest of singing birds.

In the experience of this now-restored penitent, as always, the renewal of his experience in God resulted in vital evangelism.

Chapter V

The Sinner's Repentance and God's Response

"Draw near to God and He will draw near to you. Cleanse your hands, you sinners; and purify your hearts, you double-minded" (Jas. 4:8).

The hands spoken of here obviously represent the overt acts of sin committed; nor is James speaking ambiguously. Rather, he clearly suggests six specific sins of which his readers are guilty, and from which their hands require cleansing if they are to recover their lost relationship with God.

These Christians are Guilty of Futile, Sinful Striving

What is the source of quarrels and conflicts among you? Is not the source your pleasures that wage war in your members? You lust and do not have; so you commit murder. And you are envious and cannot obtain; so you fight and quarrel. You do not have because you ask with wrong motives so that you may spend it on your pleasures (Jas. 4:1-3).

The condition of these spiritually carnal Christian Jews is reminiscent of Isaiah's description of ancient Israel: "But the wicked are like the tossing sea, for it cannot be quiet, and its waters toss up refuse and mud. There is no peace, says my God, for the wicked" (Isa. 57:20, 21).

The expression of the spiritual and moral disease is not as important as the disease itself. The wars and fightings—or better, brawlings, as the margin has it—the vain strife for things unattainable, the death-dealing blows against fellow Christians, the silence of God in relation to their prayers; these are all but the open external running sores that aggravate the body, distress the mind, and render its putrefaction a reproach before the world. Isaiah prophesied to Israel of a like condition: "The whole head is sick and the whole heart is faint. From the sole of the foot to the head there is nothing sound in it. Only bruises, welts, and raw wounds, not pressed out or bandaged, nor softened with oil" (Isa. 1:5b, 6).

What an accurate picture of many contemporary Christians! Brawlings in the home, in the church business meetings, in conferences and assemblies; strife for positions, prominence or preeminence, even in the body of Christ. Greediness for better and more material comforts and luxuries; murderous blows by subtle insinuations or questionable accusations against the reputations or characters of fellow Christians. Frenzied but futile prayers with fastings and howlings that would shame the false prophets of Baal at the challenge of Elijah on Mount Carmel. All of this, and little wonder at the dead silence of an insulted and sadly-offended righteous God.

But the deadly, cancerous germ that produces the putrefaction does not remain hidden. James is a faithful spiritual physician. He skillfully diagnoses the disease. "You lust . . . that you may spend it on your pleasures" (Jas. 4:2, 3). Upon the impure altars of their inner spiritual beings there continually burns the false fire of sinful passion, the flames of which greedily lick up the illegitimate sacrifices faster than they can be fed into it, and then hungrily cry for food for the flames that cannot be sufficiently supplied. Saint Augustine rightly observed that "man has salt on his tongue for God." The waters that issue from the material fountains of this world can only temporarily slake physical thirst, and the temporal, or material water cannot slake spiritual thirst. Jesus said to the Samaritan woman, concerning the well of Jacob: "Everyone who drinks of this water shall thirst again; but whoever drinks of the water that I shall give him shall never thirst; but the water that I shall give him shall become in him a well of water springing up to eternal life" (John 4:13, 14). Again, how true the words of St. Augustine: "The mind of man will never rest until it rests in thee [God]." And the author of Hebrews cites the remedy: "There remains therefore a Sabbath rest for the people of God . . . Let us therefore be diligent to enter that rest" (Heb. 4:9, 11a).

These Hebrew Christians are Indicted
For the Sin of Spiritual Fornication

"You adulteresses, do you not know that friendship with the world is hostility toward God? Therefore whoever wishes

to be a friend of the world makes himself an enemy of God"
(Jas. 4:4).

Worldly alliances, entanglements and commitments to
organizations that prohibit the use of Christ's name, questionable alliances with unprincipled individuals or organizations, intermarriage of Christians with those who deny the
claims of Christ upon their lives, indulgence in godless
worldly amusements and sinful pleasures, adoption of the
principles and practices of the world as the norm of Christian conduct, reliance upon and placing of hope for world
peace in humanistic international alliances, conformity to
worldly ideals and practices of immodesty or extravagance
in attire and life styles of the ungodly, are among the modern
counterpart sins of Christians, against which James cried
out in the Christian Israel of his day. The line of demarcation between the unconverted world and the church has been
so nearly erased in the present day that few are now able
to recognize the boundary. The hour has arrived for a new
delineation between the kingdom of Satan and the kingdom
of God. God is a jealous God and will not share His glory
with another. Martin Marty sees the erosion to be such as
to have erased practically all vital Christian distinctions from
worldliness in America.[1]

Sinful Pride Comes in for Its Indictment
At the Hands of This Inspired Apostle

James declares that "God is opposed to the proud, but
gives grace to the humble" (Jas. 4:6). Pride is the keystone
sin of the spiritual nature. Remove it and the whole edifice
constructed against God will collapse. Maintain it and God
is barred from the life. It is that which exalts the self against
God and leaves no room for Him in the life. Death to the
sinful proud self is an absolute prerequisite to the new life
in Christ. Jesus said, "Unless a grain of wheat falls into the
earth and dies, it remains by itself alone" (John 12:24b). So
many of us abide fruitlessly alone in our snug Christian professions simply because we have never died to self. We are

---

[1]Martin E. Marty, *The New Shape of American Religion* (New York:
Harper and Bros. Publishing, 1958-9), Chapter 4, "America's Real
Religion: An Attitude."

peculiar hybrids, so to speak, resulting from a cross between the Christian faith and the spirit of a godless age rendering us sterile and incapable of spiritual reproduction. We abide sadly alone, remaining impotent in the face of a defiant and aggressive world. Sinful pride holds the citadel of self for Satan.

It was this self-righteous, paralyzing pride that prevented the "elder son," in the parable of Luke 15, from the appropriation and enjoyment of his father's blessings. Hear the sad acknowledgement of this spiritually-starved elder son to his father: "Look! For so many years I have been serving you, and I have never neglected a command of yours; and yet you have never given me a kid, that I might be merry with my friends" (Luke 15:29). Then hear the father's mildly rebuking reply: "My child, you have always been with me, and all that is mine is yours" (v. 31). Pride paralyzes faith and thus prevents appropriation of blessings provided. It clogs the fountain of living waters and converts our lives into barren desert wastes. Pride must go before revival can come. The writer will never forget an observation of his early Christian life when he witnessed a fashionable lady of the world, whose soul had been awakened by God, earnestly seeking peace with God. In the midst of her earnest quest she was suddenly arrested by the violent assertion of the proud, sinful self. After a moment's hesitation and reflection on the opinion of another, she was heard to repeatedly exclaim, "What would Doctor Shepherd think if he should see me here?" Then, defeated in her quest for God by the fear of one Doctor Shepherd's opinion, she sadly arose from the place of prayer, and like the rich young ruler, "went away sorrowfully."

The Sin of Slander
Falls Under the Stroke of Divine Indictment

"Do not speak against one another, brethren" (Jas. 4:11a).

There is no more deadly sin among Christians than the sin of evil speaking. It invariably deals a double death-blow. It deals out blighting death to the spirit of the speaker, and it unmercifully cuts down in cold blood the one spoken about. More hopes have been blasted, more reputations ruined, more confidences destroyed, more damage done to the kingdom of God by this foul fiend of the carnal spirit than perhaps any known enemy of God. And to think that it is one of the commonest sins of professed Christians! Bishop A. B. Simpson once said,

> I had rather play with forked lightning, or take in my hands living wires with their fiery current, than to speak a reckless word against any servant of Christ; or idly repeat the slanderous darts which thousands of Christians are hurling on others to the hurt of their souls and bodies. You may often wonder, perhaps, why your sickness is not healed, your spirit filled with the joy of the Holy Ghost, or your life blessed and prosperous. It may be some dart which you have flung with an angry voice, or in some idle hour of thoughtless gossip, is pursuing you on its way, as it describes the circle which always brings back to the source from which it came, every shaft of bitterness, and every idle and evil word . . . There is nothing which hinders, chokes the channel of prayer and ties God's hands like malice, unforgiveness and bitterness locked up in the hearts of God's professed Christians.

The noted Methodist evangelist of another generation, Beverly Caradine, relates that the greatest revival he ever witnessed started with two women coming forward and asking the pastor's forgiveness for having spoken unkindly of him. Such confession always prepares the way for revival. The account is reproduced here for the reader's benefit.

> It broke the hard crusty feeling which had settled over the meeting. From that started a half dozen more confessions just like them, and like a flash the heavens were opened. The scenes which followed would be impossible to describe: hundreds shouting, waving, crying, laughing . . . The altar was filled with weeping, praying seekers. Salvation rolled, heaven and earth came together. All by asking forgiveness and getting the hindrances out of the way.

The story is told of a very critical and slanderous woman who was visited by a neighbor lady in her community on a

Monday morning. Soon the slanderous woman called the attention of her visitor to another neighbor's washing on the line outside the window. Said she, "As usual it is poorly laundered and quite unclean." Upon this the visitor arose, and removing her handkerchief from her purse, she drew it across the windowpane, leaving a clean path behind. Then looking through she remarked, "Your neighbor's clothing is perfectly clean; the dirt is on your own windowpane."

Thus, so often our vision of others and of life itself is blurred by the impurities in our own lives. Jesus said, "Blessed are the pure in heart, for they shall see God" (Matt. 5:8). David, when seeking restoration to the favor of God, prayed, "Create in me a clean heart, O God, and renew a steadfast spirit within me" (Ps. 51:10).

The Sin of Presumption is Indicted by God

Come now, you who say, "Today or tomorrow, we shall go to such and such a city, and spend a year there and engage in business and make a profit." Yet you do not know what your life will be like tomorrow. You are just a vapor that appears for a little while and then vanishes away. Instead, you ought to say, "If the Lord wills, we shall live and also do this or that" (Jas. 4:13-15).

Presumption is among the commonest of sins within the Church. So many of our Christian services are conducted presumptiously. We venture out into the day's activities without taking time for private devotions; our children are sent forth into the godless environment of many of our public schools without the blessing of the family altar; important business is transacted and far-reaching personal and church decisions are made, after which we ask God's blessings upon our decisions. If all goes well, we compliment ourselves. If the outcome is unfavorable to our liking, we blame divine providence. On the wall of a doctor's waiting room there appeared the words: "In time of trouble, and not before, God and the doctor we adore. But when the trouble is over and all is righted, God is forgotten and the doctor is slighted." For many Christians God is little more than a "trouble-shooter"; a sort of emergency recourse, or a temporary city of refuge, when in reality He desires to be the constant companion of our lives.

W. H. Griffith Thomas writes most poignantly on the peril of presumptuous sins among self-righteous Christians.

> Nothing is easier than self-righteousness and self-deception in religion. It is well-nigh impossible to enjoy outward privileges without presuming upon them . . . The greater the knowledge, the greater the danger of being content with merely a nominal Christianity. It is one of the most solemn truths that without any real change of heart we may know a great deal of Christian truth, may even be occupied with Christian work, and closely associated with Christian people, knowing with great familiarity religious phraseology and living largely in a Christian atmosphere, and yet all the while may be without the new life that comes from the Spirit of God. The danger of such a position is far greater than that of willful and deliberate sin. Our Lord was constantly warning His hearers against such presumption (Matt. 7:22, 23; Luke 13:26, 27). The greater the privilege the greater the peril. The higher the delight the more imperative the duty. Let us ever pray the Psalmist's prayer: "Keep back Thy servant from presumptuous sins."[2]

It has been said that man's natural course is to bypass God in the strength and vitality of youth as quite unnecessary; then gloat over human success and independence from God in the security of middle life; but finally turn and blame God for the reverses and insecurity of declining years. Presumptive independence stands condemned among our most glaring sins.

The Sin of Omission is Condemned

In his epistle, the apostle James tells us, "Therefore, to one who knows the right thing to do, and does not do it, to him it is sin" (Jas. 4:17).

---

[2]W. H. Griffith Thomas, *St. Paul's Epistle to the Romans:* A Devotional Commentary" (Grand Rapids: Wm. B. Eerdmans Publishing Company, 1946), pp. 91, 92.

It is shocking to discover in the gospels that Christ has much more to say about, and far greater condemnation of, the sins of omission than the sins of commission.

In the great arraignment by Christ, as recorded in Matthew 25:31-33, 41-45, it is not the sin of adultery, of robbery, of drunkenness, or even of overt dishonesty that condemns the assembled multitudes, but rather the sin of the failure to have done what was required by God. "Then He will answer them, saying, 'Truly I say to you, to the extent that you did not do it to one of the least of these, you did not do it to Me. And these will go away into eternal punishment' " (Matt. 25:45, 46a).

The parable of the talents teaches the same lesson of divine condemnation on the sin of omission. Even the rich man in hell, as depicted in Luke sixteen, has but one charge brought against him, that he had failed to do his duty to his fellow man while on earth, the condemned sin of omission. "Child, remember that during your life you received your good things, and likewise Lazarus bad things; but now he is being comforted here, and you are in agony" (Luke 16:25b).

On the occasion of the delivery of the "Great Commission" to His disciples, Jesus' promise of His accompanying presence with them is conditioned upon their obedience to His command to go into all the world and make disciples of all nations. We have no right of claim to His presence if we fail to do His will as revealed for our lives.

Of these sins of fleshly strivings, spiritual fornication, sinful pride, slander, presumption, and omission the hands must be cleansed if we are to expect spiritual renewal in this age. On a church bulletin board there appeared the following pertinent exhortation: "Repent now and avoid the rush on the Judgment Day."

God's Response to Man's Repentance

"Draw near to God and He will draw near to you" (Jas. 4:8a).

What is the divine sequel to penitent man's approach to God? James hastens to answer this question: "He [God] will draw near to you" (Jas. 4:8a).

Modern practical materialism has affected much of man's thought about God, as the great philosopher Aristotle's concept of God influenced thought about God in his day. Aristotle resolved his concept of God into an impersonal magnetic force which was always passive and never active. So materialistic thought today would bid us adjust ourselves to certain fixed and unalterable laws with the desired consequences guaranteed. Not so with a correct concept of personal Christian theism. God is a person who can "sympathize with our weaknesses" (Heb. 4:15a), and is capable and ready to respond to our sincere entreaties. Blinded by our worship of illusory materialism, *the here* and *now* of our temporal world, we lose sight of the God who is personal and eternal. How well it has been said that

> . . . we have not merely to comply with an unconscious and impersonal law, but to follow the motions of a quickening Spirit. It is not merely a matter of conforming ourselves to the fixed laws of the universe. That is the creed of Stoicism, of Calvinism, which is baptised Stoicism, and of modern science. It is too simple, because we have to do not with mechanical law but with the living God. For the Word of God . . . is God Himself in action.[3]

When we have met the conditions of revival in submission to God—denial of the authority of Satan in our lives, in genuine repentance and humility—then "He who is coming will come, and will not delay" (Heb. 10:37b). Or as Malachi puts it: "The Lord whom you seek will suddenly come to His temple . . . behold, He is coming, says the Lord of hosts" (Mal. 3:1b).

There are many encouraging evidences of approaching spiritual renewal. God waits on sinful men to repent of their sins and return to Him for help. The call comes today as of old, if

> . . . My people who are called by My name humble themselves and pray, and seek My face and turn from their wicked ways, then I will hear from

---

[3]W. R. Inge, *The Study Bible*, John Stirling, ed., "Hebrews" (London: Cassell and Co. Ltd., 1926), p. 8.

heaven, will forgive their sin, and will heal their land (2 Chron. 7:14).

Malachi's message to Israel is equally true for us today. "Return to Me, and I will return to you; says the Lord of hosts" (Mal. 3:7b).

"Draw near to God, and He will draw near to you." The greatest need of this hour is a renewed manifestation of God. He will return when we return. The Father waits for the prodigal's return. Restoration to the Father's favor and our lost spiritual inheritance is conditioned upon our return to God.

A recent scientific report in a popular magazine discusses the agricultural possibilities of the Sahara, the greatest desert waste of the entire earth. It is said, by this authority, that chemical analysis of the soil of the great Sahara Desert reveals it to be one of the most fertile areas on the face of the globe. The only deficiency is moisture. But, says this authority, there are exhaustless supplies of water beneath the sands of the Sahara, if they could only be brought to the surface for irrigation purposes. That this may yet be accomplished is believed to be a possibility, with the result that the greatest waste area of the earth, stretching across North Africa for a distance of upward of four thousand miles from east to west, and nearly a thousand miles from north to south, may be converted into one of the most fertile agricultural areas known to man.

However this may be, it is certainly true that the only possibility of reclaiming the spiritual desert wastes of the Church and the lives of multitudes of her numbers in our day is to be found in a tapping of the exhaustless resources of the divine Spirit. To the Samaritan woman Jesus said, "Everyone who drinks of this water [the material water of Jacob's well] shall thirst again; but whoever drinks of the water that I shall give him shall never thirst; but the water that I shall give him shall become in him a well of water springing up to eternal life" (John 4:13b, 14). If we will but bore through the *hard pan* and *rock of indifference, lethargy* and *unbelief* of professing Christendom, and release upon the church and the world a mighty floodtide of the water of life, then our generation will experience that mighty spiritual purification and animation that will reclaim our waste areas and cause our generation to blossom as the rose. It is doubtful if any previous generation has ever had such great potentialities for reclamation as the present. The resources of our generation are practically exhaustless, but without God they are as devoid of spiritual value as is the great Sahara Desert of agricultural value. Animated by the Spirit of God in a mighty spiritual revival, this generation may yet become the most glorious and productive the world has ever known. The question is, "Will we repent and return to God?" When we do, revival will become a reality!

After ten days of earnest prayer and preparation by the one hundred and twenty disciples:

> Suddenly there came from heaven a noise like a violent rushing wind, and it filled the whole house where they were sitting. And there appeared to them tongues as of fire distributing themselves, and they rested on each one of them. And they were all filled with the Holy Spirit (Acts 2:2-4a).

The result of this floodtide of blessing was the conversion of some three thousand unbelievers.

Again when the apostles had been released from prison and had joined the church in prayer, we read of them: "And when they had prayed, the place where they had gathered together was shaken, and they were all filled with the Holy Spirit, and began to speak the word of God with boldness" (Acts 4:31).

Once while serving as a missionary in Africa, an urgent call came to the author to conduct a revival in a girl's boarding school. Moral and spiritual conditions were at a deplorable level. Few if any of the students or African teachers were professing saving faith in Christ. Disciplinary problems were distressing the missionaries. For a week the gospel messages were delivered twice a day, and prayer for revival was offered to God. All efforts appeared to be fruitless, however, as the hearts of students and teachers alike were apparently locked against God. Undaunted, all the workers entered a determined effort of fasting and prayer. In the four o'clock service of the following day, everything appeared as hopeless of revival as before. At the close of the message, a time of quiet waiting before God followed and then as suddenly and as powerfully as on the day of Pentecost, a mighty sweeping presence of the Holy Spirit flooded the room. An attractive young lady who was the recognized leader of the student body was suddenly smitten by the Spirit with a deep sense of conviction and repented of her sin. In an instant, without urging or exhortation, every student and.teacher was on their knees crying to God for saving mercy. For some two hours the writer witnessed one of the greatest penitential prayer meetings it has ever been his privilege to see. At the close of that prayer meeting not a student or teacher remained outside the saving mercies of Christ. Nor did the moral and spiritual influence of that revival end with the service of that day. Spiritual and moral fruit continued.

For more than a quarter of a century a barren desert of ecclesiastic sterility prevailed in America and Western Europe. The humanistic ideal of the inevitable perfection of humanity had pervaded the thought of statesmen, educators, and much of the clergy alike. The First World War occurred and shook the foundations of this philosophy. Ten years later, recovery was in progress when the great depression and then the Second World War struck the mortal blow to man's blind optimism. The great Korean War further emphasized the awful depth of human depravity, followed by the Vietnam fiasco. With European and Asiatic civilizations largely in ruins and America in jeopardy, men began, at last, to realize that there could be found no security in the temporal order. Thus, once again, as always under such circumstances, it was recognized that if there was to be found any hope and security, it must be found in the spiritual and not in the material realm. This recognition turned the thoughts of men to God and opened the door for a new divine visitation. Evangelist Billy Graham came forth in response to God's call and has played a leading role in calling the minds and hearts of Americans, as also the rest of the world, back to God. Spiritual hunger and evidence of revival are seen in many parts of the world today.

In his little book, *God Came to Gujerat,*[4] Floyd Banker graphically portrays the mighty manifestation of God in India that began under the ministry of Dr. Paul S. Rees in Akola, Berar in 1951, a movement that reached deep into the

----

[4]Floyd Banker, *God Came to Gujerat,* 2nd ed. (Syracuse, New York: The Wesley Press, n.d.).

heart of India. This revival started with the confession and repentance of missionaries and national Christians.

Africa has felt the mighty touch of God in some of her apparently most hopeless areas. For three years, from 1929-1931, a sweeping revival moved throughout Northern Sierra Leone, one of Africa's previously most unresponsive areas, resulting in the conversion of thousands of pagans. This revival started with the repentance and confession of the church, and even the ministry. Powerful spiritual revivals visited the campuses of Wheaton, Houghton and Asbury Colleges in the sixties. These all began with confessions, repentance and restitution.

The author had the privilege of engaging in three gracious revival campaigns outside the United States in the nineteen fifties. Two of these campaigns were conducted in the Bahama Islands. On the first occasion the messages were directed primarily to the Christians of the existing churches. The Spirit faithfully applied the pungent truth and spiritual awakenings followed. Services were conducted in taverns, in the open air and in the regular churches. People were converted in all of these locations and conditions. Three years after the first campaign in the Bahama Islands a bartender testified that a man had been converted in his tavern and had never returned there, but had continued a faithful Christian to that date. A leading minister of the city verified this account. In another tavern a backslidden Christian dramatically smashed his flask of whiskey on the floor in the midst of carousing spectators and walked outside where he knelt in a gateway nearby with the members of the evangelistic team and gave his heart to Christ. Three others immediately followed him in yielding their lives to Christ. Revival was begun in the great old tourist capital of Nassau and later reached large proportions. A month after the evangelistic party's return to the States, a Christian leader from Nassau wrote:

> When you were here in December you started a fire, and it has developed into a Holy Ghost revival. Our nightly audiences are above 2,000. There is no church in the city large enough for the crowds, so we are having the services in a city park.

Subsequently, information received from a visiting evangelist to that city indicated that he had witnessed many conversions. From the Island of Eleuthera a leading minister wrote, concerning this evangelistic crusade: "Everyone is still talking about the blessed time of refreshing your team brought to Eleuthera. The spirit of revival still exists." From a leading minister in Nassau came this report:

> Echoes have come from many directions of this city, and from the out islands, of a spiritual awakening as a result of the Christian example and consecrated life of this Commission [the evangelistic team] while they ministered to the spiritual needs of those with whom they came in contact.

During a city-wide evangelistic crusade conducted by the author in 1955 in Mexico City, under the auspices of the Maranatha Evangelical Association, great evidence of spiritual hunger was witnessed in the churches. More than five hundred souls sought the Lord for spiritual restoration or initial salvation. The same spiritual hunger and response to the gospel of Christ was in evidence all the way from the poorest people in the slums to the materially prosperous Protestant churches of that great old city. Scores of hungry souls were gathered into the Kingdom of Christ because they were willing to return to God. A man from the Yukon Peninsula who was more than ninety years of age chanced to visit his Christian daughter in Mexico City during this revival campaign. During a great movement of the Spirit in the Prince of Peace Presbyterian Church on a Sunday morning he came to know Christ as his personal Saviour. On the last Sunday morning service of this gracious campaign in the famous Ganti Street Methodist Church, more than one hundred and fifty persons found Christ as Saviour.

There can be no question about the reality of revival when men are awakened to a sense of their need, and when they are willing to meet the divine conditions requisite to God's manifestations to their souls. "From the days of your fathers you have turned aside from My statutes, and have not kept them. Return to Me, and I will return to you, says the Lord of hosts" (Mal. 3:7a).

Said Jesus: "I am the way, and the truth, and the life; no one comes to the Father, but through Me" (John 14:6).

CHAPTER VI

The Vision That Transforms

"I saw also the Lord"

There probably was never a greater hour of need for moral and spiritual revival in the Kingdom of Judah than on the occasion of Isaiah's vision, as that vision is recorded in Isaiah 6:1-8, which reads thus:

> In the year of King Uzziah's death, I saw the Lord sitting on a throne, lofty and exalted, with the train of His robe filling the temple. Seraphim stood above Him, each having six wings; with two he covered his face, and with two he covered his feet, and with two he flew. And one called out to another and said, "Holy, Holy, Holy, is the Lord of hosts, the whole earth is full of His glory." And the foundations of the thresholds trembled at the voice of Him who called out, while the temple was filling with smoke. Then I said, "Woe is me, for I am ruined! Because I am a man of unclean lips, and I live among a people of unclean lips; for my eyes have seen the King, the Lord of hosts." Then one of the seraphim flew to me, with a burning coal in his hand which he had taken from the altar with tongs. And he touched my mouth with it and said, "Behold, this had touched your lips; and your iniquity is taken away, and your sin is forgiven." Then I heard the voice of the Lord, saying, "Whom shall I send, and who will go for us?" Then I said, "Here am I. Send me!"

The golden key that unlocks the message of this vision is contained in the prophet's words, "I saw also the Lord." It matters little whether this vision constituted Isaiah's original call to the prophetic office, as some hold, or whether it came at a later period in his life, according to the views of others. In either event it was an illuminating spiritual vision in an hour of dire need that transformed the life and outlook of the prophet and changed the future course of the kingdom, if not all history. Real visions are always transforming. Peter quoted Joel's prophecy on the day of Pentecost: "And it shall be in the last days, God says, that I will pour forth of My spirit upon all mankind; and your sons and your daughters shall prophesy, and your young men shall see visions, and your old men shall dream dreams" (Acts 2:17).

From Joel's prophecy it is clear that the vision is a preview of future and as yet unrealized possibilities, and that it is characteristic of youth, while the dream is a reconstruction of past experience in some form, and is characteristic of old age and decline. The first projects itself imaginatively into the future and beholds challenging possibilities; the second reconstructs past experiences and reclines with a deep sense of satisfaction in the golden yesterdays, idealizing the past. Nor does this mean that the number of years lived determines the outlook on life. It has been well said that one is not old until one ceases to grow. Cessation of growth may occur in early life, or it may never occur. This is an individual characteristic, and something that may be determined by personal attitudes and outlook on life. Somewhere it is recorded that "two prisoners looked out through prison bars; one saw mud, the other saw stars." Good advice is given in the following homely couplet. "As you ramble on through life, Brother, whatever be your goal; Keep your eye upon the doughnut, And not upon the hole!"

The poet, George Washington Doane, caught the significance of the transforming power of a vision and penned the following lines under the caption of "Life Sculpture."

> *Chisel in hand stood a sculptor boy*
> *With his marble block before him,*
> *And his eyes lit up with a smile of joy,*
> *As an angel-dream passed o'er him.*
>
> *He carved the dream on that shapeless stone,*
> *With many a sharp incision;*
> *With heaven's own light the sculpture shone,—*
> *He'd caught that angel-vision.*

Children of life are we, as we stand
  With our lives uncarved before us,
Waiting the hour when, at God's command,
  Our life-dream shall pass o'er us.

If we carve it then on the yielding stone,
  With many a sharp incision,
Its heavenly beauty shall be our own,—
  Our lives, that angel-vision.[1]

There are no less than six aspects of the prophet Isaiah's vision, as recorded in this passage. We shall examine each of these aspects.

The Prophet's Vision Reflects the Times
And Conditions of His Day

These times and conditions are suggested in the words, "In the year of King Uzziah's death." This was indeed a momentous year. The circumstances are highly significant. Uzziah had probably reigned over the Southern Kingdom for about fifty-five years. This was the longest reign of any king of Judah. The early days of his rule were marked by beneficent reforms and great prosperity. The kingdom had been greatly improved morally, spiritually, religiously, socially, economically, and politically by this king.

Then, as so often happens, the king grew proud and self-reliant, and consequently decline followed. Moved by impatience at the priest of God, this once great and righteous king intruded into the Holy Place of the temple and offered sacrifice to God in the priest's stead. The anger of the Lord was manifest against him, with the result that he was smitten with the curse of the dread disease of leprosy. From that hour Uzziah knew himself to be a doomed man. His self-confidence waned. Gradually he lost his influence over the kingdom. The altars to heathen deities that he had earlier destroyed were restored and the pure worship of Jehovah was corrupted. Economic, social, moral, and political corruption rapidly replaced the earlier reforms of his reign. Powerful, militar-

---

[1]George Washington Doane, "Life Sculpture," in *One Hundred and One Famous Poems with a Prose Supplement,* rev. ed. (Chicago: The Cable Company, 1929), p. 136.

istic, pagan nations began to threaten the very existence of the kingdom of Judah.

Saddest of all was the fact that the priests and prophets of Jehovah showed little concern for the welfare of the kingdom. Apostasy had paralyzed the spiritual nerve of the kingdom. Then one day the long-feared but inevitable occurred. King Uzziah died! This announcement seems to symbolize the passing of the last ray of hope for Judah. Demoralized, destitute of the help of Jehovah through her apostasy, threatened by militaristic powers from without, and now deprived of her king and with no promise of a competent ruler to lead her forth to reform and renewed hope, Judah faced a dark future.

It was in this deep, dark hour that the young prophet went into the temple to pray. Of all the prophets of Judah, Isaiah appears to have been the only one sufficiently concerned about the welfare of his people to present the condition before the Lord in prevailing prayer. That he was possessed of a deep sense of personal responsibility before God for the welfare of the kingdom appears evident. That he saw the utter hopelessness of the situation without the undertaking of God is equally evident.

To face dark and foreboding reality without faith for victory over it is devastating pessimism. To face such reality and deny its existence is delusive blind optimism. But to face such reality and admit it to be all that it claims for itself, and then turning from it to God in faith, claim victory over the situation, is true Christian realism. Isaiah was such a realist. He denied nothing of the dark situation that characterized the kingdom of Judah, but looking beyond these circumstances he "saw the Lord." Happy is the man who can see beyond the present foreboding circumstances of life to behold victory and a promising future.

The Prophet's Vision Reflected
The Presence of the Living God

"I saw also the Lord . . . Mine eyes have seen the King, the Lord of hosts" (KJV).

Had the prophet's vision been limited to the conditions and circumstances of his times he would have sunken down into utter despair. Had the Hebrew young men seen only the fiery furnace, they would have perished in its flames. Had Daniel seen only the den of hungry lions, he would have fallen an easy prey to their ravages. Had Job seen only his pitiable plight on the ash heap, he would have hopelessly perished there. Had Paul and Silas seen only the damp, dark, unsanitary interior of their Philippian prison inner-cell, they would have resigned themselves to their apparent hopeless situation. Had John seen only the apparent hopelessness of his Patmos exile, he might have suffered the fate of Napoleon on St. Helena. But not so with true faith in God.

As the Hebrew young men beheld the God able to deliver them from the fiery furnace; as Daniel believed in the God able to lock the lions' jaws; as Job beheld the God able to resurrect him from the dead; as Abraham saw the God able to restore his lost hopes; as Paul and Silas rejoiced in the God who could unlock prison doors; and as John envisioned a limitless new world of freedom in the Great Revelation; so the young prophet Isaiah finally prayed past the discouraging circumstances of his times in the kingdom and caught a vision of the eternal God who was greater than all the problems and obstacles confronting that kingdom. The prophet's vision of God was multifold.

The prophet saw the sovereign God ruling. "I saw the Lord sitting on a throne." The earthly throne of Judah was worse than vacant. King Uzziah was dead and no worthy successor was in prospect. The kingdom was without a trustworthy ruler. No one could predict the future. All appeared utterly hopeless and the people in the kingdom of Judah were helpless. Defeat and destruction seemed to be inevitable.

How often this situation has recurred in history, and how often it has recurred in the life and experiences of the church and individual Christians. Just when the worst has come and it seems that there is no way of escape, that all is lost, then someone prays the desperate prayer of faith, as Isaiah prayed, and God in His eternal omnipotent rulership suddenly appears and changes the entire outlook.

Selfish ambitious men have arisen at periods of human history to wrest the world from God's hands and rule it. Alexander the Great marched across the stage of time with his armies of conquest. But when, in A.D. 323, this would-be world ruler lay dying in a drunken stupor in the ancient city of Babylon, with his empire soon to deteriorate and disappear, God was still securely on His throne in heaven controlling the on-moving universe, and directing the course of human history. In his day, Napoleon Bonaparte marched his armies forth to the conquest of the world, in defiance of the rulership of God. However, when this would-be world ruler sat pining away in his tiny island prison on St. Helena, and his name was forgotten by men, God, the eternal King, remained serenely seated on the throne of glory.

In the twentieth century Mussolini in his turn arose and threatened to reestablish the ancient Roman Empire and extend his dominion over the world. But when his worst was done and he finally hung by his toes, while the soldiers who had once marched under his command now marched by and in disdain spat on his dead body, God remained undisturbed on His universal and eternal throne. Likewise, Hitler went forth to the conquest of earth's millions, defiant of God and man. But when Hitler's day was done and men had forgotten his glory, God's power and glory remained unimpaired. Japanese nationalistic Shinto arose and asserted its violent efforts for world conquest and dominance. There were the dark days of Pearl Harbor, Corredigor, the Death March, Hiroshima and Nagasaki, and then the defeat of Japan and the Emperor's renunciation of his divinity—and God was still there.

In succession, Joseph Stalin stepped forth to dethrone God by his atheistic communism, and again, as before, the world stood in trembling and fear lest his threat be made good. But ere long, vast multitudes marched by Stalin's coffin and viewed for the last time the remains of the man who defied God. Then, as reaction set in against Stalin's Communist Party leadership, his successors renounced him, removed his statue from the Kremlin and degraded his name to the level of criminal. Khrushchev had his day of defiance of God and threat of atheistic Communist world dominance, and then he suddenly faded into oblivion. Mao Tse-tung, with his threat of world dominance had his day and then passed from the stage of action in disrepute by his own followers.

God sits on the throne of the universe and laughs at the folly of men and devils who would attempt to dethrone Him. "Thy throne, O God, is forever and ever" (Heb. 1:8).

Likewise, in man's life today, when domestic failures, financial collapse, failing health, moral and spiritual defeat, loss of friends or loved ones, disappointments, or disillusionments—when any of these or one of a thousand other adverse conditions would threaten to wreck our lives, let us remember that God still occupies the throne of the universe. If having seen our problems, we too can pray and look beyond them to see "the Lord sitting on a throne," then we are assured of the transforming effect of that vision in our lives.

The prophet saw God in His exaltation: "I saw the Lord sitting on a throne, lofty and exalted." Men may stoop to conquer. Questionable political finagling may be indulged in to gain desired ends. Political wire-pulling and immoral criminal bribery may be employed, sometimes even within the body ecclesiastic, but God never gains His ends by immoral means. The ideal of a God exalted in holiness, honor, justice, and righteousness is the greatest incentive to holy living ever afforded mankind. We shall have spiritual and moral renewal in our day when we have a new vision of the exalted character of divinity—a vision that will make clear the distinction between a holy God and sinful mankind.

The prophet beheld God in His authority and power. "I saw . . . the Lord of hosts." This expression, "Lord of hosts," is a military term. In her demoralized and dejected condition, with militaristic nations threatening her very existence, what greater need could Judah have had than that of an efficient divine military leader who could assure her of certain victory? In all the battles of the ages, and in the lives of individuals, when men have recognized the leadership of the Lord and obeyed His commands, He has led forth to victory. To His disciples, just before His ascension, Jesus said: "All authority has been given to Me in heaven and on earth. Go therefore and make disciples of all nations . . . and lo, I am with you always, even to the end of the age" (Matt. 28:18b-20b). Our assurance of His presence and power rests in our obedience to His commands.

The prophet's vision included the thrice holy Triune God: "And one called out to another and said, 'Holy, Holy, Holy, is the Lord of hosts' " (Isa. 6:3a). In direct proportion to our loss of the concept of God's holiness do we lose our concept of the sinfulness of sin. Sin can only be known aright as it is seen against the backdrop of the holiness of God. Sin and holiness are antithetical. To lose the keen sense of the significance of one is to lose the true significance of the other. We shall not experience a deep conviction for sin with a consequent abhorrence of sinfulness in this or any other day until we have had a revelation of the holiness of God.

The prophet envisioned God's glory. The celestial beings exclaimed, "the whole earth is full of His glory" (Isa. 6:3b). Only a moment before, weighed down with the crushing burden of his apostate people, and overshadowed by the dark cloud of divine disfavor, Isaiah had beheld a world filled with gloom. But now that he has caught a vision of God in true perspective, he beholds a world filled with divine glory. At first he had viewed it from man's perspective, and it was dark and foreboding indeed; but now having gotten his prayers through to God, he beholds the world from God's perspective, and it is all glorious.

The seventy-third division of the Psalms represents the Psalmist as viewing the world from the human perspective, until he all but decided to capitulate to the way of sinful men, believing the best was to be found there. In the seventeenth verse is found the key to his salvation: "Until I came into the sanctuary of God; then I perceived their end" (Ps. 73:17). Here his perspective is changed as he enters the sanctuary of God, prays, and gets the divine perspective. The motto, "Prayer Changes Things," is not so much true as is the statement that prayer changes man's view of situations. Thus, the prophet's altered perspective transformed "gloom" into "glory." Likewise our hope of revival lies in an exchange of our human perspective for the divine perspective. Gloom can never bring revival. Divine glory can never fail to revive hopes and produce spiritual revival.

The prophet also envisioned God's holy wrath: "And the foundations of the thresholds trembled at the voice of Him who called out, while the temple was filling with smoke" (Isa. 6:4). Smoke, as the term is used in the Scriptures, has usually symbolized divine wrath. Nor can sin ever appear in the presence of a holy and righteous God without stirring His just wrath. Sin is ever highly inflammable in the presence of the holy fire of God. The author of the letter to the Hebrews declares, "Our God is a consuming fire" (Heb.

12:29). The voice of God shakes the movable, and the smoke of His divine wrath evidences consumed sin when it is revealed by the fiery brightness of His holiness. God is by His very holy nature ever angry with sin, and it is this divine wrath against sin that produces deep conviction in the heart of the sinner.

The Prophet's Vision Reflected the Spiritual and Moral Undoneness of His Own Condition in Relation to His Fellow Citizens

"Then [note the adverb of time] I said, 'Woe is me, for I am ruined! Because I am a man of unclean lips, and I live among a people of unclean lips; for my eyes have seen the King, the Lord of hosts' " (Isa. 6:5).

This threefold aspect of the prophet's vision reveals the petitioner's relationship to God. Now that the clouds of divine wrath have cleared away and God is unveiled in all His glorious holiness before the gaze of the waiting prophet, he suddenly realizes his own unworthiness to stand in God's presence. For the first time (apparently) in his life, Isaiah realizes that his personal relationship with God is not right. He cries out: "Woe is me, for I am ruined [lost]" (Isa. 6:5a). If his sudden and awful realization were expressed in our modern machine age, perchance it would read, "Woe is me! for I am out of gear." The real problem confronting the prophet in the midst of his personal and national circumstances was the fact that there was a vast gulf between man's desperate condition and the all-sufficiency of God to meet that need. There was no connection between the exhaustless power of the "divine dynamo" and the dire need of His people on earth. Sin had short-circuited the divine power. The lights were out in the kingdom and men were helplessly groping their way in the fearful inky blackness of a sin-benighted world. "I am lost!" was the cry of this spiritually-awakened soul.

How utterly lost, hopeless, and helpless, a person thus awakened by the celestial vision suddenly realizes himself to be. It was under such circumstances that the spiritually-awakened Psalmist cried out: "I am a stranger with Thee

. . . Turn Thy gaze away from me that I may smile again, before I depart and am no more" (Ps. 39:12, 13). And it was under similar circumstances that the spiritually arrested and awakened persecutor of the Christians, Saul of Tarsus, to whom the light and glory of God's effulgence appeared on the Damascus road, "trembling and astonished said, Lord, what wilt thou have me do?" (Acts 9:6, KJV).

During one of the earliest revivals conducted by the writer, an unusual experience of this nature came to light. Attending and supporting this God-favored meeting in a rural community was a highly-respected couple who were members of a church in a nearby town. At about midway in the series of meetings, this farmer's wife ceased to attend the services. Presently, inquiry was made, and the husband gave the information that his wife was in a very seriously disturbed state of mind, and that for several days she had secluded herself in her room and had refused to eat and could not sleep. Frankly, he was worried about her condition.

That evening in the church special prayer was offered in her behalf. Shortly after the opening of the service, this lady entered the church and requested permission to speak. With a radiant countenance she related her experience of having joined the church at the age of seventeen years, and then faithfully served in the church during all the subsequent years of her life. She had judged herself to be a true Christian; however, during this revival series she had suddenly awakened to the realization that she had never experienced a vital saving relationship with God. This discovery had nearly driven her reason from its throne, until that very evening at the same time prayer was offered for her in the church she had experienced a glorious revelation of the redeeming Christ with the accompanying unspeakable peace that His presence brings. Like the prophet Isaiah, she had a vision of the ineffable glory of God, and then in the light of that glory discovered herself spiritually undone, until a vital saving relationship was established with God through Christ.

Essential to spiritual renewal in this, or any generation, is a revelation of the holiness of God with the resultant discovery of man's spiritual lostness. Until man discovers himself spiritually undone, he will not acknowledge his need of God, nor will he seriously seek after the Lord.

Again, this aspect of the prophet's vision revealed the petitioner in relation to himself. A personal consciousness of sin before God elicits from the prophet the frank and honest confession: "I am a man of unclean lips." Like the penitent King David, when suddenly awakened by the prophet Nathan's parable, who cried out, "I know my transgressions," so Isaiah now awakened and, illumined by the revelation of God to his heart, cries out, "I am a man of unclean lips." He sees himself as he is in reality, mirrored in the divine effulgence, and is made to abhor his defiled condition. Like the leper of old, as he approached the inhabited village, the prophet cried out, "Unclean, unclean," "I am a man of unclean lips!" His confession was personal and it was specific. "I am a man of *unclean lips.*" This kind of confession will produce a divine response, and the prophet's experience was no exception to this rule.

God's illumination and revelation of the exceeding sinfulness of the human heart may be likened to the functions of an X-ray technician in relation to human disease, as contrasted with the work of a photographer. It is the photographer's purpose to present the most pleasing likeness possible of the subject. He spares no pains in his efforts to present his subject in the most advantageous light possible, even to the point of sheer flattery. Such is not the purpose of the X-ray technician. Rather, completely disregarding externalities, he focuses the penetrating rays of his X-ray on the internal malady, develops the picture and presents it to the physician or surgeon as a directive for the skilled practitioner's procedure in remedying the malady. When this picture of the cancerous internal condition is developed, it is not the sort of likeness that one would wish to frame and display in his living room for the admiration of his friends. That would be the function of the photographer and not the X-ray technician. God is a spiritual X-ray technician and not a spiritual photographer. "Man looks at the outward appearance, but the Lord looks at the heart" (1 Sam. 16:7b).

It seems that the prophet Jeremiah was such a spiritual X-ray technician in quest of the moral malady that was destroying the spiritual vitality of his people when he uttered those words: "The heart is more deceitful than all else and is desperately sick: who can understand it?" (Jer. 17:9). And then speaking for God, the prophet continues: "I the Lord search the heart, I test the mind, even to give to each man according to his ways, according to the results of his deeds" (Jer. 17:10).

The writer once had the following experience, which was both amusing and pathetic. He had parked his car near a large African market on a very clear, cloudless day, and was returning from a nearby store after completing a business transaction. Several small, perfectly nude, African children were dancing near the car, while curiously observing their moving images as reflected in the side of the car. Presently a very old, wrinkled, bent, white-haired African woman made her appearance, slowly shuffling her bare feet along the dusty path. For a moment she stood curiously watching the children, and then turning about she suddenly stood face to face with herself clearly mirrored in the side of the well-polished black car. For a moment she shaded her fading vision with her hand, then straightening her poor old bent form in realization that at last she had seen herself, she threw up both hands and exclaimed, "Great God, is that what I look like?" Upon this she whirled about and ran down the dusty path as fast as her feet would carry her. Likely, she had never seen herself in a mirror before. One glimpse of her reflected appearance was sufficient to cause her to flee in horrifying fear.

So it is with the unclean heart revealed for the first time in the clear light of God's manifest presence. The convicted sinner must either cry for mercy or flee from the presence of God. "I am a man of unclean lips," the prophet confessed.

Finally, the prophet saw himself in relation to his social environment: "I live among a people of unclean lips."

Paul said, "not one of us lives for himself, and not one dies for himself" (Rom. 14:7). It was the first murderer who said to God, "Am I my brother's keeper?" (Gen. 4:9). While man is an individual, and is morally responsible for all his decisions and acts as an individual, at the same time, he is a social being who bears responsibility for the condition and conduct of his fellows. There is a certain sense in which he is responsible for their condition and conduct, as well as his own. Isaiah, here, seems to be saying, "I have not been personally what I should have been, else the kingdom of Judah would not be in the condition in which it is now. Because I have not been what I should have been in my relationship to God, I have allowed myself to become partaker of the sins of my fellows." "I am a man of unclean lips, and I live among a people of unclean lips." Long association with evil without protest will eventually accustom a person to his evil environment, and in time wear down his resistance to that evil. Such was Lot's experience in wicked Sodom, and such seems to have been the prophet Isaiah's experience. While living among wicked men, one needs to take care to retain one's spiritual and moral identity.

Then there is another sense in which the prophet was responsible for the evils of the kingdom. He was God's appointed messenger to Judah. As such, he vicariously shared their guilt. It was in this respect that Isaiah says of the Messiah, "The Lord has caused the iniquity of us all to fall on Him" (Isa. 53:6b). And it is with this in mind that Paul says of Christ, "He made Him who knew no sin to be sin on our behalf" (2 Cor. 5:21). We cannot innocently dwell in the midst of sin without presenting the condition to God in prayer for His divine remedy.

The Prophet's Vision Reflects the Divine Provision of Atonement for Sin

No sooner had the waiting prophet made his confession of sin than the divine response was forthcoming: "Then one of the seraphim flew to me, with a burning coal in his hand which he had taken with tongs from the altar. And he touched my mouth with it and said, 'Behold, this has touched your lips; and your iniquity is taken away, and your sin is forgiven.' " Again the response of God to the prophet's prayer of confession is several-fold.

First, the restored penitent's remedy was immediate. Its immediacy is suggested by two factors. First, the adverb of time used by the inspired writer, "then," indicates that as soon as the confession was complete God's remedy was forthcoming.

Second, the words, "Then one of the seraphim flew to me," suggest that the remedy was transported by the speed of a winged celestial messenger. Malachi's words concerning the Messiah are applicable at this juncture: "The Lord, whom ye seek will *suddenly* come to His temple" (Mal. 3:1). Again, the author of the letter to the Hebrews speaks confidently of God's response to man's faith: "Therefore, do not throw away your confidence, which has a great reward. For you have need of endurance, so that when you have done the will of God, you may receive what was promised. For yet in a very little while He who is coming will come, and will not delay" (Heb. 10:35-37). Paul adds his testimony to the faithfulness of God in reponse to man's confessed need in the Thessalonian letter thus: "Faithful is He who calls you, and He also will bring it to pass" (1 Thess. 5:24). Finally, of the great historic Pentecostal occasion we read: "When the day of Pentecost had come ... *suddenly* there came from heaven a noise like a violent, rushing wind, and it filled the whole house where they were sitting. And there appeared to them tongues as of fire distributing themselves, and they rested on each one of them. And they were all filled with the Holy Spirit" (Acts 2:1-4a).

When man's part is done in meeting the divine conditions of salvation, he need not fear that God will fail in His part of the covenant. Peter declares, "The Lord is not slow about His promise" (2 Pet. 3:9).

This divine provision was both living and life-giving. This fact is suggested by the notation concerning the seraphim: "with a burning coal in his hand" or "a *live* coal" (KJV). It was not a burned out, dead ember that he brought to the prophet, a formal symbolism of religion, but a living, burning, glowing coal of fire that required handling with metal tongs. As a living coal, it provided spiritual life for the soul of the penitent prophet. As a burning coal, it purged the death-dealing sin of his soul. Elsewhere, Isaiah represents God as saying: "I will also turn My hand against you and will smelt away your dross as with lye, and will remove all your alloy" (Isa. 1:25). And Malachi, speaking for God, says: "And He will sit as a smelter and purifier of silver, and He will purify the sons of Levi and refine them like gold and silver, so that they may present to the Lord offerings in righteousness" (Mal. 3:3). John the Baptist declared to his generation. "As for me, I baptize you in water for repentance; but ... He Himself will baptize you with the Holy Spirit

and fire . . . and He will thoroughly clean His threshing floor
. . . but He will burn up the chaff with unquenchable fire''
(Matt. 3:11, 12). Again, we have the declaration of the author
of the letter to the Hebrews: ''Our God is a consuming fire''
(Heb. 12:29).

*The animating and purifying coal of fire was taken from
the altar of sacrifice:* ''with a burning coal in his hand which
he had taken from the altar with tongs.'' As all the ancient
animal sacrifices typified or foreshadowed the ultimately-
real sacrifice that God was to make of His Son Jesus Christ
for the sins of the world, so this altar from which the
seraphim took the live coal foreshadowed and thus signified
Calvary's altar-cross on which Jesus Christ was to offer His
life in atonement for the sins of the world. In the determi-
nant council of divinity, Christ's atonement had been as really made from the time of man's Fall as it was when finally
consummated in His words on Calvary: ''It is finished.'' And
thus the divine provision for the sin of the prophet, Isaiah,
as for all sin in all ages, was the sacrifice of Christ as symbolized by the ''burning coal . . . from the altar.''

*The divine provision was efficacious for the penitent's
release from his sin:* ''He touched my mouth with it and said,
'Behold this has touched your lips; and your iniquity is taken
away, and your sin is forgiven.' '' It is significant that this
divine provision, the living coal, was applied at the very point
of the prophet's recognition of his need and his consequent
confession. He had confessed, ''I am a man of unclean lips,''
and the celestial messenger immediately applied the living
coal to his mouth and said, ''Behold, this has touched your
lips; and your iniquity is taken away, and your sin is forgiven.'' God always forgives and cleanses such sin as is confessed. He does not forgive or cleanse unconfessed sin. John
declares: ''If we confess our sins, He is faithful and righteous
to forgive us our sins and to cleanse us from all unrighteousness'' (1 John 1:9). But said the Psalmist: ''If I regard
wickedness in my heart, the Lord will not hear'' (Ps. 66:18).

*Finally, the heavenly messenger assures the prophet of
cancelled sin:* ''Your iniquity is taken away.'' How like the
promise of God is this that assures us that ''As far as the
east is from the west, so far has He removed our transgressions from us'' (Ps. 103:12). Nor is the prophet to be left with

a polluted nature; rather, the divine remedy is applied to the *sinful nature* of his soul. Says the messenger of salvation: "your iniquity is taken away." With Toplady, the penitent soul can sing, "Be of sin the double cure, save from wrath and make me pure." This man found in the divine atoning provision what Christ was to provide when, "that He might sanctify the people through His own blood, [He] suffered outside the gate" (Heb. 13:12).

The Prophet's Vision
Reflects His Divine Call to Service

"Then I heard the voice of the Lord, saying, 'Whom shall I send, and who will go for us?' Then I said, 'Here am I. Send me!' "

Now that redemption has become a gracious reality in the prophet's experience, he is ready for service. The divine call comes clear and the redeemed prophet's reply is immediate. Redemptive revival in the lives of God's people must ever precede evangelism. When the church has a new vision of redeeming divine reality, the world will learn of it in aggressive evangelism. The church will then be quick to say, "Here am I, send me," when she has first said, "Woe is me! for I am ruined," and is then touched with the living coal from God's altar.

CHAPTER VII

The Meaning of the Cross of Christ

"There they crucified Him" (Luke 23:33).

Luke 23:13-37 records the culmination of Christ's condemnation unto death on the Cross of Calvary. The crucifixion of Jesus Christ represents one of the most significant events of all human history. Christ's Cross divides history into two related and yet distinct eras. It separates the era of bondage from the era of liberty, the era of darkness and shadows from the era of light and new hope, and the era of promise from the era of fulfillment. Christ's Cross represents the meeting place of Law and Grace, of bondage and freedom, of condemnation and justification, of wrath and mercy, of despair and hope, of death and life. The first yields to the second in each instance at the Cross. Paul declared that "the law has become our tutor [better, a truant officer or a child guardian] to lead us to Christ, that we may be justified by faith" (Gal. 3:24). God's Law apprehended, arrested, and judged man a sinner worthy of condemnation and then delivered him to Christ, the divine Judge, fettered and sentenced to everlasting death by execution. Christ compassionately and mercifully looked upon man's hopeless and pitiable plight, stepped down from His judgment seat, and voluntarily offered Himself to the Father in death upon Calvary's Cross as an acceptable substitute for condemned man. He did this to satisfy the justice of divine wrath against humanity's sin and to reconcile God to man.

No member of *homo sapiens* ever experienced reconciliation to God independent of the Cross. Before that historic event men were saved by anticipation of Christ's Cross, by faith in the coming Messiah, through the types and shadows that pointed to the Cross—"a shadow of good things to come" (Heb. 10:1; cf. Col. 2:17). Since the event of the Cross, men have been saved by reflective faith—by looking back to the Cross. Christ's Cross is the central focus of human history. Thus the Cross of Jesus Christ stands as the inextricable symbol of the Christian faith.

The words recorded by Luke, *"There they crucified Him,"* direct the reader's attention to four considerations of Christ's Cross, namely: the *place* of the Cross; the *people* responsible for the Cross; the *purposeful meaning* of the Cross; and the *person* of the Cross. Here we shall first consider the *place of the Cross in redemption.*

The Place of Christ's Cross

The Cross represents a place in time and space.

The adverb of place, *there,* suggests more than a grammatical meaning. It points to a time and place in history where a Divine-human act and event of immeasurable significance took place. The crucifixion account in the gospels is no myth cunningly devised in the vivid imagination of some religious leader who sought to procure the emotional responses of men in obedient faith to a new religious authority. Nor can the claim be substantiated that it is a disguised borrowing from some Greek or Roman religious mythology of the first Christian century. The gospel records present an authentic account of the crucifixion of a man whose name was Jesus Christ, who claimed identity with God, on a hillock outside the city walls of Jerusalem, which place bore the name of Calvary of Golgotha, and which was the designated location of the execution of common criminals. This event took place during the Judean governorship of Pontius Pilate in the approximate year of A.D. 29 or 30.

The Cross represents a place of utter rejection.

The author of the letter to the Hebrews says "that he [Jesus] might sanctify the people through His own blood, suffered outside the gate" (Heb. 13:12), or outside the gates and walls of the sacred city of Jerusalem. As the "sin offering" of the ancient Israelites was required to be burned outside the camp of Israel, so Christ, in fulfillment of that type, was made the "sin offering" for all men when He was sacrificed outside the city walls. He was utterly rejected as the promised Messiah by the Jews. How pertinent are the words of John: "He came to His own [His own domain, or the world of His own creation (cf. John 1:3)]; and those who were His own [His own people] did not receive Him" (John 1:11). His rejection was aggravated by the fact that He was made the associate of the meanest of criminals, in the experience of His crucifixion. Isaiah prophetically declared that He "was numbered with the transgressors," the import of which appears to be that His name was entered on the death warrant with those who were worthy of such an ignominious execution as crucifixion.

Golgotha signifies, in the crucifixion experience of Jesus Christ, His utter rejection—religious, social, and national—by the race of which He was humanly born and by the people whom He came to save.

The Cross represents a place of unspeakable horror

Golgotha, or Calvary, means the place of a skull. It may have been so named because of the numerous unburied skulls of previously executed criminals which were strewn about over the area. Tradition has it that crucified criminals were not infrequently left on their crosses to be stripped of their flesh by vultures, in which case their skeletons remained unburied.

Other accounts indicate, however, that Calvary got its name from the physical resemblance of the hillock to a human skull, with the excavated tombs representing the facial cavities. Mounted on the center cross, between the two coarsely cursing thieves who agonized in the tortures of death atop the skull-hill, the Saviour was confronted with man's last and greatest enemy—*death.*

The Cross represents a place of frightening loneliness

Indeed, the two thieves were there. The soldiers were there. The curious multitudes were milling about. Mary and a few disciples lingered sympathetically but fearfully in the nearby shadows. As the shades of death closed about Him, and human strength waned, all the world and humanity were shut out from the Saviour's consciousness. Finally, the light of the sun went out and inky blackness enshrouded the hill, while the Saviour's extreme self-consciousness severed His last conscious contact with the world outside of Himself.

For the instant of death the Father's face was lost from view. In this moment of utter aloneness, which is the most awful experience known to man, those words were wrung from the lips of the suffering Saviour, "My God, My God, why hast Thou forsaken Me?" (Mark 15:34). Of this fourth word from the Cross, G. Campbell Morgan has said that we have here the greatest explanation of the atonement ever given to man, and that beyond this explanation, we dare not go. The poet caught the meaning of Christ's frightful existential encounter there on the Cross and penned those lines: "It was alone the Saviour died, on dark Gethsemane." The experience of Jesus Christ on the Cross in this darkest of eternity's moments represents the deepest meaning of the unauthentic man and His consequent nullity. It represents the moment when sinful man, without the supporting presence of God, encounters death utterly alone. It speaks eloquently, but awfully, of what it means for a soul to be lost. Here, more than at any other time, Christ takes the lost sinner's place. Such an experience is indeed the experience of the atheist, a person who has been declared to be "a man without invisible support." How different is the Psalmist's encounter with death, supported as he was by God's presence: "Even though I walk through the valley of the shadow of death, I fear no evil; for Thou art with me; Thy rod and Thy staff, they comfort Me" (Ps. 23:4).

Thus, Christ's Cross holds the central place in human history and in human experience; both as a judgment on sin and a provision of salvation from sin, and as the meaningful integrating factor and force in the universe. There is a very real sense in which our universe is both Christocentric and Cross-centered. The Cross of Christ gives meaning to existence in the universe.

The People Responsible for Christ's Death on the Cross

"There *they* crucified Him" (Luke 23:33).

The pronoun "they" suggests a plural responsibility for Christ's crucifixion. The record reveals that responsibility.

The Jewish religionists of Christ's day were responsible for the Cross. Foremost among those responsible for Christ's execution by crucifixion were the most religious people of His day. Peter boldly, directly, and explicitly charged the Jewish rulers with the crucifixion of Jesus Christ (Acts 2:23, 36; 4:10). The gospel narrators represent the Jewish rulers as having planned and plotted Christ's crucifixion in the most painstaking and unjust manner. They induced one of His disciples, Judas, to betray Him for a paltry monetary reward. They deceptively apprehended, illegally tried, and unjustly condemned Christ in their ecclesiastical court before dawn on Friday. They produced false testimony through bribery against Him. They employed political leverage against Pilate to secure the death sentence of Christ in the governor's court. They subtly insinuated Pilate's political insecurity with Rome, should he fail to yield to their insistent demands for Christ's crucifixion: "If you release this Man, you are no friend of Caesar" (John 19:12), they threatened.

Even when Pilate had weighed the evidence and rendered the honest, impartial, and official decision of his judgeship, to the effect that he had found "no fault in Him," the Jewish rulers cast justice to the wind and insistently pressed their demands for Christ's death.

Moved by a demonically-inspired jealous hatred of the Christ for the power and popularity which He enjoyed with the multitudes, and deeply stung by the matchless wit and wisdom of His utterances and His cutting rebukes of their pious hypocrisy, these anger-blinded Jewish rulers pushed their claims for Pilate's sentence of death against the innocent Christ. The transparency of their hypocrisy was evident to the governor, for this shrewd Roman official knew that "because of envy they had delivered Him up."

And so has insincere, selfishly-motivated, legally-dead, or blindly-fanatical religious leadership repeatedly crucified afresh on the Cross of selfish interests, the Christ of God. Thus, false religion has made its contribution to the crucifixion of Jesus Christ. It bears a large responsibility for His Cross!

The political representatives of Christ's day and country were responsible for the Cross. Pilate possessed the authority to decide the execution or acquittal of Jesus Christ. He was in no way ignorant of the nature and merit of the case before him. His own examination of the man on trial, in the light of all evidence presented, had thoroughly convinced him of the innocence of Jesus Christ. He had found Him a just man with no cause of death in Him. His conviction and formal judicial pronouncement were firmly grounded.

Added to the foregoing was the solemn warning of Pilate's wife. Her warning in a dream seems to have been intended as a protective overshadowing of the decision of the lower court of Pilate by God's higher universal court of final appeal. "Have nothing to do with that righteous Man" Pilate's wife wrote to him in a hurried note, "for last night I suffered greatly in a dream because of Him" (Matt. 27:19). Political pressure won the day over reasoned justice and the court of the Judean judge, and the innocent victim was sacrificed to the irrational demands of the envy-mad Jewish mob.

The military also bore its responsibility for Christ's Cross. With no interest whatsoever in the justice or injustice of the trial and sentence of Jesus Christ, the Roman soldiers, at Pilate's command, marched Jesus away in a most ruthless manner to the hill of horrors. There, in a totally disinterested and merciless manner, they nailed His hands and His feet to the Cross and comfortably positioned themselves to watch Him die suspended between two wretched thieves who were crucified with Him.

Some forms of military policing and even defensive warfare, if such can be satisfactorily defined, appear to be inescapable necessities in the present world order. It was this consideration, in part at least, that led Luther to his view of the dual necessity of Law and Grace and his concept of the "two kingdoms," the kingdom of Law and the kingdom of Grace, in sinful man's present state.

Notwithstanding the foregoing apparent inescapable conclusion concerning the present order, it is nevertheless an observable fact that military life and activity tend to destroy the higher idealism of the participants and to reduce them to morally irresponsible robots. This tendency is well exemplified in an article, written by a veteran soldier, bearing the title "Murder Is My Business," which appeared in a popular magazine at the close of the Second World War. When man's reverence for the sacredness of life has been brainwashed or propagandized out of him, and he has been reduced to an instrument for the destruction of life, he has become something less than human. And so with General Sherman we are compelled to admit that "war is hell!" The

Roman military crucified Christ, and the military is ever in danger of destroying the best that is in humanity.

The economic interest bore its share of responsibility for the Cross. It may appear to be only by inference that the soldiers, at the foot of Christ's Cross gambling for His garments, can be identified with the commercial interests of their day. Their conduct, however, can hardly be considered less than commercial. Again, Judas, one of Christ's own disciples, had hoped to profit economically and commercially by selling His Master at the common market price of a slave. Disillusioned of his hopes that Christ would establish an earthly kingdom wherein he might continue his office and embezzlement, as he had done as treasurer of the apostolic company, Judas finally decided on another plan. Outside Jerusalem was a parcel of land containing a vein of clay especially valuable for fine pottery making. If he could obtain enough money from the betrayal-sale of Christ to procure the purchase of this plot, he could establish himself in the pottery business and thus obtain wealth and security that would compensate for his now-blasted hopes of ill-gotten gain through embezzlement in the treasureship of Christ's promised future kingdom. After all, would not Christ escape from His would-be captors after the bargain was made with the Sanhedrin and the betrayal money was safely in Judas' bag, as He always had escaped from His enemies before? Such was the false hope of the disciple who commercialized on his Master. When finally Judas realized that Christ was condemned to die on the Cross, his mind could not bear the strain of the personal responsibility that rested upon him, and thus in remorseful despair, he took his own life on the very parcel of land from which he had sought material gain. That thirsty clay that promised to yield him ill-gotten profit received his life blood into its pores. Thus Judas and the gambling soldiers represent those who would make gain at the expense of Christ's sufferings and death on the Cross. Is it less a travesty on the Cross of Christianity when a contemporary church invites businessmen to become members at an Easter Sunday service on condition of their promise to pay a stipulated annual amount into the church's treasury, but without reference to a personal commitment to Christ? Is the commercialized blind-barter that characterizes so much of the contemporary spirit of Christmas a less reprehensible act of commercializing the Cross?

The ignorant populace was involved in the responsibility for the Cross. His Cross stood by a prominent thoroughfare. Above it on a plaque was written the charge that procured His condemnation—"This is Jesus, the king of the Jews." That all might know and understand, the charge was written in the three great languages of the Empire—Hebrew, the language of religion; Greek, the language of culture; and Latin, the language of law and government. Thus beholding and reading, the milling masses taunted, "He saved others; he cannot save Himself." And so he was judged by the insensible and irrational populace to be an imposter—a professed King without a kingdom, a would-be ruler without authority to command an army that could save Him from His own enemies. And so the indifferent populace, too, helped to nail Christ to the Cross, just as the ignorant and thoughtless indifference of the masses still drive the nails into the hands and feet of the Christ on the Cross.

There is a collective responsibility involving the whole human race's implication in the dastardly deed of the Cross. The Apostle declared that "Christ died for our sins, according to the scriptures." The beloved disciple John announced that "God so loved the world, that He gave His only begotten Son, that whoever believes in Him should not perish, but have eternal life" (John 3:16). Thus, all stand guilty and condemned for their part in the tragedy of the Cross, until they repent and are saved by the God-man who conquered the Cross.

Finally, God Himself assumed His responsibility for Christ's Cross. This almost has the ring of blasphemy until we realize that it was God, in Christ, reconciling the world unto Himself there on the Cross. This fact Paul boldly declared to the Corinthian Church (2 Cor. 5:19). It was indeed the blood of God Himself, in the person of His Son, the God-Man, that was shed on the Cross. It was by "the determinate counsel and foreknowledge of God "that Christ was taken by wicked hands and slain (Acts 2:23, KJV). But the will of the Father was expressed in the will of the Son when Christ declared that it was for the very purpose of suffering on the Cross that He had come (John 10:18). Thus Christ declared that He had come to do the will of the Father, and that it was His purpose to voluntarily lay down His life for man's redemption. Consequently, we conclude that the whole universe of personal beings, devils, men, and God, were involved in the Cross of Christ. Man's wickedness made the Cross necessary; God's love made it possible; and Christ's salvation made it redemptive—a redemptive provision as universal as the salvation needs of lost humanity (John 3:16).

The Purpose and Person of the Cross in Redemption

"There they *crucified Him*" (Luke 23:33).

Unless the Cross of Christ can be shown to have had a justifying purpose, it may be judged as totally unworthy of the permissive will of a loving and just God. We believe that such a purpose is demonstrable.

The crucifixion of Jesus was purposefully planned.

The practice of execution by crucifixion was not employed by the Jews. It had been practiced by the Chinese, the Hindus, the Syrians, the Egyptians, the Persians, the Africans, the Greeks, and the Romans. The approved Jewish methods of execution were strangulation and stoning. Under the Roman rule, however, there was but one condition under which the Jews were permitted to execute the death penalty. Josephus informs us that if a Gentile ventured beyond the Court of the Gentiles into the Jews' sacred precincts of the temple, he could be slain on the spot, even without the necessity of a trial. Otherwise, the Sanhedrin could only recommend the death sentence, which could be executed by the Roman government only.

Two principal types of crosses were used for the purpose of crucifixion. First, there was the "X" cross. The feet of the "X" cross was planted in the earth or embedded in the rock, and then the victim's hands and feet were tied or nailed to the "X" bars.

The "T" cross seems to have been more commonly used for execution than was the "X" type. It was more likely a "T" cross on which Christ was crucified. Here, likewise, the hands and feet of the victim were tied or nailed to the crossbar and the upright beam respectively. A sort of saddle was also fastened to the upright beam which bore in part the weight of the victim's body. Across the top of the upright beam was a wooden plaque on which was written the crime of the condemned. On this cross the condemned man was usually left until he was judged to be dead. On occasion he lived from two to three days, while the merciless sun beamed its rays upon him, and the vultures sometimes tore away his flesh while the life was still in his body. If it became necessary to remove the bodies of the crucified from the crosses before the Sabbath to prevent the desecration of that Holy Day, as in the case of Christ, then the legs and the thighs of the yet-living crucified victims were broken with heavy hammers to prevent their escape after removal. This cruelty was spared the Christ, as the soldiers judged Him to be dead before removal from the Cross. The certainty of His death before removal also bore witness against a possible subsequent charge that Christ never really died, with the consequent charge that His professed resurrection was only a farce— that in fact He recovered and escaped.

The ignominy of the death to which Christ was subjected is further emphasized by the fact that only slaves who had committed the meanest crimes were crucified on crosses. Christ had been valued at the price of a slave by His own disciple, Judas, and He was subjected to the inglorious death of a slave instigated by the Jews, but executed by the Roman government at the persistent demands of the Jews. Thus He endured the most awful physical suffering, degradation, and disgrace, as a social outcast and common criminal.

The Person of the Cross is essential to the Christian faith.

The crucifixion occurred in a conspicuous place, on an eminence beside a thoroughfare, clearly marked with the crime for which the victim was crucified, that all might see.

The cross that bore the body of Jesus Christ was firmly planted in the earth beneath Him, which fact may suggest the incarnation of God's Son in the human flesh, and consequently His perfect humanity and His resultant kinship to all men on earth. The upright beam of Christ's Cross that projected into the open heavens may be understood to signify His perfect, infinite, divine nature. Here the two natures, the divine and the human, were represented as perfectly united in the God-Man. When thus viewed, Christ qualified to become the perfect and unique Mediator between God and man, since He adequately represented both divinity and humanity.

The outstretched arms of the crucified Christ on the vertical beams of the cross, terminating as they did in open space, seem to suggest the extended mercy of God, and the efficacy of Christ's atonement, to all men from all time through all time—mercy bestowed upon the penitent thief, and offered to the impenitent thief alike. Thus Christ was the "Lamb who has been slain" in the purposeful provision of God, that He might "take away the sin of the world" (Rev. 13:8; John 1:29).

The Person of the cross was God's Son and man's Saviour. "There they crucified *Him.*"

The *person* crucified on the *central cross* is of the utmost significance to the Christian faith for all time, as that person was the long-expected Messiah. His work of spiritual deliverance could only be accomplished by His victory through and over death. The person of the center cross was the unique God-Man—perfect God and perfect man. It was only by His perfect representation of the person of divinity and the person of humanity that Jesus Christ could make an adequate atonement for sin that would satisfy God and deliver man (Isa. 53:5-11).

The Christ of the center Cross was the Lord of Glory humiliated to the position of a wretched suffering slave. It was by dipping to the deepest depth of humanity's suffering in His crucifixion experience that Christ could qualify to become the perfect High Priest of all people.

The person of the center cross was the world's greatest example of righteousness. In His life He had taught righteousness or justice as the very essence of the Christian faith. In His death on the Cross He exemplified the principle He had taught by providing justification for man before God through His substitutionary self-sacrifice for the sins of all mankind.

The person of the center cross was the world's greatest teacher. The greatest lesson He ever taught was the lesson of love manifested for sinful humanity in His sufferings and death to provide redemption for all—the innocent suffering for the guilty.

In conclusion, the death of Christ on Calvary's Cross was more than the death of a martyr, or a righteous man for a worthy cause, or even a ransom for the sins of many. His death was a voluntary, vicarious (or substitutionary), and ultimately victorious death to provide salvation from sin, and reconciliation to God, for all who will repent and appropriate by faith the provisions of His death on the Cross (see John 10:10-18). The Cross of Christ means a suffering, but victorious Saviour who provided salvation for all.

The final purpose and power of the Cross of Jesus Christ have their highest expressions in Christ's own words, which were spoken in the context of the Cross: "And I, if I be lifted up from the earth [upon the Cross], will draw all men to Myself" (John 12:32). The exhibition and demonstration of God's redemptive love in His suffering Son on the Cross for fallen, sin-enslaved, helpless, and otherwise hopeless humanity, hold the greatest appeal for the sinner's return to the Father that the world has ever witnessed. The Cross stands in the midst of time and eternity as the focal point of all history. It represents God's love revealed at its highest. It is the mighty redemptive act of God toward which the awakened sinful soul is all but irresistibly drawn.

Chapter VIII

The Triumph of Christ's Resurrection Over Death

*"But now Christ has been raised from the dead,
the first fruits of those who are asleep"* (1 Cor. 15:20).

The Reality of the Resurrection of Jesus Christ

In the Gospel according to St. Luke 24:1-8 is found the clearest account of the resurrection of Jesus Christ anywhere recorded in the New Testament. In verses 5 and 6 of this record the angels are represented as having asked the highly-significant question: "Why do you seek the living One among the dead?" These messengers then continued: "He is not here, but He has risen."

If the crucifixion of Jesus Christ represents the greatest tragedy of human history, His resurrection represents the greatest victory and the most glorious event of eternity. If the crucifixion of the Son of God was earth's darkest hour, the morning of His resurrection was eternity's brightest moment. The resurrection of Jesus Christ is the greatest recorded miracle of the Bible and the greatest miracle of eternity. It is the abiding miracle of eternity, for He lives forever. It was promised by the prophets, accomplished by Christ Himself, proclaimed by the Apostolic Church as the central fact of the gospel, and it is the central theme of the New Testament. As it was the principal burden of the Apostolic witness, so it was the main object of unbelieving Jewish hatred and opposition. In his preface to the Acts of the Apostles, Luke declares that to the apostles Jesus "presented Himself alive, after His suffering, by many convincing proofs, appearing to them over a period of forty days, and speaking of the things concerning the kingdom of God" (Acts 1:3). What are the proofs of Christ's resurrection to which Luke alludes?

Primarily and foremost among the evidences of His resurrection is the very essential divine character of the

Christ. Peter grasped this principle when he proclaimed Christ's resurrection in his great sermon on the day of Pentecost thus: "God raised Him up again, putting an end to the agony of death, since it was impossible for Him to be held in its power" (Acts 2:24). The divinity of Christ was the guarantee of His resurrection from the dead. If He was God, He must be victorious over death. If he was not God, then there could be no resurrection. He was God. He arose! Said He, "I am the resurrection, and the life" (John 11:25).

A second attestation to Christ's resurrection was His own prediction concerning that glorious event. In Luke's record Jesus is represented as saying: "The Son of Man must suffer many things, and be rejected by the elders and chief priests and scribes, and be killed, and be raised up on the third day" (Luke 9:22). And again, in the Gospel according to John, Christ declares, concerning His death and resurrection, "For this reason the Father loves Me, because I lay down My life that I may take it again. No one has taken it away from Me, but I lay it down on My own initiative. I have authority to lay it down, and I have authority to take it up again" (John 10:17, 18). These predictions found their glorious fulfillment on the morning of Christ's resurrection from the dead.

A further attestation to Christ's resurrection from the dead was the fact of the empty tomb. How significant are the words of the young man arrayed in white garments who met the women at the tomb of Jesus: "Do not be amazed; you are looking for Jesus the Nazarene, who has been crucified. He has risen; He is not here; behold, here is the place where they laid Him" (Mark 16:6). Had the enemies of Jesus stolen away His body, they would have produced it later to silence the preaching of the resurrection. Had His own disciples stolen away the body of Jesus, they would not have died preaching what they knew to be a falsehood. Every precaution had been taken by the Roman government to prevent trickery or falsification, but in spite of official precautions, Divinely outwitted Roman authority and robbed it of its prize through the greatest miracle of eternity.

Again, the reality of Christ's resurrection was attested by an angel sent from God in heaven who consoled the distraught women with the words, "Do not be afraid; for I know that you are looking for Jesus who has been crucified. He is not here, for He has risen, just as He said. Come, see the place where He was lying" (Matt. 28:5, 6). As far as we know the function of the angels, they are but messengers of God. A greater and more important message than this borne to the sorrowing women at the tomb by the angel freshly commissioned of God, man has never received.

The unbelieving, pagan Roman guards themselves bore witness to Christ's resurrection from the dead. We hear these frightened political servants reporting the absence of Christ's body from the grave to the chief priests of the Jews. Immediately the Sanhedrin called a council before which the guards were summoned to testify. After due deliberation the council

> gave a large sum of money to the soldiers, and said, "You are to say, 'His disciples came by night and stole Him away while we were asleep.' And if this should come to the governor's ears, we will win him over and keep you out of trouble." And they took the money and did as they had been instructed (Matt. 28:12-15).

There is every evidences from this account that the Jews were convinced of the sincerity and validity of the testimony of these guards to the resurrection of Jesus Christ from the dead. Their bribes but emphasized the fact of their conviction of His resurrection.

Among the most telling evidences of the resurrection of Jesus Christ were His several post crucifixion-resurrection appearances. Luke summarizes these appearances thus: "He also presented Himself alive, after His suffering, by many convincing proofs, appearing to them over a period of forty days, and speaking of the things concerning the kingdom of God" (Acts 1:3). The Scripture narrators give us no less than eleven of these specific appearances. Those to whom He appeared are designated as Mary Magdalene, "the other women," two disciples on the way to Emmaus, Simon Peter, the astonished disciples in the absence of Thomas, the disciples with Thomas present, the seven disciples at the Sea of Galilee, above five hundred brethren on a mountain in Galilee, James, the Lord's brother, the disciples with the commission, and His last appearance to His disciples on Mt. Olivet just preceding His ascension. Thus these many personal witnesses to His living presence subsequent to His crucifixion, death and burial bear a powerful testimony to the validity of Christ's victory over death.

The Christian Pentecost was by no means the least attestation to Christ's resurrection from the dead. Said Jesus to His disciples before His crucifixion: "It is to your advantage that I go away; for if I do not go away, the Helper shall not come to you; but if I go, I will send Him to you" (John 16:7). In Luke's record in the Acts of the Apostles we read of the fulfillment of this prediction of Christ: "And when the day of Pentecost had come . . . they were all filled with the Holy Spirit" (Acts 2:1a, 4a). Christ's "going away," or ascension, was a specific requisite to the descent of the Holy Spirit. Without His resurrection from the dead, there could have been no ascension to the Father. The descent of the Holy Spirit on the day of Pentecost in fulfillment of Christ's promise is one of the most conclusive evidences anywhere afforded of Christ's resurrection from the dead.

The appearance of the ascended Christ to the dying martyr, Stephen, gave eloquent testimony to His resurrection from and victory over death. Christ's revelation to the mad persecutor, Saul, on the Damascus road forever convinced that fanatical Jew of the reality of Christ's resurrection from the dead. In fact, Benjamin Robinson of the University of Chicago states that it was this profound conviction, that Christ was alive from the dead, that completely altered the character and the conduct of the persecutor Saul and made out of him the great world evangelist, Paul.[1] "I am Jesus whom you are persecuting" was the reply of Christ to the startled query of Saul, "Who art Thou, Lord?" and Christ's reply forever settled and satisfied the mind of the great apostle concerning the Lordship of Jesus through the resurrection from the dead. In his lonely exile on Patmos John received "The Revelation of Jesus Christ" (Rev. 1:1a), the risen and living Lord, that settled whatever questions may have haunted his mind and inspired him to record that great-

---

[1]Benjamin W. Robinson, *The Life of Paul* (Chicago: University of Chicago Press, rev. 1928), pp. 54-58.

est of all revelations preserved for our edification as the last book of the New Testament.

Added to the "many proofs" of Christ's resurrection from the dead as recorded in sacred writ, are the evidences of the transforming power of the living Christ in the lives of countless millions of all nations throughout the past two thousand years of the Christian era. St. Augustine, Luther, Calvin, Wesley, Moody, and Graham, to mention only a few of the marvels of the transforming grace of the living Christ, stand as uncontestable witnesses to the fact that Christ arose from the dead and thus conquered sin, death and the grave. Millions today stand forth to testify that Christ lives and transforms them from creatures of darkness and despair to children of light and hope. And we, children of God through the redeeming grace of Christ, together lift our voices in the words of the hymn, "You ask me how I know He lives? He lives within my heart." There is no better supported event in the history of mankind than Christ's resurrection from the dead. Blackstone, one of the world's greatest legal authorities, has been reported as having said that the resurrection of Jesus Christ is the best established fact of history.[2]

The Nature of the Resurrection of Jesus Christ

"But now Christ has been raised from the dead, the first fruits of those who are asleep" (1 Cor. 15:20).

Upon mention of the resurrection of the dead the question arises in the minds of many as that question was anticipated by the Apostle Paul in his letter to the Corinthians. "But some one will say, 'How are the dead raised? And with what kind of body do they come?" (1 Cor. 15:35). Fortunately we are not left without a satisfactory answer to this perplexing problem. Both the gospel narrators and the apostle Paul give us guidance in our quest for the solution of the nature of the resurrection of the dead. Paul says that Christ is "the first fruits of those who are asleep." By this we understand Paul to mean that not only is the resurrection of Christ from the dead the assurance of the believer's resurrection, but as

---

[2]W. E. Blackstone, *Jesus Is Coming* (New York: Fleming H. Revell Company, 1932).

Christ was raised so shall the believer come forth from the dead. "For as in Adam all die, so also in Christ all shall be made alive" (1 Cor. 15:22).

The nature of Christ's resurrection was *identical.* The word *identical* is not intended to imply the reformation of the same chemical elements that composed the material body of Christ prior to His death; rather, the import of His identical resurrection is that it was "true to fact; not exaggerated." In other words, the physical form of the body of the Son of God as it was known to His disciples before His death came forth from the tomb in which He had been incarcerated, indwelt and animated by the same vital divine-human personality that informed that body before death. There were accusations that His disciples had stolen His body away, that in reality He had never actually died on the cross, but that He had swooned under the impact of His intense sufferings and then subsequent to removal from the cross He had been spirited away. As opposed to these groundless accusations the scripture record furnishes uncontestable evidence of His identical resurrection. The women came and "found the stone rolled away from the tomb, but when they entered, they did not find the body of the Lord Jesus" (Luke 24:2, 3). Mark takes special pains to note concerning the stone, that "it was extremely large" (Mark 16:4). It would seem that Mark grasped the unusual significance of the removal of this stone from the tomb of Christ. It is significant that when the soldiers had taken the body of Christ down from the cross and placed it in the tomb, they were careful to execute the official instructions in the most detailed manner. The stone placed against the opening of the tomb that held Christ's body was "sealed" by the official Roman stamp. Matthew records: "Pilate said to them, 'You have a guard; go, make it as secure as you know how. And they went and made the grave secure, and along with the guard, they set a seal on the stone" (Matt. 27:65, 66). It was a most serious offense to break this seal, other than by official Roman instruction or sanction. The Roman guards had no such permission. They would not have imperiled their lives by giving such permission to others. The removal of the stone was clearly an indication of intervention from an authority and a power that transcended official Rome—the miraculous power of God.

Again, we read of the deliberate manner in which Christ had removed and orderly arranged His funeral shroud before His departure from the tomb. John relates concerning his own approach to the empty tomb on Sunday morning: "and stooping and looking in, he saw the linen wrappings lying there"; and then says our narrator concerning the approach of Peter, "and [as he] entered the tomb; . . . he beheld the linen wrappings lying there, and the face-cloth, which had been on His head, not lying with the linen wrappings, but rolled up in a place by itself. Then entered in therefore the other disciple also, who had first come to the tomb, and he saw, and believed" (John 20:5-8). Nothing can be clearer than that the manner in which they found the grave clothes in the empty tomb of Christ was sufficient evidence to convince these disciples that Jesus Christ was no longer a victim of death. Thus, the removed stone, the orderly arranged grave clothes, the tomb devoid of the body of Christ, and the reappearances of Christ to His disciples bespeak for Christ His identical resurrection from death and the tomb.

The Resurrection of Jesus Christ was in Physical Form. Subsequent to His resurrection, Jesus Christ invited a doubting Thomas to thrust his hand into His spear-pierced side and his fingers into the nailprints of His hands. He sat at meat and ate with those disciples who had known Him before His death, and now recognized the identity of His physical form with the Master they had known before the crucifixion, thus giving evidence that it was He who had died on the Cross who now partook of food with them.

To say that the resurrected body of Jesus Christ was identical in physical form with that He bore before the crucifixion is not to say that there came forth from the grave of Christ, or that there will come forth from the graves of the righteous dead in the resurrection of the just, the identical elements that were placed in the grave. This would be easy enough as a divine miracle in certain instances where the body had either not yet suffered decomposition or where the identical elements had not been scattered afar. However, the burial of a child of God at sea where the elements of his body may be widely diffused through consumption by aquatic animal life, and even assimilated into other physical organisms, or the scattering and subsequent diffusion of the elements of the body following a cremation, present exceedingly perplexing problems to the theory of the restoration and resurrection of the identical elements. Furthermore, according to physical science the chemical elements in the body of a living person change physiologically many times during the course of a lifetime. Since all of those elements have at some time been informed in the individual's body, the question may be fairly asked, "Which of the elements in the several bodies one has had in a lifetime are to come forth in the resurrection?

Again, to take the view that the identical chemical elements reappear in the resurrection is to presuppose a fundamental dualism, a position which will not stand in the light of sound Biblical Christian idealism. Thus, we conclude that the resurrected body of Christ was *identical* in form with that body which He bore prior to His death. And since He is "the first fruits of those who are asleep," it is but logical to conclude that the bodies of the righteous dead will be identical in form with their earthly bodies, though not of material substance. Concerning the nature of the resurrected body, the Apostle Paul declares:

> But God gives it a body just as He wished, and to each of the seeds a body of its own . . . There are . . . heavenly bodies and earthly bodies, but the glory of the heavenly is one, and the glory of the earthly is another . . . So also is the resurrection of the dead. It is sown a perishable body, it is raised an imperishable body; it is sown in dishonor, it is raised in glory; it is sown in weakness, it is raised in power; it is sown a natural body, it is raised a spiritual body. If there is a natural body, there is also a spiritual body . . . As is the earthy, so also are those who are earthy; and as is the heavenly, so also are those who are heavenly. And just as we have borne the image of the earthy, we shall also bear the image of the heavenly (1 Cor. 15:38-49).

Then, as if to make the nature of the resurrected body more understandable to his Corinthian readers, the Apostle continues:

Now I say this, brethren, that flesh and blood cannot inherit the kingdom of God; nor does the perishable inherit the imperishable. Behold, I tell you a mystery; we shall not all sleep, but we shall all be changed, in a moment, in the twinkling of an eye, at the last trumpet; for the trumpet will sound, and the dead will be raised imperishable, and we shall be changed. For this perishable must put on the imperishable, and this moral must put on immortality. But when this perishable will have put on the imperishable, and this mortal will have put on immortality, then will come about the saying that is written, "Death is swallowed up in victory. O Death, where is your victory? O Death, where is your sting?" (1 Cor. 15:50-55).

Thus the greatest Christian thinker since Christ, by a few masterful strokes of his pen, forever signs the death warrant of the age-old error of the essential dualism of mind and matter.

The Resurrection of Jesus Christ was Final and Permanent. It is of importance, concerning the nature of Christ's resurrection, that death was for Him a real experience of history never to be repeated. Christ, by His resurrection from the dead, and Paul, in his interpretation of that miraculous event, forever establish the validity of spiritual personalities as the ultimate substances and real existences in the universe. For Christ and for Paul material forms were contingent upon and determined by spiritual personalities. Deterministic materialism must ever fall under the shattering blows of sound Christian personal idealism.

Briefly, to summarize, the resurrection of Jesus Christ was the "first fruits" from the dead and thus afforded a preview of redeemed man's resurrection from the dead. The resurrection, while identical as to form and person, is not a re-formation of the identical chemical elements that compose the temporal body. The resurrected body is a glorified, celestial body which the Apostle Paul designates "a spiritual body." Christ's resurrection provisionally and potentially brought an end to man's greatest enemy, death. If in Him we believe and live, we shall never die, in the strict sense of that word *death*. His resurrection affords a hope that extends beyond the article and experience of death. The life of the true spiritual personality as lived in and through faith in the resurrected Son of God ultimately transcends the experience of death. The real meaning of the resurrection of Jesus Christ is that personal, spiritual personality is the *ultimately real* substance in the universe. "Because I live, you shall live also," are the reassuring words of Christ to His followers. A faith-union with the immortal personality of Christ is the guarantee of the believer's immortality and resurrection.

The Significance of the Resurrection of Jesus Christ

The resurrection of Jesus Christ validates and gives significance to His oral teachings and claims, His miracles and acts of mercy, and His death on the Cross. Had not Christ arisen from the grave, His death would have spelled the denial of everything that He claimed for Himself and that He claimed to have done for others. It is the resurrection of Jesus Christ from the dead that differentiates the Christian religion from every other religious system in the world. No other religion, living or dead, has claimed for its founder a resurrection from the dead.

It is the resurrection from the dead that gives meaning to Christ's atoning death on the cross. Without the resurrection, Christ should have been but a martyr for a good cause. Through the resurrection, Jesus Christ proved Himself to be the Lord of the universe. Paul says of the resurrected Christ: "who was declared with power to be the Son of God by the resurrection from the dead, according to the Spirit of holiness, Jesus Christ our Lord" (Rom. 1:4). It is Matthew who records the supreme claim of Christ subsequent to His death and resurrection: "And Jesus came up and spoke to them saying, 'All authority has been given to Me in heaven and on earth' " (Matt. 28:18).

The resurrection of Jesus Christ signifies His victory over Satan. The long and vicious battle between the evil personality of Satan, the enemy of God and all righteousness, and the Son of God, Jesus Christ, came to its final end when, in anticipation of His resurrection from the dead, Christ uttered those final words on the cross: "It is finished." His

resurrection from the dead was but a verification of that
utterance on the Cross. The death-blow had been struck to
Satan. Satan's power was provisionally and potentially
destroyed when Christ stepped out of the tomb on that first
Easter morning. He had descended into the very region of
spiritual darkness to lay hold upon, overpower, and extricate
from the Devil his usurped powers. Thus since that first
Easter morning Satan has had no authority over man, except
as man has denied the claims and rights of Jesus Christ to
be Lord and Master of his life, and has willfully submitted
himself to the authority of the vanquished enemy of God and
man.

The resurrection of Christ signifies victory over sin.
Man's greatest enemy through the ages has been sin. It
robbed him of his original fellowship with God and banished
him from the presence of the Divine. It brought upon him
a million ills and woes that crushed him under the burden
of their weight. It sent him despairing to death and the grave.
It robbed him of his hope of immortality. Sin, more than any
one thing, has deprived life of its meaning. But when Jesus
Christ came forth from the grave, He came forth a victor
over that age-old enemy of man—*sin.* He had in His death
and resurrection made provision for the elimination of the
guilt, the burden, the consequence, and the nature of sin. The
very cause of death itself, sin, was destroyed in the resurrection of the Son of God.

*The resurrection of Jesus Christ signifies victory over
death.* The warning of God to the first human pair was a
warning against this potential enemy, death. Speaking of the
forbidden fruit, God said: "Ye shall not eat of it, neither shall
ye touch it, lest ye die" (Gen. 3:3, KJV). Man disobeyed and
consequently died. It was primarily a spiritual death, but
ultimately a physical, and potentially an everlasting death.
That initial sin disposed the posterity of Adam to sin, and
as a result of the sin of Adam and his posterity, death became
a universal experience. Paul solemnly declares: "Therefore,
just as through one man sin entered into the world, and death
through sin, and so death spread to all men, because all
sinned" (Rom. 5:12). Thus death became the universal experience of man because all men fell under the curse of sin. Little wonder that death has ever been man's greatest object

of fear. Little wonder that all his days he stands in jeopardy of that merciless enemy, death. But Christ, who "tasted death for every man," likewise destroyed death for every man. Said Christ, "I am the resurrection, and the life; he who believes in Me shall live even if he dies" (John 11:25). No more magnificent description of Christ's victory over this greatest of all enemies is found anywhere than that given us in the Revelation of John. Said Jesus, as recorded by John, "Do not be afraid; I am the first and the last, and the living One; and I was dead, and behold, I am alive forevermore, and I have the keys of death and of Hades" (Rev. 1:17, 18). Faith in the resurrection of Jesus Christ destroys man's fear of death and assures him of life beyond the grave.

The final significance of the resurrection of Jesus Christ is His assurance of immortality to His believing children. Said Christ: ". . . because I live, you shall live also" (John 14:19). Someone has remarked most suggestively: "One day he said with the absoluteness of God: I am the resurrection and the life," and in that challenge to the power of death, he flung a bridge of assurance from trembling human hearts between the here and the hereafter."

Thus the resurrection of Jesus Christ is an incontestably-established fact of history—the greatest miracle of eternity. His resurrection was a final proof of the transcendence of divine, spiritual personality over the world of nature, and His resurrection signifies His final and complete victory over the age-long enemies of God and man—Satan, sin, and death. And the resurrection of Jesus Christ is the assurance of the resurrection and immortality of every believing child of God. Little wonder that the poet sang: "Up from the grave he arose, with a mighty triumph o'er his foes; He arose the victor from the dark domain, and He lives forever with His saints to reign . . ."[3] Here is the central significance of the resurrection of Jesus Christ.

------

[3]Robert Lowry, "Low in the Grave He Lay," *Hymns of the Living Faith*: "Official Hymnal of the Wesleyan-Methodist Church of America" (Syracuse, NY: Wesleyan-Methodist Publishing Association, 1951@, Light and Life Press), No. 117.

CHAPTER IX

The Meaning of Christian Faith

*"Now faith is the assurance of things hoped for,
the conviction of things not seen"* (Heb. 11:1).

Jesus exhorted His followers to "Have faith in God" (Mark 11:22). One may lose physical sight and gain visions of indescribable beauty not apparent to the optical sense. One may lose the use of the auditory organs and still gain audience with the celestial. One may lose the natural touch and still feel the gentle breezes of God's Spirit on his soul. One may lose his temporal possessions and still be an heir to the unsearchable riches of God. One may lose earthly friends and still enjoy the companionship of the eternal God. One may lose physical health and still enjoy eternal life. But no one can lose faith and have anything of value left. Edgar Guest, the beloved American poet, grasped this fact and penned those significant lines in his verse entitled "Faith in Faith," (better titled, "Faith in God.")

Each must stand in the court of life
  And pass through the hour of trial;
He shall tested be by the rules of strife,
  And tried for his self-denial.
Time shall bruise his soul by the loss of friends
  And frighten him with disaster,
But he shall find when the anguish ends
  That of all things faith is master.

So keep your faith in the God above,
  And faith in the righteous truth;
It will bring you back to the absent love
  And the joys of a vanished youth.
You shall smile once more when your tears are dried,
  Meet trouble and swiftly rout it,

For faith is the strength of the soul inside,
And lost is the man without it.[1]

The indispensability of faith to human existence and man's relationship with God is clearly set forth in the letter to the Hebrews as follows:

> Now faith is the assurance of things hoped for, the conviction of things not seen. For by it the men of old gained approval. By faith we understand that the worlds were prepared by the word of God, so that what is seen was not made out of things which are visible. By faith Abel offered to God a better sacrifice than Cain, through which he obtained the testimony that he was righteous, God testifying about his gifts, and through faith, though he is dead, he still speaks. By faith Enoch was taken up so that he should not see death; and he was not found because God took him up; for he obtained the witness that before his being taken up he was pleasing to God. And without faith it is impossible to please Him, for he who comes to God must believe that He is, and that He is a rewarder of those who seek Him (Heb. 11:1-6).

In this great passage faith is described, *first*, as the "*assurance* [or substance] of things hoped for, the *conviction* of things not seen." *Second,* faith is exemplified, both humanly, in that by it "the men of old gained approval," and in its divine creativity, in that by faith "the worlds were prepared by the word of God." *Third,* faith for redemption from sin is exemplified in Abel's act of faith, "through which he obtained the testimony that he was righteous." *Fourth,* the ultimate resurrection victory of the righteous is prefigured in Enoch's faith by which "God took him up; for he obtained the witness that before his being taken up he was pleasing to God." And *finally* there is clearly set forth the indispensability of foundational faith, "He who comes to God must believe that He is"; and of functional faith, "and that He is a rewarder of those who seek Him."

------

[1]Edgar A. Guest, "Faith in Faith," *Flames of Faith,* William L. Stidger, compiler (New York: Abingdon Press, 1922), pp. 165, 166.

The differentiation between faith and belief has been expressed succinctly thus: "Belief is assent to testimony, and faith is assent to testimony united with trust. Faith is an active principle; it is an act of both the understanding and the will. The distinction between belief and faith is that between 'believe me' and 'believe on me.' "[2]

Further, faith may exist in varying degrees. Such is clearly exemplified in the case of Abraham as recorded by Paul in Romans 4:19-21; and in Paul's exhortation to Christian charity in Romans 14:15. The varied states of mind with regard to the acceptance of a proposition as true, as analyzed by Paul Glenn, is helpful.[3] He observes that the mind, when presented with a proposition may, *first*, either utterly "reject the proposition as lacking sufficient evidence to merit its consideration; or *second*, it may remain in a state of "doubt" or suspended judgment, feeling that it indeed has evidence, but insufficient evidence upon which to accept the proposition as true; or *third*, it may proceed to what the logicians call a state of "suspicion," or an inclination in favor of the acceptance of the proposition as true; or *fourth*, the mind may advance to "opinion" in favorable regard to the proposition; or *fifth*, it may advance to conviction; with evidence at hand, it may arrive at "certitude," and thus rest on the assurance of the reliability and reality of the proposition. While in "opinion" the mind is still open to change, in "certitude" the mind has finally closed on the proposition as true, and thus in the soul's quest for God the heart sings, "I can, and I will and I do believe that Jesus saves me now." Thus the penitent sinner attains certain salvation through faith.

Though every state of the mind with regard to the divine proposition of human salvation, as analyzed by logic, may be found represented in the Scriptures, it is this final state of certitude through faith alone that produces the soul rest in the saving and sanctifying mercies of God in Christ. It is to this certitude through faith that the author of the Epistle to the Hebrews alludes when he writes: "There remains therefore a Sabbath rest for the people of God. For the one

---

[2]*The Westminster Dictionary of the Bible*

[3]Paul J. Glenn, *Dialectics*: "A Class Manual in Formal Logic" (St. Louis, MO: B. Herder Book Company, 1929), p. 315.

who has entered His rest has himself also rested from his works, as God did from His. Let us therefore be diligent to enter that rest" (Heb. 4:9-11a).

It was this consideration of the mind's feverish quest for certitude, attainable only through the rest of faith, that inspired the immortal utterance of St. Augustine: "The mind of man will never rest until it rests in Thee [God]." And it was the poet's contemplation of this blissful state of mental and spiritual certitude that made possible, through the final expulsion of doubt, those reassuring lines: "Now rest, my long divided heart; Fixed on this blissful center, rest: Nor ever from thy Lord depart, With him of every good possessed."[4]

The Apostle John grasped this glorious finality of faith and employed the word *know* to express the positive concept of religious certainty no less than a total of sixty times in his combined New Testament writings. The word is used in this sense approximately thirty-seven times in the gospel that bears his name, and twenty-two times in the epistles.

Perhaps the idea reached its highest concept in John's definition of eternal life: "And this is eternal life, that they may *know* Thee the only true God, and Jesus Christ whom Thou hast sent" (John 17:3).

It should be obvious that faith, to be genuine, must have an object. Without an object it ceases to be faith and may become but fruitless wishful thinking. Jesus supplies that necessary object of religious faith in His exhortation to His disciples: "Have faith *in God*" (Mark 11:22). Thus, God, the Father of our Lord Jesus Christ, the personal, living, spiritual, responsive Christian God, is ever the necessary object of man's religious faith. An exhortation to believe without supplying an object of faith is as futile as exhorting a traveler famishing of thirst on the barren desert waste to drink and slake his thirst when there is no water to drink. As God is the ultimate object of man's religious quest, so He is the object of man's religious faith. Jesus said, "Have faith in God." True faith in God always leads to religious certitude.

---

[4]Philip Doddridge, "O Happy Day, That Fixed My Choice," *Hymns of the Living Faith* (Syracuse, NY: The Wesleyan Methodist Publishing Association, 1951), No. 242.

Faith may be best understood by the following fourfold analysis: *natural* (or intellectual) faith, *evangelical* faith, *fiduciary* faith, and *achieving* faith.

There is natural, or intellectual faith. "He who comes to God must believe that He is" (Heb. 11:6a).

This kind of faith is best designated "belief," since it is passive rather than active, in its relation to God. However, it may well be called "faith," since it involves the totality of man's life in relation to himself, his family and friends, life in the universe, and even his acceptance of the existence and providence of God. One great Church father expressed the importance of faith to life in his words, "I do not seek to know that I may believe; but I seek to believe that I may know."

Man was created to believe in himself, his fellows, in life, and in God. Faith is as natural to a person as breathing. This natural faith is the essential basis of all life and living. It is the foundation of every human activity, of the social structure, of economic life, political organizations, and of the domestic life. Without this natural faith, it would be impossible for man to continue existence; Nor does any person exist without natural faith.

This faith is indispensable to man's salvation in Christ, but in itself it is inadequate for personal salvation. Jesus said that "the demons also believe, and shudder," but theirs is not the active faith of obedience. Belief is a necessary foundation for man's salvation, but it is not productive of the actual experience of salvation or the superstructure of the Christian life.

There is evangelical faith. "By grace you have been saved through faith; and that not of yourselves; it is the gift of God" (Eph. 2:8).

While there has been much controversy among scholars over the antecedent of "the gift of God" in Ephesians 2:8, some contending the word "faith" and others "grace" to be the antecedent; grace, rather than faith, would seem to be more consistent with the Scriptures in general. Furthermore, since faith is man's active response to God's initiative, it cannot be considered a "gift" unless we assign the act of man's believing to God. Such an assignment would, of course, be a form of divine determinism, and that can never be reconciled with Scripture or Christian ethics.

Furthermore, faith has no meaning except in an active subject-object relationship. In other words, faith, like love, does not exist in the abstract. Consequently, God could not bestow a non-existent abstraction upon man. Certainly there is a general sense in which faith, as all of man's capacities and abilities, is the gift of God. Lungs and the atmosphere breathed are God's natural gifts to man, but God does not do the breathing for him. That is his responsibility, and failure to exercise that responsibility means death. So faith is a person's responsible function if he is to appropriate the saving grace of God. Thus it is "grace" and not "faith" that is God's gift.

While belief, or an intellectual assent to God and His promises, is necessary to a person's salvation, it requires a personal active, appropriating, evangelical faith in the merits of Christ's atonement to procure personal salvation. It is not simply belief about Christ, but a present active faith in the merits of Christ's death on the cross that saves. Inseparably connected with faith is submissive obedience to God's will. Said Christ, "If any man is willing to do His will, he shall know . . ." (John 7:17).

But as certainly as one is saved by faith in Christ, just so certainly does one experience heart purity by faith. In his defense of the Gentiles at the first general Christian council at Jerusalem, Peter declared: "He [God] made no distinction between us and them, cleansing their hearts by faith" (Acts 15:9). Christ provided purity from the sinful nature in the Christian's heart (Heb. 13:12), but only the Christian's faith in that provision of Christ can make the heart clean from sin. When evangelical faith functions for man's cleansing, he can then sing:

> *Oh, now I see the crimson wave,*
> *The fountain deep and wide;*
> *Jesus, my Lord, mighty to save,*
> *Points to His wounded side.*
>
> *I see the new creation rise.*
> *I hear the speaking blood;*
> *It speaks! polluted nature dies—*
> *Sinks 'neath the crimson flood.*

I rise to walk in heav'n's own light,
Above the world and sin;
With heart made pure and garments white,
And Christ enthroned within.

Amazing grace! 'tis heav'n below,
To feel the blood applied;
And Jesus, only Jesus know:
My Jesus crucified.

The cleansing stream I see, I see!
I plunge, and O it cleanseth me;
O praise the Lord, it cleanseth me,
It cleanseth me, yes, cleanseth me.[5]

There is fiduciary faith. "The righteous man shall *live* by faith" (Rom. 1:17b).

Many have possessed intellectual or natural faith, or belief, and have exercised evangelical faith for forgiveness and cleansing, who have failed to maintain a constant fiduciary faith in Christ. Fiduciary faith is the faith of the child in the parent, the faith by which the Christian maintains his personal saving relationship with Christ. It is for fiduciary faith that Paul prays in the Ephesian letter: "That Christ may *dwell* in your hearts through faith" (Eph. 3:17).

The three Hebrew young men exercised fiduciary faith in God. When faced with the fiery furnace, they said:

> If it be so, our God whom we serve is able to deliver us from the furnace of blazing fire; and He will deliver us out of your hand, O king. But even if He does not, let it be known to you, O king, that we are not going to serve your gods or worship the golden image that you have set up (Dan. 3:17, 18).

It was this kind of faith that characterized Daniel when he was faced with the lions' den (Dan. 6:24). Likewise David reflected his fiduciary faith when he uttered those immortal words, "Even though I walk through the valley of the shadow of death, I will fear no evil, for Thou art with me;

---

[5]Phoebe Palmer, "The Cleansing Wave," *Hymns of the Living Faith* (Syracuse, NY: Wesleyan Methodist Publishing Association, 1951), p. 313.

Thy rod and Thy staff, they comfort me" (Ps. 23:4). When we learn to trust the person of God for the faithfulness of His character alone, and not fluctuate with the exigencies of life, then we have fiduciary faith. Such faith anchors the soul in the midst of the fierce storms of life.

There is achieving faith. "He who comes to God must believe . . . that He is a rewarder of those who seek Him" (Heb. 11:6).

Achieving faith is that faith by which the Christian takes from the hand of God the answers to his prayers. This was the faith of Elijah when he prayed for rain (Jas. 5:17, 18), the faith of Jacob at Peniel, the faith of Abraham for a son, and the faith of Hannah for a child. It was achieving faith by which George Muller established and maintained his great orphanage in England; and it was this faith that established such great Christian works as the China Inland Mission, the Sudan Interior Mission, the Christian and Missionary Alliance Mission, and the World Wide Evangelization Crusade. It should not be assumed that all Christians have achieving faith in the same degree. This is a faith that requires time and experience to develop. The young Christian cannot expect to exercise the achieving faith of a mature servant of God. Achieving faith grows with experience and exercise.

The author was once invited to assist in a revival in a Friends Church where the lady pastor and her assistants had been conducting evangelistic meetings for five weeks, in faith for revival, but without visible results. The church was packed beyond capacity with people evidently deeply convicted of sin, but there had been no visible turning to God. The workers were tired and worn from long effort, but would not give up faith for revival. At the close of the author's sermon on this particular night, it appeared futile to give an invitation to accept Christ, but from a sense of duty the effort was made, and a small boy responded, gave himself to Christ, and was graciously converted. This event seemed to touch the hearts of the impenitent, and suddenly a pent-up flood of penitential tears was released. By midnight twenty-six young people were converted who had never before known the Lord. From this service a far-reaching spiritual awakening broke upon the church and community. Many years later the pastor of this church informed the author that the substantial membership of the present church was the product of that revival. When the defenses are down and the heart craves for God, "He . . . will come, and will not delay" (Heb. 10:37b).

After years of apparently fruitless service in South Africa, a friend in England wrote Mary Moffat asking her what she might send her as a present that would be useful to their work in Africa. Knowing there were no Christians to take communion, nor any apparent potential converts, Mary replied, with a great display of faith, "Send us a communion service." Some three years later supplies from England arrived at the Moffat mission station on a Saturday. Among those supplies was the communion set which she had in faith requested.

In the meantime a spiritual awakening had occurred among the Africans and the following Sunday a number of new converts were served the Christian communion for the first time. Thus Mary Moffat's faith was rewarded, even when she believed against all evidence.[6]

Someone has related a dream in which he died and went to heaven. There he was ushered into a great storeroom where many wrapped and labeled parcels were stacked. When he inquired of the angel the meaning of these packages, he was informed that they were the answers to the prayers of God's children who had become impatient and lost faith before the packages were delivered. Jesus said: "Have faith in God."

----

[6]Clara McLeister, *Men and Women of Deep Piety* (Syracuse, NY: Wesleyan Methodist Publishing Association, 1920), pp. 339, 340.

Chapter X

The Reality of Spiritual Restoration

"Draw near to God and He will draw near to you. Cleanse your hands, you sinners; and purify your hearts, you double-minded. Be miserable and mourn and weep: let your laughter be turned into mourning, and your joy to gloom. Humble yourselves in the presence of the Lord, and He will exalt you. Do not speak against one another, brethren. He who speaks against a brother, or judges his brother, speaks against the law, and judges the law; but if you judge the law, you are not a doer of the law, but a judge of it. There is only one Lawgiver and Judge, the One who is able to save and to destroy; but who are you who judge your neighbor? Come now, you who say, 'Today or tomorrow, we shall go to such and such a city, and spend a year there and engage in business and make a profit.' Yet you do not know what your life will be like tomorrow. You are just a vapor that appears for a little while and then vanishes away. Instead, you ought to say, 'If the Lord wills, we shall live and also do this or that.' But as it is, you boast in your arrogance; all such boasting is evil. Therefore, to one who knows the right thing to do, and does not do it, to him it is sin" (James 4:8-17).

The people to whom James wrote the epistle that bears his name had lost their way from the reality of Christian faith. To them the Christian faith had become but a meaningless name and a powerless form; they must either find their way back to God and to the vitality of their experience in Christ or they would soon sink into spiritual and even nominal oblivion. The crux of their problem is clearly stated and the remedy is set forth with equal clarity in the epistle of James, chapter four, verse eight: "Draw near to God and

He will draw near to you. Cleanse your hands, you sinners; and purify your hearts, you double-minded.''

These are no idle words or meaningless platitudes. They are the burning indictments of a true prophet to his people in the deep dark hour of their moral and spiritual declension. They are the inspired apostle's clear call for spiritual revival to his people, and to deficient Christians in every day.

The effects of sin with its consequent guilt have usually disposed many to flee from the conscious presence of God, rather than to remain in or approach to the holiness of the divine presence. Apprehended of God after the first disobedience against the divine will, Adam confessed, ''I was afraid . . . so I hid myself'' (Gen. 3:10b). When the divine command came to the prophet Jonah to preach to the wicked Ninevites, and his spirit rebelled against that command, the record states that ''Jonah rose up to flee to Tarshish from the presence of the Lord'' (Jonah 1:3a). When the prodigal son had demanded his inheritance and declared his independence of his father, it is said of him that ''not many days later [he] . . . went on a journey into a distant country, and there he squandered his estate with loose living'' (Luke 15:13). Divorced from God and bent on spiritual and moral dissipation, sinful man seeks refuge from the divine disapproval by flight into one or another of the many defenses. He cannot remain long under the Father's surveillance when his heart is not right with God.

It is not unusual for man to exchange orthodox Christian principles and practices for heterodox views and questionable moral indulgences, when unconfessed sin beclouds his relationship with the Father. Modern cults have enjoyed a shocking recrudescence in America and other parts of the modern world during recent decades. Examination reveals that for the most part the adherents of these counterfeit religions are apostates from evangelical Christian churches. Seldom are converts made directly from among non-Christians to heterodox cults. It is not new nor strange that Christians who have lost their way from God through sin should in their spiritual desperation resort to the ''palmist,'' the ''spiritualist medium,'' ''the Jehovah Witnesses,'' ''Mormonism,'' ''Christian Science,'' or one of the many pagan Oriental sophisticated ''theosophical'' or ''mental culture'' cults. It will be remembered that when the Lord refused to answer King Saul, and he faced impending tragedy at the hands of the enemy Philistines, Saul in desperation and destitution resorted to the Witch of Endor in false hope for help where he met his tragic doom.

The writer was amazed at the candid statement of a noted spiritualist medium, in a city where he was pastoring, when he stated that a pastor of one of the largest churches of that city frequently came to him to receive messages from the "outerspace world." Thus it would appear that even the ministry may lose contact with God and in distress turn to Satan's counterfeits. It was reported that there were several ex-ordained ministers of evangelical churches in the service of Father Divine of Harlem, New York. A Christian African merchant of the writer's personal acquaintance withdrew from his church communion and identified himself with the Mohammedan religion which permits polygamy, just because this once-bright Christian merchant desired to take a second wife, which practice Christianity condemned, but which Islam permits. He changed his Christian beliefs and practices for a false religion in an attempted justification of his immoral conduct. The sad declension from the Christian faith to the denial of its essential truths by the late world-renowned Bishop James Pike that finally led him to gross demon-inspired spiritualism is a well-known example of the inevitable results of departure from God.

But there are many other attempted escape mechanisms into which man would try to flee from the presence of an offended God. Among these is rationalism. One need only investigate the personal history of some of the world's greatest inventors of false and damaging systems of philosophy, such as Friedrich Nietzsche (1844-1900), Arthur Schopenhauer, Sigmund Freud, or the contemporary existential atheist, Jean Paul Sartre, to discover that their philosophies were attempted escape mechanisms from dreadful personal realities. The whole naturalistic evolutionary hypothesis is an invented escape mechanism in an attempt to evade man's moral responsibility to God. If God is not creator and providential governor of the universe, then man may more comfortably live as a practical naturalistic atheist. Naturalistic materialism that denies the personality and reality of God, whether that be of the Marxian brand or otherwise, is but a futile attempt on the part of man to escape the reality of God and man's moral responsibility.

Projectionism is likewise a common refuge of man from the consciousness of guilt wrought by a sense of God's disapproval. The testimony of the first recorded sinner reflects this advice. Apprehended by God, Adam is heard to say, "The woman whom Thou gavest to be with me, she gave me from the tree, and I ate" (Gen. 3:12b). Saul became guilty of the same projectionism when rebuked by Samuel (1 Sam. 15:14-23).

But none of these, or any other escape device, will enable sinful man to elude the reality of a holy and just God. Said the Psalmist, "If I ascend to heaven, Thou art there; If I make my bed in Sheol, behold Thou art there" (Ps. 139:8). It is not until sinful man, like Hagar of old, acknowledges and faces the reality of God and exclaims, "Thou art a God who sees" (Gen. 16:13), that revival and return to God begin. Francis Thompson's classic poem, "The Hound of Heaven," vividly depicts the futility of sinful man's attempt to escape the pursuit of a loving, but offended, God.

> *I fled Him, down the nights and down the days;*
> *I fled Him, down the arches of the years;*
> *I fled Him, down the labyrinth ways*
> *Of my own mind; and in the mist of tears*
> *I hid from Him, and under running laughter.*
> *Up vistaed hopes I sped;*
> *And shot, precipitated,*
> *Adown Titanic glooms of chasmed fears,*
> *From those strong Feet that followed, followed after.*
> *But with unhurrying chase,*
> *And unperturbed pace,*
> *Deliberate speed, majestic instancy,*
> *They beat—and a Voice beat*
> *More instant than the Feet—*
> *"All things betray thee, who betrayest Me."*
> *I pleaded, outlaw-wise,*
> *By many a hearted casement, curtained red,*
> *Trellised with intertwining charities;*
> *(For, though I knew His love Who followed,*
> *Yet was I sore adread*

Lest, having Him, I must have naught beside).
But, if one little casement parted wide,
The gust of His approach would clash it to.
Fear wist not to evade, as Love wist to pursue.
Across the margent of the world I fled,
And troubled the gold gateways of the stars,
Smiting for shelter on their clanged bars;
Fretted to dulcet jars
And silvern chatter the pale ports o' the moon.
I said to Dawn: Be sudden—to Eve: Be soon;
With thy young skiey blossoms heap me over
From this tremendous Lover—[1]

But the question then arises, How may man with the consciousness of sin in his life draw near to God? How can he get free from the guilt of sin? How can sinful man approach a holy and righteous God? This question has several answers in the fourth chapter of James.

Sinful man's initial step in his return to God is submission. "Submit therefore to God" (Jas. 4:7a).

So long as man attempts to solve his own problems, to fight his own battles, to heal his own spiritual wounds, to cure his own spiritual diseases, to satisfy his own spiritual thirst, to still his own spiritual restlessness; so long as he seeks within himself the answer to these or other human desires or needs, he will strive in vain. Occasional mirages of clear fountains of fresh, cool water will appear on the desert of our wasted lives to lure us on, but time and human effort will prove them to be the false illusions that they are. And alas, each unfinished tower of Babel to heaven, each dry-well of disillusioned hopes, will but further deepen the despair of man apart from God. When we are willing to admit personal defeat, throw down our weapons of rebellion, surrender our humanly-devised purposes and plans; in short, when we make a final and unconditional surrender of ourselves to Christ and allow Him to master and govern our lives, then, and only then, will we find our victory in Christ. Among His

---

[1]Francis Thompson, "The Hound of Heaven," *Readings in Religious Philosophy*, Geddis MacGregor and J. Wesley Robb, eds. (Houghton-Mifflin Company, 1962), p. 26.

last earthly utterances Christ declared, "All authority has been given to Me in heaven and on earth" (Matt. 28:18b). It is noteworthy that the Book of Acts makes one hundred and ten references to the Lordship of the risen Christ. *Lord* is the most important word in Acts. The Apostle Paul declares Christ to be, "with power . . . the Son of God by the resurrection from the dead" (Rom. 1:4). Submission to Christ's lordship in our lives is the first prerequisite to His saviorship in our lives. He cannot, and He will not save until we submit. The order is submission, then salvation. His will in our individual lives, the authority of His word as the rule of our conduct, and His personal governorship over all the affairs of our lives must be recognized and obeyed if we are to know Him in peace. And until we know Christ in peace, we do not know Him as Savior. Christ is the Prince of Peace.

Man's return to God is the denial of the right of Satan to exercise authority over his life. "Resist the devil and he will flee from you" (Jas. 4:7b).

Sinning man is a subject of Satan's kingdom. It is not easy to acknowledge that our sins are Satanic impositions upon us; that, as Paul puts it, "Do you not know that when you present yourselves to someone as slaves for obedience, you are slaves of the one whom you obey, either of sin resulting in death, or of obedience resulting in righteousness?" (Rom. 6:16). It is hard for sinful man to admit that he is not his own master—the instigator and executor of his own deeds—that he is the slave of Satan. However, such is the case, and the reality of this deplorable and humiliating situation must be frankly faced. Jesus said, "the ruler of the world is coming, and he has nothing in Me" (John 14:30b). All Satanic claims had been so completely denied by the Son of God that Satan had no authority in His life. Complete victory in the life of the Christian demands full surrender to Christ who has conquered Satan, with a complete and final denial of all rights of Satan to any part or place in our lives. It has been well said that the reason some people have so much sin in their lives that they do not want is because they have some darling sin that they are not willing to give up. The final resistance and rejection of Satan comes when our lives are fully surrendered to Christ who conquered Satan at the Cross. This is graphically depicted by John in Revelation 1:17b-18: "I am the first and the last, the living One; and I was dead, and behold, I am alive forevermore, and I have the keys of death and of Hades."

Man's return to God is a genuine heartbreaking sorrow for sin committed against God. "Be miserable and mourn and weep: let your laughter be turned into mourning, and your joy to gloom" (Jas. 4:9).

The flippancy with which death-dealing sin is treated today, even among many Christian people, is utterly appalling. Even the basic sins of unbelief and the rejection of God's will that nailed Christ to Calvary's cruel cross, are excused as indications of inescapable human weakness, rationalized as respectable marks of the modern scientific mind, or made objects of gross and refined jests from pulpit and pew, on the street, in the press, by the sophisticated remarks at the banqueting table, and over the radio and television alike. Some professed Christians who once would have shuddered with a revolting sense of horror at the gory, inhumane brutality seen on the television screen, or whose sense of modesty or purity would have suffered shock at the seductive conduct of certain Hollywood stars, or would have recoiled from the death-dealing effects of the liquor and drug traffic as from the venomous fangs of a hooded Indian Cobra, can now relish such with impunity. Among these professed Christians not a few have become so spiritually stupefied, having had their finer spiritual sensibilities benumbed if not deadened, that they can watch into the late hours of the night, or the wee hours of the morning, with a sense of greedy enjoyment, these same sins on their televisions with apparent absence of moral compunction. Many a modern church is laughing its way to hell at the televised vaudeville of the devil that feeds the perverted passions of an apostate people, while their children are being cultured in crime and immorality by the corner drugstore comics and criminal brutality of violent films. These and a multitude of other cunning devices are employed by the Wicked One to decoy the church from her spiritual heritage and mission into the way which seems right to a man, but the end of which is "the way of death" (Prov. 14:12).

It is not easy for the perverted professing soul to turn from the vaudeville of religious sham and pretense, recognize and accept the disapprobation of God on the sin of insincerity and subject his soul to the chastening rod of God; but it is necessary if he would save himself from this perverted generation. "Be miserable and mourn and weep: let your laughter be turned into mourning and your joy to gloom" (Jas. 4:9). Said Jesus, "Blessed are those who mourn, for they shall be comforted" (Matt. 5:4). In his spiritual destitution and desperation the Psalmist prayed:

> I have become dumb, I do not open my mouth, Because it is Thou who hast done it. Remove Thy plague from me; because of the opposition of Thy hand, I am perishing. With reproofs Thou dost chasten a man for iniquity; Thou dost consume as a moth what is precious to him; Surely every man is a mere breath. [Selah. Hear my prayer, O Lord, and give ear to my cry; Do not be silent at my tears; For I am a stranger with Thee, A sojourner like all my fathers. Turn Thy gaze away from me, that I may smile again, Before I depart and am no more (Ps. 39:9-13).

Every great revival in human history has been characterized by conviction for sin that wrought affliction of soul and deep sorrow of spirit, before spiritual victory in God came. The prophet Zechariah foresaw such a spiritual awakening for the house of David and exclaimed:

> And I will pour out on the house of David and on the inhabitants of Jerusalem the Spirit of grace and of supplication, so that they will look on Me whom they have pierced; and they will mourn for Him, as one mourns for an only son, and they will weep bitterly over Him, like the bitter weeping over a first-born. In that day there will be great mourning in Jerusalem (Zech. 12:10, 11a).

Sin is no light matter and requires a frank recognition of its hideousness, and genuine sorrow for its commission. Until we are broken, and until we are willing to break with sin, God will remain at a distance from us. "If I regard wickedness in my heart, the Lord will not hear" (Ps. 66:18). "He who conceals his transgressions will not prosper, But he who confesses and forsakes them will find compassion" (Prov. 28:13). "A broken and a contrite heart, O God, Thou wilt not despise" (Ps. 51:17b). It has been said that repentance is heartbreak for sin, but that saving faith is heartbreak with sin.

Man's return to God is in genuine humility. "Humble yourselves in the presence of the Lord, and He will exalt you" (Jas. 4:10).

There is such a thing as a humility that is proud of itself, and there is an appearance of humility that is the expression of a secret subtle pride of the wicked heart. The secret pride of the heart is one of the most deceptive and deadening of all known sins.

Confession of sin to God is self-humiliation. It is taking the witness stand against oneself. The acknowledgement of our ins or faults to our fellows is self-humiliating, since it is a depreciation of ourselves in the estimation that others may have of us. Restitution is self-humiliating, since it requires the self to take back stolen property or make amends for wrongs or injustices that it has inflicted on others. Acknowledgement of bitter or uncharitable feelings toward another is self-humiliating, since it unmasks the true self and exposes its hideous nature to our fellows who may have a better opinion of us. The sinful pride of the human heart clogs more fountains of spiritual blessings, and pours more deadly poison into the stream of life than any other known sin. It is an identical twin with the sin of unbelief.

An African story is told of a family of antelope. Among the fawns was a young buck with a beautiful coat of glossy hair and a handsome rack of long spreading horns. He was the pride and envy of all the young antelope. In due time his recognized superior beauty motivated him to an attitude of such superiority and disdain for his inferior fellow-antelope as to awaken jealousies and dislike for him in the minds of others. Proudly he strutted his way among the herd, until in the late dry season when water became hard to find. Daily the water descended in the drinking holes until at last this proud young buck found it impossible to reach the water by reason of his spreading rack of horns that prevented the descent of his head into the water hole. At last his beautiful coat faded and his well-rounded body became emaciated from thirst, and he fell dead by the side of the trail, a victim of his own pride, while the herd passed disdainfully by. "Pride goes before destruction and a haughty spirit before stumbling" (Prov. 16:18). God has great regard for humility. "Humble yourselves in the presence of the Lord, and He will exalt you" (Jas. 4:10). The Psalmist said: "He does not forget the cry of the afflicted" (Ps. 9:12b). Isaiah exclaims:

> For thus says the high and exalted One who lives forever, whose name is Holy, I dwell on a high and holy place, and also with the contrite and lowly of spirit in order to revive the spirit of the lowly and to revive the heart of the contrite (Isa. 57:15).

James declares: "God is opposed to the proud, but gives grace to the humble" (Jas. 4:6b). And Peter joins with the exhortation: "clothe yourselves with humility toward one another, for God is opposed to the proud, but gives grace to the humble. Humble yourselves, therefore, under the mighty hand of God, that He may exalt you at the proper time" (1 Pet. 5:5b, 6). The way to spiritual renewal is ever the way of self-effacement.

CHAPTER XI

The Plight of the Carnal Believer

"Therefore leaving the principles of the doctrine of Christ, let us go on unto perfection" (Heb. 6:1a, KJV).

"Pursue after . . . the sanctification without which no man will see the Lord" (Heb. 12:14).

The author of the letter to the Hebrews has depicted vividly the condition of the imperfect Christian, and God's remedy for that condition. While this divine word picture embraces verses 12-29 of the 12th chapter of Hebrews, we shall here limit our consideration to verses 12-17, and verses 22, 24 and 29. The message reads thus:

> Therefore, strengthen the hands that are weak and the knees that are feeble, and make straight paths for your feet, so that the limb which is lame may not be put out of joint, but rather be healed.
> Pursue after peace with all men, and after the sanctification without which no one will see the Lord. See to it that no one comes short of the grace of God; that no root of bitterness springing up causes trouble, and by it many be defiled; that there be no immoral or godless person like Esau, who sold his own birthright for a single meal. For you know that even afterwards, when he desired to inherit the blessing, he was rejected, for he found no place for repentance, though he sought it with tears . . .
> But you have come . . . to Jesus the mediator of a new covenant and to the sprinkled blood, which speaks better than the blood of Abel . . . For our God is a consuming fire (Heb. 12:12-17, 22, 24, 29).

The Jewish Christians, whether at Jerusalem where James remained as pastor, or Jewish Christians in the dispersion, to whom this epistle was written, were a people who by this time had largely lost their spiritual vision and divine grace. The church stood sadly in need of spiritual renewal and restoration to the favor of God.

This letter to the Hebrew Christians, written by an unknown author, likely between A.D. 64 and 67, vividly depicts their sad spiritual plight. In chapter 12:12-17, this author's exhortations suggest that these people were discouraged; *"strengthen the hands that are weak"*; that they had become prayerless; *"the knees that are feeble"*; that they had suffered moral declension; *"make straight paths for your feet"*; that broken fellowships within the church had become their experience, as suggested by his words: *"pursue after peace with all men"*; and that they had either lost or had failed to advance to that purity of heart and life provided for them; *"pursue . . . sanctification, without which no one will see the Lord."* This author then warns his readers against three grave dangers. *First,* there is the danger of falling completely from divine favor; "See to it that no one come short of the grace of God" [Mar. fall from the grace of God]: *second,* the danger of the carnal poisoning of their spiritual lives; "that no root of bitterness [poison] springing up cause trouble, and by it many [the whole body] be defiled"; and *finally,* he warns against the fearful and irreparable state of total apostasy, as exemplified by the sad plight of Esau when he had equated the material with the spiritual and exchanged the latter for the former (Heb. 12:15, 16).

The purpose of this letter to the Hebrew Christians was clearly to encourage them to continue in the Christian faith and life at a time when they were sorely tempted to forsake Christ and Christianity and return to Judaism, which was now the empty shell of their former faith. In chapter 10:32-39, it is made clear that they had been genuinely converted to Christ: "after being enlightened" (v. 32a); that they had been subjected to very severe trials: "you endured a great conflict of sufferings" (v. 32b); that they had lost heavily of their material possessions by becoming Christians: "accepted joyfully the seizure of your property" (v. 34); that they were tempted to forsake Christ: "do not throw away your confidence, which has a great reward" (v. 35); and that they were in great need of renewed faith and steadfastness: "For you have need of endurance, so that when you have done the will of God, you may receive what was promised" (v. 36).

The real problem confronting these Hebrew Christians was that they, like so many present-day Christians, had failed to go on to perfect love, or Christian holiness, as is made clear in chapter 6:1: "let us press on to maturity, not laying again a foundation of repentance from dead works and of faith toward God."

A common objection offered to the doctrine and experience of Christian perfection is that such an experience would preclude further growth. This objection fails to grasp the real meaning of Christian perfection in that it conceives the experience to be an end in itself, rather than a means to a greater end. "Christian perfection" is not to be confused with "absolute perfection." The first is a perfection of motive; the second, a perfection of performance. The first is attainable through grace in the present life. Christian perfection is preparatory to a normal growth and development in grace, but never an end in itself. An illustration may help to an understanding of the practical function of Christian perfection.

A gardener prepares the soil and plants his seed in straight rows. The sun warms and the spring showers moisten the soil, creating conditions favorable to germination. A week later the plants make their healthy appearance in straight rows in the apparently-clean soil. The gardener is elated as his neighbors compliment him on his promising garden.

After a few days, with further showers and warm sunshine, obnoxious weeds make their appearance in the garden, threatening to sap the soil-food from the plants and overgrow them, with the consequence of dealing death to this promising garden. The gardener becomes alarmed and prepares to extract the weeds from the garden. But his wife protests, saying that should he extract the weeds from the garden, it will be rendered "perfect," and thus will not realize further development nor come to fruition. Quite naturally the gardener might conclude that his wife was a likely subject for the psychiatrist. He would likely reply that the removal of the weeds would but eliminate the hindrances and free the plants for normal growth and development. Likewise, sanctification purifies the Christian believer's heart of the disease germs of carnal impurities and thus frees the believer from these hindrances to growth in grace for a normal development in the Christian life.

Defects of the Carnal Christian

The first defect of the carnal Christian is a thoroughgoing case of discouragement. That debilitating spiritual malady is graphically depicted in the author's exhortation to "strengthen the hands that are weak" (v. 12a). Weymouth's translation has it "drooping hands." Discouragement has probably robbed more people of their faith and courage, and consequently their Christian victory, sheared more people of their strength, and beclouded the future outlook of more souls than any other known spiritual malady. Discouragement is a disease the germs of which breed rapidly in the impure heart. It is an extremely contagious disease capable of incapacitating for service a whole contingent of the Lord's army, and thus giving the enemy an easy victory. Discouragement is Satan's most effective weapon.

The second defect of the carnal Christian is dissuasion from prayer (v. 12b). While the Authorized Version reads, "the feeble knees," and Weymouth likewise translates it "palsied knees." When discouragement becomes effective in the Christian life, prayer ends. The knees will no longer bend in prayer; instead they tremble, like a palsied person, in fear. Fear supplants prayer. Their prayerlessness has disposed them to draw back in fear: "if he shrinks back, My soul has no pleasure in him" (Heb. 10:38b). While kneeling is not the only posture of prayer represented in the Scriptures, it is apparently the most frequently represented. It is suggestive of true humility, and a recognition of the proper relation of man the creature to God the Creator. Spiritual power declines in proportion to diminishing prayer. A prayerless Christian or church is spiritually powerless against the impact of Satan and his temptations.

The third defect of the carnal Christian is impaired moral conduct: "make straight paths for your feet, so that the limb which is lame may not be put out of joint, but rather be healed" (v. 13). This defect of immature Christians bespeaks declension in moral conduct. Their discouragement and prayerlessness have led to careless living, with the consequent that they no longer live by the rule of right conduct.

They are leaving behind them ways that are crooked, and thus difficult for the weaker members of the body of Christ to understand and follow. This bad example tends to discourage and dissuade the weaker brethren from the way of righteousness: "that the limb which is lame may not be put out of joint, but rather be healed"; or as Weymouth reads: "so that what is lame may not be put entirely out of joint but rather be restored." One commentator significantly remarks: "smooth paths containing no stumblingblocks that may injure the lame . . . if they do not remove the stumblingblocks from the paths, lameness may become dislocation."[1]

The fourth defect of the carnal Christian is dissension in fellowship. "Pursue after peace with all men" (v. 14a); or in Weymouth's translation: "strive for peace with all men." When the church becomes discouraged, ceases to pray and suffers moral declension, the fellowship and peace of that church will soon be displaced by jealousies, bickerings, rancor, strife, and factions. When carnal impurity ferments in the unsanctified heart, the dove of peace departs from the sanctuary of the soul. Concerning this condition and its cause James wrote: "What is the source of quarrels and conflicts among you? Is not the source your pleasures that war in your members?" (Jas. 4:1).

Three Dangers Facing the Carnal Christian

The first danger that threatens the carnal Christian is falling from grace. "See to it that no one comes short of the grace of God" (v. 15a). Weymouth reads: "carefully see to it that none fails to avail himself of the grace of God." But the marginal reading of the Authorized Version is particularly specific: *fall from the grace of God.* The surest way to fall from grace and backslide in heart and life is to condone impurity in the unsanctified heart. The Ephesian church is an apt example of this condition. Hear Christ's charge against this backsliding church: "I have this against you, that you have left your first love. Remember therefore from where you have fallen, and repent and do the deeds you did at first" (Rev. 2:4a, 5a).

------

[1]J. R. Dummelow, ed., *A Commentary on the Holy Bible*: "Complete in One Volume" (New York: The Macmillan Company, rep. 1951), p. 1028.

The second danger facing these Christians was carnal poisoning: "that no root of bitterness springing up cause trouble, and by it many be defiled" (v. 15b). Weymouth is illuminating: "that no root bearing bitter fruit spring up and cause trouble among you, and through it the whole brotherhood be defiled."[2] Because the ancient Oriental medicine man sometimes concocted his poisonous drugs from bitter herbs, even as primitive pagan medicine men do today, they came to associate bitterness with poison. The two words became synonymous. A certain type of this bitter poison was used to execute criminals. The Greek "hemlock" is typical. It was by the drinking of the hemlock that Socrates was executed. When the condemned man drank the bitter poison, it often produced convulsions as it spread through the body, and then deadening paralysis, putrefaction of the bloodstream, and finally death followed. Thus, the author of this letter suggests that impurity of heart is a bitter poisonous root, capable of springing forth into an active injection of its deadly venom into the spiritual bloodstream of the victim, thus making the whole body violently sick with resultant spiritual paralysis and death. This impure working in the soul of the unsanctified believer is somewhat like the effect of the poison of certain serpents on their victims. One type of serpent venom causes a coagulation of the blood with resultant deathly sickness and ultimate putrefaction of the blood. Another type, however, affects the nervous system, and causes rapid paralysis, rendering the victim helpless in the presence of its captor.

The author has watched the deadly African Mamba stealthily crawl upon its unwary victim, usually a rodent, and sinking its pin-point fangs into the victim's flesh, inject the death-dealing venom into its system. After a brief and futile effort to flee the enemy, the victim would lose its equilibrium, stagger and then fall in a helpless state of paralysis while the serpent crept patiently up to swallow its prey.

In a church business meeting one night on the writer's pastorate a strong policeman, who had subdued many incor-

---

[2]Richard Francis Weymouth, *The New Testament in Modern Speech* (New York: Harper & Brothers, Publishers, n.d.), p. 550.

rigibles in his day, was suddenly overcome with a raging storm of anger over a disagreement on plans for a church building. Though a believer for many years, he was an unsanctified Christian who had never gone on to heart purity. With reason temporarily dethroned by the evil passion of anger, he stalked out of the church, never to return. Subsequently a man stumbled upon his dead body on a dark street of the city, where he had been stricken by a heart attack without ever finding his way back to divine grace, as far as was known. The impurity of wrath and resentment injected its venom into his soul and spiritually paralyzed him in the death grip of anger.

A girl who was once a student in the author's classes informed him that her mother had died some years earlier of a heart attack induced by an uncontrolled fit of anger while she was reprimanding the high school principal for giving her daughter a lower grade than she thought she should have had. Such was the effect of sin's assertion of itself in the life of Judas, with the terrible consequences of betrayal and suicide.

The third danger confronting the carnal Christian is total apostasy: "that there be no immoral or godless person like Esau, who sold his own birthright for a single meal" (v. 16). One authority observes that "Esau's defect was a want of appreciation of spiritual blessings. He despised his birthright (see Gen. 25:24), which implied not merely material advantage, but the spiritual heritage of the covenant promise."[3] The word profane, as here used, is the antithesis of hallowed or sacred, and consequently it means unspiritual, or secular or common. Esau's spiritual sensibilities were so far deadened that he could equate the spiritual with the secular, and was unable to distinguish between their essential values. He had lost his spiritual sensibility and discernment. Thus total apostasy may not be so much the withdrawal of God's favor and presence from the soul as the inability to any longer perceive spiritual realities. Esau had sold his birthright upon which the blessing was contingent. He sought and failed to retrieve the blessing because he did not have the birthright.

---

[3]Dummelow, *A Commentary on the Holy Bible,* p. 1028.

It is impossible to obtain the blessings of salvation without a spiritual birthright—a right relationship with God. Moral impurity, if allowed to remain in the heart and assert itself, will deaden and ultimately destroy the spiritual sensibilities and leave the soul incapable of sensing, responding to, or perceiving God.

God Offers a Threefold Remedy
for the Carnal Christian

The first remedy is an earnest desire to be made free from the sinful nature. "Pursue after . . . the sanctification without which no one will see the Lord" (v. 14). Again the author of the letter to the Hebrews exhorts: "let us press on to maturity" (Heb. 6:1). Until the dangers of moral impurity are recognized and abhorred, and the soul longs for cleansing more than for anything else, there is little hope for an experience of heart purity: "you will seek Me and find Me, when you search for Me with all your heart" says the Lord to Israel through the prophet (Jer. 29:13). "Blessed are those who hunger and thirst for righteousness, for they shall be satisfied," said Christ (Matt. 5:6).

The second remedy is appropriating faith in the sanctifying provisions of the atonement: "you have come to Jesus the mediator of a new covenant and to the sprinkled blood, which speaks better than the blood of Abel" (Heb. 12:22, 24). Again, this author writes: "Therefore Jesus also, that He might sanctify the people through His own blood, suffered outside the gate" (Heb. 13:12). Christ's death on the cross atones for sins committed and provides cleansing from the inward sinful nature. Said the prophet: "In that day a fountain will be opened for the house of David and for the inhabitants of Jerusalem, for sin and for impurity" (Zech. 13:1).

The third remedy is the fiery baptism with the Holy Spirit: "our God is a consuming fire" (Heb. 12:29). By virtue of the atoning provisions of Christ's death the Holy Spirit cleanses the Christian believer's heart from moral pollution by the purifying fire of the Holy Spirit's presence and nature. Said John the Baptist: "I baptize you in water for repentance, but He who is coming after me is mightier than I . . . He Himself will baptize you with the Holy Spirit and fire" (Matt. 3:1). On the day of Pentecost the soul purification of the disciples was accomplished when "there appeared to them tongues as of fire distributing themselves, and they rested on each one of them" (Acts 2:3). Again the apostle wrote: "that my offering of the Gentiles might become acceptable, sanctified by the Holy Spirit" (Rom. 15:16b). The Holy Spirit is the divinely-revealed Person of man's soul cleansing. Peter declared, concerning the household of Cornelius, that their hearts were purified by faith through the mighty baptism of the Holy Spirit (Acts 15:8, 9).

As the bright rays of the sun kill the disease germs of a severe, debilitating, and decimating epidemic, thus arresting its progress and purifying the atmosphere, likewise the revealed presence of the holiness of God to the impure heart of man will destroy the disease germs of the heart's inner pollution and heal the sin-diseased soul, making it pure, healthy, and victorious. Real spiritual progress begins when the inner sinful nature is purified. Jesus said: "Blessed are the pure in heart, for they shall see God" (Matt. 5:8); and the author of this letter exhorts: "Pursue after . . . the sanctification without which no one will see the Lord." Spiritual purity is God's provision for spiritual progress in His followers now, and their preparation to enter heaven hereafter. When the honest, seeking soul cries out with the Psalmist of old, "Create in me a clean heart, O God," that person will soon experience the fulfillment of Christ's promise: "The pure in heart . . . shall see God" (Matt. 5:8), and "The one who calls you is faithful and he will do it" (1 Thess. 5:24, NIV).

Chapter XII

The Prayer That Prevails

"The effective prayer of a righteous man can accomplish much" (James 5:16).

To understand this assertion in relation to its context, it is necessary to read the entire passage from verses thirteen through twenty.

> Is anyone among you suffering? Let him pray. Is anyone cheerful? Let him sing praises. Is anyone among you sick? Let him call for the elders of the church, and let them pray over him, anointing him with oil in the name of the Lord; and the prayer offered in faith will restore the one who is sick, and the Lord will raise him up, and if he has committed sins, they will be forgiven him. Therefore, confess your sins to one another, and pray for one another, so that you may be healed. The effective prayer of a righteous man can accomplish much. Elijah was a man with a nature like ours, and he prayed earnestly that it might not rain; and it did not rain on the earth for three years and six months. And he prayed again, and the sky poured rain, and the earth produced its fruit. My brethren if any among you strays from the truth, and one turns him back; let him know that he who turns a sinner from the error of his way will save his soul from death, and will cover a multitude of sins.

Christ's exhortation, at all times "[men] ought to pray and not lose heart" (Luke 18:1b), is exceedingly pertinent. The importance of prayer in human experiences has made of it a universal characteristic of mankind. That much praying, even among Christians, is little more than wishful thinking, is evident from its frequent fruitlessness.

James strikes at the very crux of the matter and prescribes the kind of prayer that is effective in the words of our text: "The effective prayer of a righteous man can accomplish much."

Prevailing (Effectual) Praying is Specific

The word *effectual* (as used in the KJV) assumes a cause sufficient to afford the necessary incentive and power to attain the desired end. In other words, as James used the word *effectual* in this passage, he assumes a specific object of prayer that gives both direction and force to the prayer. Much prayer is without value because it is without any specific objective—it is aimed at no mark in particular. James says: "You ask and do not receive, because you ask with wrong motives, so that you may spend it on your pleasures" (James 4:3).

In chapter 5:13-19 James clearly sets forth certain objectives of prayer. Let us briefly examine these objectives.

The prayer object of affliction. "Is anyone among you suffering? Let him pray." Perhaps no Biblical writer was better qualified to write on the subject of prayer than James, pastor of the Jerusalem church. Tradition has it that he was called the horny-kneed apostle from his much kneeling in prayer.

That the apostle means something quite different from physical illness, by the word *affliction*, is evident from the subsequent verse in which he exhorts prayer for the *sick*.

Among the common afflictions that are worthy objects of prayer is discouragement. Perhaps no more effective weapon for defeating God's children has ever been designed by the enemy than discouragement. And strange it is that not infrequently this malady follows great spiritual victory. Almost immediately following his great victory over the prophets of Baal, Elijah found himself dejectedly alone by the brook beseeching God to let him die. Following the victory of Nineveh's repentance, Jonah likewise succumbed to dejection and prayed for death. Again, it is the moment of the sense of greatest aloneness that constitutes man's severest temptation. It was so with Christ when on the Cross in that excruciating moment, as He met sin's ultimate issue, He cried out, "My God, My God, Why hast Thou forsaken Me?" (Matt. 27:46b). It was so with Job in his awful aloneness.

Is any afflicted by the unendurable sense of a unique temptation, "let him pray." Said the Psalmist, "Even though I walk through the valley of the shadow of death, I fear no evil; for Thou art with me" (Ps. 23:4a).

Numerous other afflictions, such as lack of self-confidence, an under-evaluation of one's abilities and capabilities, restrictive influences upon one's religious liberties and activities, physical handicaps or mental limitations; any of these or one of a thousand other afflictions may be greatly ameliorated or even eliminated by prayer. "Is any among you afflicted? Let him pray."

The prayer object of illness. "Is anyone among you sick? . . . the prayer offered in faith will restore the one who is sick, and the Lord will raise him up" (James 5:14a).

Liberal theology, modern psychiatry, and a number of current cults have of recent date placed much emphasis upon the therapeutic value of religion for the physically or mentally ill. For the most part, these agencies have worked on the principles of auto-suggestion, hypnotism, Mesmerism, elimination of the malady by denial (Christian Science), mental transcendence or psychic radiation — all of which differ radically from the intervention of a personal God correcting the physical malady in response to the prayer of faith exercised for healing by one of His children.

From the days of the Apostles to the present, the Church has never been without a certain degree of emphasis upon divine healing. The book of Acts is replete with such instances. It is reported that in recent times the Church of England has recognized the special office of divine healing.

Certainly there is no warrant here for capitalizing on divine healing through the publicizing of healing meetings in a sort of assembly-line fashion as is done by certain faith healers. In fact the order recommended by James is quite the opposite. Says the Apostle concerning the sick: "let him [the sick] call for the elders of the church, and let them pray over him, anointing him with oil in the name of the Lord" (James 5:14). Thus James recommends that the ill person assume the initiative in calling the elders to pray for him.

Prayer for healing is a less difficult prayer for God to answer than prayer for the conversion of a sinner. The latter involves the will of the individual, which God always respects; whereas in the former, God could answer irrespective of the will, since He is dealing primarily with the temporal and material rather than the spiritual.

James recommends that the ill person assume the initiative in calling the elders to pray for him. How different is this procedure from that of so many modern faith healers who advertise their meetings as healing meetings accompanied with promises of certain miraculous physical restoration for all who attend with physical maladies.

James' injunction to anoint the sick with oil has been frequently misunderstood, and deserves special notice here. The oil used by the Hebrews of Bible times was chiefly olive oil. It has a variety of uses, including food (2 Chron. 12:40; Ezek. 16:13; 1 Kings 17:12; Lev. 2:1, 4-7); as a cosmetic (2 Sam. 14:2; Ps. 23:5; 104:15); for anointing kings, priests, and the prophets (1 Sam. 10:1; 16:1, 13; 2 Kings 1:39; 9:1, 6); for light; for religious ritual; and as a medicine. *The Westminster Dictionary of the Bible* states that

> oil was used in medicine for mollifying wounds (Isa. 1:6; Mark 6:13). Sometimes wine was added to the oil, as was done by the Good Samaritan in the case of the wounded Israelite (Luke 10:34). Herod was put in a bath of warm oil in the hope of alleviating his disease (Josephus, *War* i. 33, 5).[1]

William Smith observes:

> The prophet Isaiah (i. 6) alludes to the use of oil as ointment in medical treatment; and it thus furnishes a fitting symbol, perhaps also an efficient remedy, when used by our Lord's disciples in the miraculous cures which they were enabled to perform (Mark v. 1. 13). With a similar intention, no doubt, its use was enjoined by Saint James (v. 14).[2]

Weymouth observes: " 'The Greek Church,' remarks Bassett, 'retains the custom of anointing, but (unlike the church of Rome) does not regard it as a sacrament, but as

---

[1] *The Westminster Dictionary of the Bible.*
[2] William Smith, *A Dictionary of the Bible.*

medicinal treatment'; as recommended by Philo, Pliny, and Galen."[3] Wesley remarks on this practice: "This was the whole process of physic in the Christian church, till it waslost through unbelief. That novel invention among the Romanists, extreme unction, practiced not for cure, but where life is despaired of, there is no manner of resemblance to this."[4] THE INTERPRETER'S BIBLE observes that it is perfectly true that the use of oil as a medicine was widespread in the ancient world (cf., e.g. Luke 10:34).[5] However, some authorities prefer to regard the case in question as sacramental rather than medicinal, a position difficult for Protestants to accept.

Adam Clarke clearly supports the medicinal position. He says:

> What is here recommended was to be done as a natural means of restoring health, which, while they used prayer and supplication to God, they were not to neglect. Oil in Judea was celebrated for its salutary qualities; so that they scarcely ever took a journey without carrying oil with them with which they anointed their bodies, healed their wounds, bruises, and so forth. Oil was and is frequently used in the East as the means of cure in very dangerous diseases; and in Egypt is often used in the cure of the *plague*. Even in Europe it has been tried with great success in the cure of *dropsy*. The *pure olive oil* is excellent for recent wounds and bruises; I have seen it tried in this way with best results. But that it was the custom of the Jews to apply it as a means of healing, and that Saint James referred to this custom, is not only evident from the case of the wounded man ministered to by the good Samaritan, Luke 10:34, but from the practice of the Jewish rabbans . . . they had . . . recourse to this as a *natural*; we find that the

---

[3]Richard Francis Weymouth, *The New Testament in Modern Speech* (New York: Harper and Brothers Publishers, n.d.), p. 565, n. 14.

[4]John Wesley, *Explanatory Notes upon the New Testament* (London: The Epworth Press, rep. 1954), p. 869).

[5]George Arthur Buttrick, ed., *The Interpreter's Bible* (New York: Abingdon Press, 1957), 12:70.

disciples used it also in this way to heal the sick, and not exerting the miraculous power but in cases where natural means were effectual . . . In short, *anointing the sick with oil,* in order to their recovery, was a constant practice among the Jews. See Lightfoot and Wetstein on Mark 6:13. Here I am satisfied that it has no other meaning than as a *natural means* of restoring health, and that Saint James desires them to use *natural means* of restoring health, and that Saint James desires them to use *natural means* while looking to God for any special blessing. And no wise man would direct otherwise.[6]

Dummelow's Commentary states:

Saint James is telling his readers that this custom was to be continued by Christian Jews, and that the confession of the sick man was to be made to the clergy ('presbyters') of the church. They would then (1) pray over him for the pardon of his sins, and (2) anoint him with oil (recognized remedy, Isa. 1:6; Mark 6:13; Luke 10:34). By these means he would obtain forgiveness of his sins, and (if it were God's will) recover from his sickness.[7]

"Wordsworth remarks that there is no indication in primitive history that *oil* was used sacramentally. It was used medically, as a means of restoration, with prayer for the due effect."[8]

Thus we conclude that the "anointing with oil" signified the use of an approved media for its curative properties in conjunction with the prayer of faith for divine intervention in the case of the sick. To paraphrase: "If anyone is ill, let him call for the minister (or spiritual leader or leaders—elders) of the church and the medical doctor, and let the doctor administer the scientific medicinal remedies while the elders

---

[6]Adam Clarke, *Clarke's Commentary* (New York-Nashville: Abingdon-Cokesbury Press, n.d.), N.T. 2, p. 827.

[7]J. R. Dummelow, ed., *A Commentary on the Holy Bible*: "Complete in One Volume," (New York: The Macmillan Company, rep. 1951), p. 1037.

[8]D. D. Whedon, *New Testament Commentary,* comment on James 5:14.

pray the prayer of faith for the effectiveness of the medicine in the cure of the sick. Such procedure God will honor in the restoration of the sick to health and his spiritual recovery, in the event he has sinned, and confesses."

The prayer object of moral fault. "Confess your sins to one another, and pray for one another, so that you may be healed" (James 5:16a).

That a fault may be the result of the impact of sin on human experience, but that it may not be a sin in itself, appears evident from this passage. Just as there are geologic faultlines in the earth resulting from earthquakes or other geological disruptions, so the disruptive impact of sin has left moral faultlines in human experience. Misjudgments of others' motives, offensive frankness in speech, mental or spiritual dullness when alertness is one's responsibility, or failure to correct an offensive habit, are but samples of a possible catalogue of faults to be found among Christians, which, while not necessarily sins in themselves, may eventuate in sin if not corrected. James' prescription for this malady is "Confess your faults . . . and pray . . . that you may be healed" (KJV). Recognition and acknowledgement are requisites to remedying the malady.

The prayer object of natural phenomena. "Elijah . . . prayed earnestly that it might not rain . . . And he prayed again, and the sky poured rain, and the earth produced its fruit" (James 5:17, 18).

The eighteenth century deists divorced God from this world and interpreted nature as a machine operated by natural laws fixed by God from creation. The nineteenth century naturalists went a step farther in denying God and making the world self-originating and developing by the supposed laws of naturalistic evolution. Twentieth century naturalists have restored God to the world as the principle of divinity (not a person) unfolding in the onmoving of nature according to its own divine natural laws. This latter view is best known as theistic evolution (a form of pantheism). In all three centuries natural law has been regarded as something fixed and unchangeable. Intelligently considered, natural law is only man's description of natural functions. Properly defined, natural law is simply God's ordinary way of doing things. He is the God of nature, whether by natural or supernatural law. Scripture and history are replete with testimonies to God's intervention and reordering of nature in cases of necessity in answer to the prayers of His people. Nature is never so fixed that God cannot change the natural order in accommodation to the needs and prayers of His children, when the occasion demands. This is what the Quaker philosopher, Elton Trueblood, designates an "open universe."

God never performs miracles for the sake of satisfying the whims of men, nor simply to exhibit His power. All miracles have a divine purpose and a moral value.

It should be observed that the arresting and altering of natural functions was not the ultimate object of the prophet's prayer. Rather this prayer that so radically affected nature was directed to the end of destroying idolatry in the land. The worship of Baal had become so rife that it appeared that the worship of Jehovah had been almost obliterated. So long as agricultural fertility and economic prosperity continued in the land, there would be no likelihood of bringing Israel to repentance and return to the true worship of Jehovah. So long as people are satisfied with the material, they will seldom manifest an interest in the truly spiritual. Elijah understood the subtle influence of material prosperity upon the people of the land, and its disposition to encourage idolatry. Therefore the prophet "prayed earnestly that it might not rain; and it did not rain on the earth for three years and six months." Consequently, the earth refused to yield her fruit, famine followed, and the material support was swept from Israel's idolatrous religious foundation. The people stood in helpless consternation before the withheld blessings and mercies of an offended God. How often has God thus been compelled to remove the foundation from idolatry before faith in it can collapse!

The famine which resulted from three and one-half years of drought prepared Israel for the challenge of her pagan religion which Elijah was about to make. When "he prayed again, and the sky poured rain, and the earth produced its fruit," the inhabitants were forced to recognize that the God of Elijah was greater than Baal. We observed a similar situation on the occasion of the deliverance of Israel from the land of Egypt.

It should be noted here that the miracle of divine intervention, in this instance, is justified by the purpose and the
results. Elijah was not praying that God would simply satisfy
his whims by demonstrating His power by a miracle in the
realm of nature. The two specific objectives involved were
"conviction for sin" and "divine mercy."

Israel was apostate and idolatrous. While Ahab was the
nominal king, Jezebel was the actual ruler of the country.
She was the daughter of a heathen king, and in her heart
she had either never been divorced from Baal worship, or
had reverted to this pagan religion. She supported by state
revenue 450 prophets of Baal ("they ate at her table," KJV).
Material prosperity characterized the kingdom, and a sense
of security and defiance of Jehovah and the true religion
prevailed under the dominant rule of this wicked queen.
Under such conditions there was no hope of spiritual revival.

Elijah prayed for three and a half years of drought that
such need and destitution might occur as to destroy the self-
sufficiency of the people and create conditions favorable to
spiritual revival. When the drought produced those conditions, Elijah was able to challenge and defeat the prophets
of Baal on Mount Carmel. Thus the miracle of drought in
answer to the prophet's prayer produced the desired effects.

Later, however, the prophet prayed for rain, and God
manifested His mercy in sending rain that fructified the fields
and restored prosperity. It was not until "he had spent everything" and "a severe famine occurred in that country," and
"he began to be in need," that the prodigal son reflected on
his loss and the abundance of his father's provision. Divine
mercy always follows human misery, when man turns from
his misery to implore God's mercy.

The prayer object of spiritual revival. With the thought
of prayer still in mind, James continues: "My brethren, if
any among you strays from the truth, and one turns him
back; let him know that he who turns a sinner from the error
of his way will save his soul from death, and will cover a multitude of sins" (James 5:19, 20).

Worthy as the foregoing objects of prayer may be, the
object of spiritual revival transcends them all. God told Paul
that His grace was sufficient, when he prayed for the removal
of the thorn of affliction. God may allow a terminal illness

to take its course in one of His children. Some faults may be left to the individual to correct by patient and persistent self-effort. God may not see fit to change the natural order in accommodation to the desires of the petitioners; but there is no circumstance under which God is unwilling to save the soul of a penitent sinner. When we lift our hearts to God in prayer for the salvation of lost men, we are always praying in the will of God. "The Lord does not wish for any to perish but for all to come to repentance" (2 Peter 3:9). "For God so loved the world, that He gave His only begotten Son, that whosoever believes in Him should not perish, but have eternal life" (John 3:16). Thus prayer for the conversion of the sinner is the climactic consideration of the Apostle in this greater prayer treatise.

Prevailing Prayer Is Emotional

James characterizes effectual praying as *fervent* (KJV). "The effective [fervent] prayer of a righteous man can accomplish much." The word *fervent*, etymologically considered, means boiling hot, or seething with fermentation.

Emotion has frequently been misunderstood in relation to religious experience. Correctly defined, emotion is the feeling-reaction of the individual to a given realization. Emotion means nothing unless it is produced by a realized situation. When so produced, it affords the power necessary for action. Matthew records of Christ that "seeing the multitudes, *He felt compassion for them,* because they were distressed and downcast like sheep without a shepherd" (Matt. 9:36). Again, in the parable of the Good Samaritan (Luke 10:25-37), both the priest and the Levite, representatives of the Jewish moral and ceremonial laws respectively, failed to come to grips with the reality of the situation presented by a robbed, wounded, and half-dead brother by the wayside. Consequently, they passed by *unmoved by any feeling of compassion.* On the other hand, it is said that "a certain Samaritan, who was on a journey, came upon him; and when he saw him, *he felt compassion*" (Luke 10:33). The Samaritan's emotional reaction was produced by the spectacle of the man's sad condition and produced in him a compassion that eventuated in the alleviation of his suffering.

So in prayer, until the reality of a situation lays hold of the consciousness of the petitioner, prayer will be devoid of any moving force. When the salvation of a soul from sin's ruinous power, or the reclamation of a derelict brother, sister, son or daughter is realized to hinge upon the effectiveness of one's petitions, an emotional reaction will be produced, giving power to prayer. "The effective prayer . . . can accomplish much." Prayers without fervor are like cold lead without ignited powder. They have no driving power in themselves.

Prevailing Prayer Is Objective

There are two general types of prayer: namely, subjective and objective. Subjective prayer may have its value in the edification of the worshiper, and even moral benefits may accrue from it.

It is, however, with objective prayer that we are here primarily concerned. Such prayer assumes the existence of a concerned and responsive God, and it is to God Himself above himself that the petitioner directs his prayer. For Elijah, God was no Tillichian "ground of being," or "depth of man's being." He was the personal governor of the universe.

The varieties of prayer are suggested by Paul in the Ephesian letter thus: "With all prayer and petition pray at all times in the Spirit" (Eph. 6:18a). Among these "*all* prayers" may be noted intercessory prayer, ejaculatory prayer, private prayer, public prayer and vocalized and silent prayer. It is not the posture, not the particular type of prayer that is of prime importance, but rather the sincerity and spirit of the prayer, plus faith in a personal God to whom it is directed. Paul's exhortation to Timothy is specific: "I want the men in every place to pray, lifting up holy hands, without wrath and dissension" (1 Tim. 2:8).

Prevailing Prayer Is Conditioned
By the Right Attitude of the Petitioner

"*The effective prayer of a righteous man* can accomplish much." The Psalmist said, "If I regard wickedness in my heart, the Lord will not hear" (Ps. 66:18). The blind man whose eyes Christ opened spoke truly when he said, "We know that God does not hear sinners; but if anyone is God-fearing, and does His will, He hears him" (John 9:31).

Any measure of personal guilt, rebellion against the will of God, hypocrisy or insincerity will destroy confidence in God and rob the petitioner's prayer of its faith and effectiveness. Prayers from unrighteous and impenitent hearts never rise to the throne of God. A specific condition for answered prayers is that the petitioner be in right relationship with God and man.

Prevailing Prayer Is Fruitful

"The effective prayer of a righteous man can *accomplish much.*"

Elijah's prayers sealed up heaven's moisture from the earth for three years, and then opened the fountain of the great deep for a mighty refreshing of the earth. The same prophet's prayers produced fire from heaven that devoured the water-soaked sacrifices on the altar, and licked up the water in the moat surrounding the altar, to the consternation of the prophets of Baal. Righteous Abraham's prayers saved Lot from the destruction of wicked Sodom. Jacob wrestled with the angel of the Lord in prayer until he blessed him and dispelled twenty years of accumulated wrath from his brother Esau's infuriated mind, causing him to meet him in peace rather than war the following day. Moses prayed and saved a whole nation from extinction by the wrath of God in the wilderness. A hundred and twenty disciples prayed in the upper room and Pentecost occurred with its initial harvest of three thousand souls. A little band of hounded Christians at Damascus prayed and the vicious persecutor, Saul, en route to that city, was arrested by Christ and transformed into the mightiest apostle of righteousness the world has ever known. John Knox's prayers caused Bloody Queen Mary to tremble and they finally saved Scotland.

Elijah was a man subject to like passions as we are, and yet he prayed. Thus, if we today pray the *"effectual fervent prayer of the righteous man that availeth much"* (KJV), we shall behold mighty transformations wrought by the power of God: "at all times they ought to pray and not to lose heart" (Luke 18:1b). Prevailing intercessory prayer would produce a spiritual revival in the church of today that would not only transform the spiritual and moral life of the church, but that would send her forth on a great mission for the evangelization of the world of this generation.

Chapter XIII

The Sanctifying Grace of Christ

"This is the will of God, your sanctification" (1 Thess. 4:3).

"Pursue after . . . sanctification without which no man will see the Lord" (Heb. 12:14).

"Jesus, . . . that He might sanctify the people through His own blood, suffered outside the gate" (Heb. 13:12).

Introduction

Full salvation in Christ has been recognized by all Christian communions as a requisite to a victorious Christian life and final entrance into heaven, though the time, manner, and agency of this experience have been points of widely-divergent opinions. Upon one point all are agreed: that to live pleasingly to God and finally enter heaven, man must be made holy. That the Bible teaches the divine provision and requirement of entire sanctification for all the disciples of Jesus Christ, not only as a requirement for entrance into heaven, but also as a provision for fellowship with God and victorious Christian living in the present life, no honest student of the Word need remain ignorant.

1. THE CONVERSION AND SPIRITUAL STATE OF THE THESSALONIAN BELIEVERS. Perhaps nowhere in the New Testament is this gracious divine provision more explicitly set forth than in Paul's first letter to the Thessalonians, chapter 5:23-24, which read thus:

"Now may the God of peace Himself sanctify you entirely; and may your spirit and soul and body be preserved complete, without blame at the coming of our Lord Jesus Christ. Faithful is He who calls you, and He also will bring it to pass."

Paul had conducted the initial Christian evangelistic campaign among the idolatrous inhabitants of Thessalonica, after he passed over into Europe on the occasion of the

Macedonian vision on his second missionary journey. This was about A.D. 51 or 52. He later wrote two letters from Corinth to this Christian church, which letters are preserved for us in the New Testament. The manner and characteristics of that great campaign at Thessalonica are set forth most graphically by the Apostle in the following words:

> For our gospel did not come to you in word only, but also in power and in the Holy Spirit and with full conviction; just as you know what kind of men we proved to be among you for your sake. You also became imitators of us and of the Lord, having received the word in much tribulation with the joy of the Holy Spirit, so that you became an example to all the believers in Macedonia and in Achaia" (1 Thess. 1:5-7).

Though these Thessalonians had been genuinely converted, they still stood in need of entire sanctification. For this second spiritual benefit in their hearts and lives Paul earnestly yearns and prays, as is expressed in his words:

> As we night and day keep praying most earnestly that we may see your face, and may complete what is lacking in your faith? So that He may establish your hearts unblameable in holiness before our God and Father at the coming of our Lord Jesus with all His saints" (1 Thess. 3:10, 13).

The Apostle's desire and prayer for the sanctification of these Christians is enforced by his deep conviction that such is God's will for them. He says, "For this is the will of God, your sanctification; that is, that you abstain from sexual immorality" (1 Thess. 4:3).

It is evident from the internal evidence of the first Thessalonian letter that the people to whom this letter was addressed by Paul were (1) genuinely converted to Christianity, and that they were living in a gracious experience of regeneration; (2) that at the time of the writing of this letter these Christians had not yet been sanctified; (3) that the Apostle Paul recognized the imperative need of their entire sanctification; (4) that God had made ample provision in the atonement of Jesus Christ for their entire sanctification in the present life; and (5) that such was God's will for them. Since a definite conversion experience ever stands as a logical and scriptural prerequisite to entire sanctification, let us note the evidence that the Thessalonians were genuinely converted to Christianity.

They had heard, believed, and obeyed the Gospel of Jesus Christ: "having received the word in much tribulation with the joy of the Holy Spirit" (1 Thess. 1:6b).

In the midst of heavy opposition and persecution from the unbelieving Jews and their fellow Grecian countrymen, these people had listened to the "good news" concerning salvation from sin, provided by the death and resurrection of Jesus Christ for all men. So welcome was this news to these benighted idol worshipers (1 Thess. 1:9) that, as in faith they received the message delivered under the anointing of the Holy Spirit, they were made to greatly rejoice in anticipation of its promises and provisions. They, like the Ephesians, had heard the word of truth, which became the gospel of their salvation (Eph. 1:15).

Nor were the Thessalonians but superficial hearers, who momentarily rejoiced in the glorious prospects of a provision which they had insufficient courage or strength of purpose to appropriate. The Apostle reflects upon their response to his preaching at Thessalonica and writes:

> And for this reason we also constantly thank God that when you received from us the word of God's message, you accepted it not as the word of men but for what it really is, the word of God, which also performs its work in you who believe (1 Thess. 2:13).

Further evidence of their ready response to this message declared unto them by the Apostle is revealed in verses nine and ten of the first chapter. They were of that class of hearers depicted by Jesus in the parable of the sower, where the seed "fell on the good soil, and yielded a crop, some a hundred-fold, some sixty, and some thirty" (Matt. 13:8). They were numbered among those of whom the author of the letter to the Hebrews wrote: "He [Christ] became to all those who obey Him the source of eternal life" (Heb. 5:9). Of them it

could be said, as Peter wrote: " . . . you have in obedience
to the truth purified your souls for a sincere love of the
brethren . . . (1 Peter 1:22a). They were not of those who,
when the bright light of the truth shines in upon their
benighted souls, instantly recoil from the divine revelation
of their unholy lives and withdraw into the denser darkness
of closed minds and rebellious hearts. Rather, they ". . .
received the word in much tribulation with the joy of the Holy
Spirit" (1 Thess. 1:6b).

They had experienced a definite change of religious affection: ". . . you turned to God from idols to serve a living and
true God, and to wait for His Son from heaven, whom He
raised from the dead, that is Jesus, who delivers us from the
wrath to come" (1 Thess. 1:9b-10).

From this review of the Thessalonians' conversion, it is
evident that they had embraced a new object of religious
affection. Says Paul, "You turned to God." This turning
represents a deliberate, intelligent and voluntary act on the
part of the Thessalonians. They had recognized in the "living and true God," as represented to them by the Apostle,
what they had ever failed to find in their idols. The God of
Christianity was moral, their idols were the very representations of immorality. The truth of the God of Christianity
was verified to them ". . . in power and in the Holy Spirit
and with full conviction" (1 Thess. 1:5). Paul could appeal
to the evidence of the truthfulness of the God whom he presented to them as that ". . . word of God, which also performs its work in you who believe" (1 Thess. 3:13b). How
unlike the dumb idols to which they had been devoted, which
both in their pretenses and their promises had brought
nothing but disappointment. As the truth of God witnessed
to their inner beings, their moral natures long dormant
awakened and responded in recognition of the divine revelation. Again, in the Christian God they experienced spiritual
vitality and fellowship, whereas in their dumb idols they had
found neither. Here there was the consciousness of a new
spiritual relationship and fellowship, which are ever the
characteristics of true religion; there had been a devotion
without recognition or response from the objects of their worship. They had "turned to God" from those that were no
gods.

When these Thessalonians "turned to God," they consequently turned "from idols." The latter was the inevitable consequent of the former. The negative turn was the natural result of the positive. They did not forsake their idols and go in search of the true God. They were among those Gentiles of whom the prophet wrote: "I WAS FOUND BY THOSE WHO SOUGHT ME NOT, I BECAME MANIFEST TO THOSE WHO DID NOT ASK FOR ME" (Rom. 10:20b). Then upon being found of God, they forsook their former life of deception. They were like Moses of old who ". . . refused to be called the son of Pharaoh's daughter; choosing rather to endure ill treatment with the people of God . . . considering the reproaches of Christ greater riches than the treasures of Egypt" (Heb. 11:24b-26a). These pagans had beheld the beauty and riches of Christ and chose Him, thus rejecting and forsaking idolatry. Their positive turn preceded the negative, which is the natural Christian order.

But yet again, these Thessalonians found in Jesus a new engrossing engagement of service, for they turned "to serve a living and true God" (1 Thess. 1:9b). It was service to a new Master from a new motive. It was a willing service inspired by the new object of their affection. Of this new service Paul could write to them his commendation for their "work of faith and labor of love and steadfastness of hope" (1 Thess. 1:3). Their new service was a love service, because it had been inspired by the God of love to whom they had been introduced and to whom they had turned.

Finally, in the new object of their religious affection they had found a new anticipation—a new hope: "to wait for His Son from heaven, whom He raised from the dead, that is Jesus, who delivers us from the wrath to come" (1 Thess. 1:10). The expectancy of Christ's return gave them a new outlook and hope from their sufferings under persecution. It is He "who delivereth" now, and who will deliver them, for whom they affectionately waited. Herein lay their "patience of hope" (1 Thess. 1:3b).

The religious experience of these Thessalonians, as reviewed by Paul in chapter one and verses nine and ten, is related to their Christian virtues of chapter one, verse three as follows: their "work of faith" consisted in their turning "unto god, from idols"; their "labor of love" consisted in their serving a "living and true God"; and their "patience of hope" consisted in their anticipation of "His Son from heaven."

These believers had experienced a definite inner divine witness to their acceptance with God: "knowing brethren beloved by God, His choice of you" (1 Thess. 1:4).

There is nothing clearer than that having heard and believed the gospel, these Gentiles received miraculous assurance of their divine election to the enjoyment of all the blessings and privileges of divine grace afforded the Jews, and that without subscription to the legalistic rites and ceremonies of the Mosaic Law. The so-called problem of "election" is well illustrated in the experience of the world-renowned missionary evangelist, E. Stanley Jones, at a certain General Conference of the Methodist Church.

Jones was officially elected a bishop of his denomination; he declined that election on the grounds that God had called him to missionary service in India and not to administrative service in his denomination. Jones was officially elected a bishop, but he declined that election. Likewise, *all* people are elected of God to salvation (John 3:16), but only those who accept their election are saved.

The forgiveness of their sins and their acceptance into the family of God, as adopted children through redemption provided in Christ, was freely attested by the Holy Spirit through His influence upon their hearts, renewing and transforming them, and bearing an inner witness to their salvation. Paul testifies to the function of the Holy Spirit in their conversion experience thus: "Our gospel . . . [came] also in power and the Holy Spirit and with full conviction" (1 Thess. 1:5). To them it had become a glorious reality that, "The one who believes in the Son of God has the witness in himself" (1 John 5:10); and "you have received a spirit of adoption as sons by which we cry out, 'Abba! Father!' The Spirit Himself bears witness with our spirit that we are children of God, and if children, heirs also, heirs of God and fellow-heirs with Christ" (Rom. 8:15b-17a). Lest there remain any doubt in their minds as to the certainty of the presence of the Holy Spirit in their regenerated experience, the Apostle adds, "God . . . gives His Holy Spirit to you" (1 Thess. 4:8b). They are not among those of whom the Apostle spoke in no uncertain tones, "But if anyone does not have the Spirit of Christ, he does not belong to Him" (Rom. 8:9b). Rather they had met the conditions of acceptance into the kingdom of God laid down by Christ in His discourse to Nicodemus: " . . . unless one is born of water and the Spirit, he cannot enter into the kingdom of God"; and again, "that which is born of the Spirit is spirit" (John 3:5b, 6b). They could say with the Apostle John: "by this we know that we abide in Him and He in us, because He has given us of His Spirit" (1 John 4:13). They had been convicted by the Spirit, born of the Spirit, received the witness of the Spirit to their acceptance with God, and were inwardly sustained by the personal presence of the Spirit in their regenerated lives. Of them it was true that "greater is He who is in you, than he who is in the world" (1 John 4:4b). And the Apostle admonishes them thus: "Do not quench the Spirit" (1 Thess. 5:19), just prior to his final prayer for their entire sanctification.

To deny the regenerative function of the Holy Spirit in the conversion experience is to deny that this experience is a work of God; and to deny the indwelling presence of the Holy Spirit in the inner life of the Christian believer is to deny the efficacy of the believer's faith in the atonement, and the vitality of his Christian experience and relationship with God. In short, to deny the presence of the Holy Spirit in the inner life of the believer is to deny that he is a Christian. To give the Holy Spirit His rightful place in the experience and life of the regenerated Christian is not to say that the individual who is genuinely saved—but not as yet sanctified holy—is baptized with the Holy Spirit, or that he is filled with the Holy Spirit. So long as the carnal self-nature remains within the Christian, that Christian is not and cannot be truly *filled with the Holy Spirit.* Only when that sinful self-nature is crucified, purified by the fiery baptism of the Holy Spirit, can the life of the sanctified Christian be said to be *filled with the Holy Spirit.* He (the Spirit) is in the hearts and lives of the regenerated, but not without an inner rival, and His domain is never complete and uncontested until that rival is expelled and destroyed through the sanctifying operation of the Holy Spirit.

The Thessalonian believers were living consistent, exemplary Christian lives. "You also became imitators of us and of the Lord . . . so that you became an example to all the believers in Macedonia and Achaia" (1 Thess. 1:6, 7). "For you, brethren, became imitators of the churches of God in Christ Jesus that are in Judea" (1 Thess. 2:14a).

The spiritual vitality that was so manifest in the conversion of the Thessalonians had not been allowed to wane; rather, it grew and abounded (1 Thess. 1:5).

Though the Apostle had been anxious lest they should have yielded to the pressure of persecution and thus lost their justified relation with God, he was reassured and made to rejoice upon receipt of good news concerning their spiritual state, as that news was brought to him by Timothy. Paul expresses his satisfaction with Timothy's report thus: "But now that Timothy has come to us from you, and has brought us good news of your faith and love . . . we were comforted about you through your faith; for now we really live, if you stand firm in the Lord" (1 Thess. 3:6a, 7, 8).

Thus, the Thessalonian believers had maintained their saving faith in Christ, and had so ordered their lives that they were examples of true Christianity. The Apostle calls them *ensamples, or examples* of the body of Christ, the church universal: "so that you became an example to all who believe." Webster defines an example as "what is taken out of a large quantity, as a sample. One or a portion taken to show the character or quality of all, a sample. That which is to be followed or imitated, a pattern. A precedent, model, or parallel case." In every respect, these believers measured up to the requirements of this definition. They were a sample or particular instance of the true Church of God in Christ, and they were a correct representation of that church to the world about them. In fact, in this latter sense their exemplification of Christianity to the world was such that the Apostle finds no occasion to apologize for their lives and conduct before the world, even though they had been so recently converted from the vileness of heathenism, as alluded to in chapter four of the first epistle. Says Paul: "in every place your faith toward God has gone forth, so that we have no need to say anything" (1 Thess. 1:8b). There was no need of apology for their conduct, nor addition to their testimony.

They had continued to walk in the light of divine truth as that light had come to them. Paul commends them: "for you are all sons of light, and sons of day" (1 Thess. 5:5a). To them the words of John are especially appropriate: "but if we walk in the light as He Himself is in the light, we have fellowship with one another, and the blood of Jesus His Son cleanses us from all sin" (1 John 1:7). By their obedience to truth and light in their regenerate lives, they were en route to that glorious experience of entire sanctification, which the Apostle was about to introduce to them.

Finally, these Thessalonian Christians had become *examples* because they had followed genuine Christian believers. Says Paul: "You also became imitators of us and of the Lord" (1 Thess. 1:6a). Again he says, "For you, brethren, became imitators of the churches of God in Christ Jesus that are in Judea" (1 Thess. 2:14a). Nor did they follow a false or misleading example. To them Paul could testify: "You are witnesses, and so is God, how devoutly and uprightly and blamelessly we behaved toward you believers" (1 Thess. 2:10).

Paul's example among the Thessalonians, as outlined above, sets forth his holy life and conduct first in relation to God, as indicated by the word "devoutly," second, in relation to the Thessalonians themselves, as suggested by the word "uprightly," and finally, in relation to his own conscience, as indicated by the word "blamelessly." Thus, these new converts, instead of backsliding from or halting at the threshold of their new religious faith, had followed the good example of the Christian lives and conduct of the Apostle and the churches of Judea, and had themselves become examples of the grace of God to their unconverted countrymen. They had caught the transparent rays from the light of the Son of God that were reflected from the lives of those that had taught them, and reflected those rays out into the darkness of the world of idolatrous men about them.

These Christians gave verbal testimony to their unsaved countrymen. "For the word of the Lord has sounded forth from you, not only in Macedonia and Achaia, but also in every place your faith toward God has gone forth" (1 Thess. 1:8).

It was important that these new converts live consistent exemplary Christian lives; but that was not enough. It was obligatory upon them that they give verbal witness to the saving power of Christ in their lives. It can hardly be properly thought that this message that sounded forth from these new converts from heathenism was in the form of sermons, or formal preaching. Nor does it appear from the internal evidence of the Thessalonian letters that they possessed any written scriptural documents, as they were dependent upon the word Paul had preached to them, and upon the apostles and the churches of Judea for their spiritual instruction and examples. Therefore, we conclude that "the word sounded forth" consisted of their personal testimonies. Such was in keeping with the purpose and plan of the Master for the spread of His Gospel. While yet with His disciples, Jesus had said to them, after speaking of His death and resurrection, and the repentance and remission of sins, "You are witnesses of these things" (Luke 24:48). Again, addressing Himself to His disciples, Jesus had said, "and you will bear witness also, because you have been with Me from the beginning" (John 15:27). To His disciples just before His ascension, Jesus said, "you shall be My witnesses both in Jerusalem, and in Judea and Samaria, and even to the remotest part of the earth" (Acts 1:8b). This may be Luke's other version of Christ's word in Luke 24:48. Thus they were to *be* Christ's witness, and they were *to* witness to Christ.

These new converts went forth bearing personal verbal testimony to the saving efficacy of Jesus Christ in their lives, and to His adequacy for the salvation of their countrymen. It is seriously doubtful whether anyone genuinely saved from sin, through faith in and commitment to Jesus Christ, can long retain his clear justified experience without bearing testimony to that experience before the unsaved. These Thessalonian Christians were not wanting in this respect.

The Thessalonian Christians possessed and exercised the three abiding Christian virtues: "constantly bearing in mind your *work of faith* and *labor of love* and *steadfastness of hope* in our Lord Jesus Christ in the presence of our God and Father" (1 Thess. 1:3).

Paul sums up the essence of Christianity, after having discoursed on and dispensed with all else considered great by men in this world, by saying, "But now abide faith, hope, love, these three; but the greatest of these is love" (1 Cor. 13:13). Thus, in chapter one and verse three Paul is crediting

the Thessalonian Christians with possession of the greatest
of the Christian virtues.

These all-important Christian virtues were no static or
mere theoretical factors in the lives of the Thessalonian converts. They possessed an active faith: "your work of faith";
an active love: "labor of love"; and an active hope: "patience
of hope in our Lord Jesus Christ." As earlier noted, their faith
wrought personal salvation in their hearts; their love engaged
them in the service of the living and true God; and their
patient steadfastness enabled them to endurance of their
present persecutions and sufferings in the fond hope of the
soon return of Jesus Christ.

Paul further commended these Thessalonian Christians
for the growth of these Christian virtues:

> Your faith is greatly enlarged, and the love of each
> one of you all toward one another grows ever
> greater; therefore, we ourselves speak proudly of
> you among the churches of God for your persever-
> ance and faith in the midst of all your persecutions
> and afflictions which you endure (2 Thess. 1:3b, 4).

In contrast, compare the Thessalonians' growth in the
essential Christian graces of *faith, hope,* and *love,* with the
failure of a once-great church in Asia Minor to continue in
those graces, and the consequent divine disapprobation that
fell upon this church. To the Ephesian Church, Jesus directed
the message:

> I know your deeds, and your toil and perseverance
> ... But I have this against you, that you have left
> your first love. Remember therefore from where you
> have fallen, and repent and do the deeds you did
> at first; or else I am coming to you, and will remove
> your lampstand out of its place—unless you repent
> (Rev. 2:2a, 4, 5).

The Ephesian Church had retained the form and pretense,
and even the practice of Christian principles; but this form
was totally devoid of content. They retained their works, but
had lost their faith; they retained their toil or labor, but had
lost their love; they retained their steadfastness but had lost
their hope. The Lord makes no mention of their faith, hope,

or love, except to charge them with having lost these virtues. The lampstand remains burnished and bright, but the oil of faith, hope, and love has burned out, leaving the lampstand depleted and the room in total darkness. Their great danger now is that the lampstand will be taken from them and their hope of re-illumination will be forever gone. They are plainly backslidden in heart, and unless they repent, even their profession and pretense of religion will be soon removed from them, and they will lapse into total apostasy.

Quite the opposite is true of the Thessalonian converts. Their lampstand remains intact, burnished and bright, with the wicks well-trimmed and the lights burning with faith "greatly enlarged," love "ever greater," "perseverance . . . in the midst of all your persecutions . . . which you endure" (1 Thess. 1:3b, 4).

The Thessalonian Christians Were Ready Candidates For the Experience of Entire Sanctification

Paul assured these Thessalonian converts that their sanctification was God's purpose thus, "For this is the will of God, your sanctification" (1 Thess. 4:3). The Apostle then proceeds to pray for them that God's holy will might be accomplished in their behalf. That prayer he expresses as follows: "Now may the God of peace Himself sanctify you entirely; and may your spirit and soul and body be preserved complete, without blame at the coming of our Lord Jesus Christ. Faithful is He who calls you, and He also will bring it to pass" (1 Thess. 5:23, 24).

First, Paul prays that sanctification may be a work of peace wrought by God Himself in the hearts and lives of the Thessalonian converts: "may the God of peace Himself sanctify you entirely." Second, Paul prays that this may be a practical experience in the believers' lives: "may your spirit and soul and body be preserved complete, without blame at the coming of our Lord Jesus Christ." Third, he declares this to be an assured experience: "Faithful is He who calls you, and He will also bring it to pass."

Would-be holy men of India have tortured their bodies, afflicted their souls and tormented their minds with every conceivable human device in fruitless endeavors to attain freedom from the consciousness of the inherent sinful nature. Western philosophers of more than two and a half millenniums have exhausted the intellectual resources of the human mind in their vain endeavors to solve the problem of sin and rid the soul of its consciousness of this inner evil nature. Egyptian Christianity early missed the mark and vainly sought holiness in one or another of monasticism's deceptive promises. Some Christians have not to the present completely rid themselves of this mistaken notion that sin is lodged in the flesh and must be routed by some human device. Even among those committed to the Pauline persuasion of God's provision for a pure heart in the believer through entire sanctification, many still try to attain holiness through works of righteousness by abstinence, attempted self-infliction of death to the carnal mind (an over-emphasis on dying out to the sinful self), observance of rules, adherence to stifling ceremonialism, or insistence upon deadening legalism. How deceptive and disappointing are man's efforts to make himself holy before God.

Entire sanctification is a work wrought by God in the soul of the believer subsequent to regeneration. It is an instantaneous act of cleansing and filling of the soul with His Holy Spirit, subsequent to which there is a continuous growth in grace and maturity in holiness of life. God is entirely holy, and when the believer's consecration is complete and entire with every reservation relinquished to Him, then God through the person of the Holy Spirit pervades the whole, and His holy personal character purifies as it pervades. Peter testifies that it was this that the disciples at Pentecost experienced, as also the household of Cornelius at Caesarea under his ministry. Said he: "And God, who knows the heart, bore witness to them, giving them the Holy Spirit, just as He also did to us; and He made no distinction between us and them, cleansing their hearts by faith" (Acts 15:8, 9).

As the dark cloud-curtain is withdrawn and the clear penetrating sunrays are admitted to the damp, disease-laden atmosphere, clarifying and purifying as it penetrates, just so the Spirit's presence illumines and purifies the diseased soul of the believer restoring health and wholeness when the inner nature is exposed without reservation to His holy presence.

Paul further asserts that sanctification is a work of peace wrought in the soul of the believer. Elsewhere the Apostle declares that "the mind set on the flesh is hostile toward God; for it does not subject itself to the Law of God, for it is not even able to do so" (Rom. 8:7). Such an evil nature of enmity against God and grace must be destroyed before inner peace can prevail. The Christ who came to make peace by the blood of His cross accomplishes this work in the believer's heart by destroying the inner enemy to grace—carnality—through the soul's sanctification.

While it is patent that sanctification has a primary meaning of consecration, or setting apart for a sacred use, it is equally evident that it has the deeper and fuller meaning of purification. Whedon's commentary is significant and helpful on this twofold meaning of the word sanctification. This authority states:

> This term [sanctify] . . . properly signifies to set apart, to remove from common use, and is often in the Old Testament used of the Levitical offerings. From this meaning of apartness from the gross and common comes the idea of consecration, purity, holiness. Hence to sanctify is to separate from sin; to bestow, by the Spirit's aid, the power of avoiding sin, and living without condemnation before God . . . Scripture and experience teach that there may be, and often is, such a measure of the Spirit's bestowal in answer to the prayer of faith, that such uncondemned state may, even after being defaulted by sin, be re-entered and more or less permanently retained. There may be a state of continuous justification, non-condemnation, undiminished divine approbation, from day to day, and of indefinite length. This spiritual power . . . is the result of a more powerful faith in a maturer Christian life . . . This is that higher plane of Christian life, that evangelical *blamelessness,* for which St. Paul here prays in behalf of his Thessalonians . . . The Apostle in the next verse assures us that God will do it! That this is to be done before death is plain from the word *preserved,* which means a continuous process previous to the coming of Christ.[1]

---

[1]D. D. Whedon, *Commentary on the New Testament* (New York: Phillips and Hunt, 1975), 4:386, 387.

That this work is entire in the sense of being a complete purification of the believer's nature is clear from the word *wholly*. "Not the whole Church," Whedon remarks, "but, as Lunemann and all the best commentators agree, the whole *personality* of the individual. He thus prays for the whole being as a unit, and then distributively for the different parts of our nature."[2]

The practicality of this divine work of grace in the believer's experience is evident from the fact that it is designed to preserve his entire being in a state of blamelessness before God. Of this purpose of divine preservation Wesley states: "Of the three here mentioned [spirit, soul, and body], only the last two are the natural constituents. The first is adventitious [or something added] and the supernatural gift of God, to be found in Christians only."[3]

Thus, Paul prays that the regenerate Christian who is indwelt by God's Spirit may be so sanctified as to be preserved in his justification before God until his soul (entire spiritual personality) and body are purified, harmonized and integrated with God's will and Holy Spirit. While this does not abrogate the sanctified man's personality in any respect, it does definitely harmonize human personality with the divine.

Paul does not imply faultlessness in the life of the sanctified believer. Faultlessness bespeaks absolute perfection—which is impossible of human attainment in this life. His prayer is for blamelessness—a state that has to do with motives rather than actions, which must always be subject to faults. The Christian may be preserved blameless in this life, and finally be presented faultless to God at the end of this life (Jude 24). The distinction between blamelessness and faultlessness may be better understood by an illustration. Let us image that a toddling child is approaching dangerously near to a precipice over which to fall would be certain death. The loving father of this child rushes to the child's rescue, but just as he is about to snatch the little one from the edge of the cliff, he slips on a stone and inadvertently

---

[2]*Ibid.*, p. 387.

[3]John Wesley, *Explanatory Notes Upon the New Testament* (London: The Epworth Press, rep. 1954), p. 763).

pushes the child over the cliff to its death on the rocks below. That loving father was blameless in his intention and endeavor to rescue his child, but he was not faultless in having unintentionally caused his child's death. Just so, though our motives may be pure and our love perfect toward God and man, we shall never attain faultlessness until this life is ended and we are finally presented to the Father by our Saviour Jesus Christ.

Finally, this experience of sanctification is assured by God: "faithful is He that calleth you" to this experience of sanctification, "who will also do it," purify and preserve his children blameless, "if we will allow it to be done." Failure to do so is to come short of God's will for our lives: "For this is the will of God, your sanctification" (1 Thess. 4:3). To refuse or fail to appropriate this grace of entire sanctification is to grieve God's Holy Spirit who is our sanctifier. To grieve the Holy Spirit is to lose God's grace and favor; from which state, unless we repent and find again God's forgiveness, we shall deteriorate spiritually and morally, and eventually lose our relationship with God and our souls in eternity without God. But we would say with the author of the epistle to the Hebrews: "But, beloved, we are convinced of better things concerning you, and things that accompany salvation, though we are speaking in this way" (Heb. 6:9). Again, with this author we would lovingly exhort: "let us press on to maturity" (Heb. 6:1); for "faithful is He that calleth you, who also will do it" (1 Thess. 5:24, KJV).

CHAPTER XIV

The Fullness of the Spirit

"They were all filled with the Spirit and began . . ." (Acts 2:4).

Introduction

The Relation of the Christian Pentecost to the Jewish Historical Pentecost.

The Pentecost of Acts 2 occurred at Jerusalem during the annual Jewish feast which, in the opinion of most scholars, commemorated the giving of the law on Mount Sinai. At the Jewish Pentecost at Sinai God wrote His law on tables of stone for the moral government of Israel. At the Christian Pentecost God renewed His moral laws on hearts of flesh for the moral government of mankind. The former was external; the latter was internal. *The former was legal; the latter was spiritual.*

The Hebrew-Jewish Feast of Pentecost signified the culmination of the harvest season, fifty days after "the putting in of the sickle" (Deut. 16:9f). The first Christian Pentecost signified the gracious fruit of the atonement of Christ, a harvest yielding in its initial stages 3,000 converts to the Christian faith. The broad inclusiveness of the participants in this Hebrew-Jewish festival, namely, "your sons and your daughters and your male and female servants and the Levite who is in your town, and the stranger and the orphan and the widow who is in your midst" (Deut. 16:11), is prophetic of the universal scope of the Gospel of Jesus Christ through the fullness of the Spirit at Pentecost (Acts 1:8). Dummelow says, "On this day the gospel harvest began; and the old Law of ordinances was superseded by the new Law of love."[1]

---

[1] J. R. Dummelow, *A Commentary on the Holy Bible* (New York: The Macmillan Company, rep. 1951), p. 820.

The Place and People of Pentecost

The actual location of the Christian disciples at the occurrence of the Spirit's effusion at Pentecost is neither finally certain nor important. That the disciples resorted to an upper room for prayer, to await the fulfillment of the promise, is clear from Acts 1:13, 14. "And when they had entered, they went up into the upper room. . . . These all with one mind were continually devoting themselves to prayer . . ." (Acts 1:13a, 14a). Some have thought that they were in the upper chamber where they ate the last supper with the Master before His crucifixion. Others, including G. Campbell Morgan, believe they were in a compartment of the temple. From Acts 2:2 it appears more likely that they were assembled in a private dwelling, possibly the home of Mary the mother of John Mark, where the church subsequently met on occasion (Acts 12:12).

Of far greater significance than the place are the persons who first experienced the baptism in the Spirit at Pentecost. This *initial baptism* in the Spirit was not the experience of non-Christian Jewish dwellers at Jerusalem, nor of the masses of non-Christian Jews gathered from the fifteen nations, as mentioned in Acts 2:9-11, for the Jewish festival. Nor was it the experience of proselytes to the Jewish faith from the Gentile world, to say nothing of the Gentile world itself. Indeed the divine effusion was to have its influence on these unconverted peoples, but not until the disciples were first inwardly purified, possessed and empowered by the Holy Spirit. Rather the *they* of Acts 2:1, who experienced this baptism in the Spirit at Pentecost were those Christian disciples enumerated in Acts 1:13, 14. This list includes such familiar characters from among Jesus' personal disciples as Peter, John, James, Andrew, Philip, Thomas, Bartholomew, Matthew, James the son of Alphaeus, Simon the Zealot, Judas the son of James, Mary the Lord's mother, and Jesus' own brothers. Indeed Luke gives the total number of believers as "about a hundred and twenty" (Acts 1:15). In His High Priestly Prayer, as recorded in the seventeenth chapter of the Gospel according to John, Jesus had prayed for these disciples. In that prayer He declared that they belonged to God, that He had kept them (except the son of perdition), and that they were not of the world, even as he was not of the world. He prayed for their sanctification through the truth, and He declared their mission was to the world. This witnessing mission of His disciples is reiterated in the commission of Acts 1:8.

Thus the recipients of the baptism in the Spirit at Pentecost were the saved disciples of Jesus Christ, separated from the world, and intended by Christ to become the living evangels of His Lordship to all men subsequent to their baptism in the Spirit. And thus their experience at Pentecost cannot be properly regarded as "the birthday" of the Christian church, as some have asserted. Christ had brought the church into existence during the days of His flesh. He had called out and saved these disciples who now waited for this baptism in the Spirit. They constituted His church before Pentecost. Rather, from an institutional and ceremonial standpoint, the Spirit's effusion at Pentecost may be regarded as the *consecration, dedication,* or *inauguration* of the church of Christ. It was the body of living believers in Christ who experienced the baptism in the Spirit as of Acts 2:1-4.[2] Upon those disciples fell, as Peter explained in Acts 2:16-18, the fulfillment of Joel's divinely-inspired prophecy.

> But this was what was spoken of through the prophet Joel: And it shall come to pass in the last days, God says, that I will pour forth of My Spirit upon all mankind: and your sons and your daughters shall prophesy, and your young men shall dream dreams; even upon My bondslaves, both men and women, I will in those days pour forth of My Spirit and they shall prophesy [preach or witness].

The Fullness of the Spirit Signifies Divine Power

"And suddenly there came from heaven a noise like a violent rushing wind, and it filled the whole house where they were sitting . . . and they were all filled with the Holy Spirit" (Acts 2:2, 4a).

---

[2]For other support of the author's position see Howard Marshall, "The Significance of Pentecost," *The Asbury Seminarian,* April 1977, pp. 17-39, and Myron Augsburger, *Practicing the Presence of the Spirit* (Scottdale, PA: Herald Press, 1982), pp. 29-37.

There appears to have been a twofold purpose in this divine phenomenon described by Luke as "a noise like a violent rushing wind." First, it was intended to stimulate the faith of the disciples for all that was to follow. Second, its purpose was to arrest the attention of the masses of people assembled in Jerusalem for the Jewish Pentecost, and thus provide audience for that inspired Apostolic preaching which was to result in the initial conversion of 3,000 people.

Power has ever been the passion of mankind. Nor does the acquisition and exercise of power appear to have been absent from God's plan and purpose for humanity. Immediately following creation we read the divine commission to our foreparents: "Be fruitful and multiply, and fill the earth, and subdue it; and rule over the fish of the sea and the birds of the sky, and over every living thing that moves upon the earth" (Gen. 1:28b). A review of man's intellectual and material achievements through the centuries would bear near conclusive testimony to the fulfillment of that commission. But there are two important realms in which persons, devoid of the grace of God, have ever failed to fulfill the commission to "subdue . . . and rule over," namely, the realms of the spiritual and moral. Solomon reflected this truth when he said, "He who is slow to anger is better than the mighty, and he who rules his spirit, than he who captures a city" (Prov. 16:32b). People have, through the exercise of their native abilities, become giants, but in the absence of divine grace, they are morally insane giants, giants who will, unless spiritually and morally conquered, inevitably destroy themselves by their own powers. It is an inner divine power that is needed to fulfill God's purpose in mankind's existence (see Eph. 3:14-17).

The Priority of Divine Power

The violent rushing wind on the day of Pentecost is directly suggestive of the dynamic of God in His relation to humanity. This "violent wind," or breath of God, is the fulfillment of Christ's words to His disciples, ". . . You are to stay in the city until you are clothed with power from on high" (Luke 24:49b). James B. Walker[3] points out that every

---

[3]James B. Walker, *God's Wisdom in the Plan of Salvation* (Butler, Indiana: Higley Press, 1958), originally published under the title, *The Philosophy of the Plan of Salvation.*

movement of God in relation to human redemption is inaugurated by an initial demonstration of His power. Such was the case at the deliverance of Israel from Egypt at the entrance of the Israelites into their promised land, at the beginning of the public ministry of our Lord, and such was the case at the inauguration of the Christian Church at Pentecost, and in each new step in the progress of the church on her triumphal march throughout the first Christian century. Likewise, at the entry of the gospel into each new land of missionary endeavor during the past 2,000 years there have been accompanying demonstrations of divine power. Paul's review of the initial entry of the gospel into the pagan city of Thessalonica well exemplifies this principle. Says he: "Our gospel did not come to you in word only, but also in *power* and in the Holy Spirit, and with all conviction" (1 Thess. 1:5a).

The Essentiality of Divine Power

Logically speaking, omnipotence is an essential note of the being of God. With the validity of this attribute, man's concept of and faith in God stands or falls. The very philosophical designation of God is the *absolute*. To deny God in this respect is only to transfer divinity to another absolute, even though that absolute may be the rationalism of man. Yet it is at this point that humanity has so frequently erred in their thinking. A revival of the denial of God's infinite power occurs in modern times in the thinking of such influential modern liberal Christian scholars as the late Edgar Sheffield Brightman of Boston University, and his theological followers. These religious philosophers seem compelled to reduce their concepts of God to the finite, before they are able to attempt a solution to the ills of the world. However, when they have thus reduced God to the finite, they neither have any solution to the ills of the world nor have they any God—not even the philosopher's god of the absolute. In limiting God they have implied something greater than God, and thus they have but made a transfer of divinity from the Judeo-Christian God to something of their own intellectual conceiving. And thus again mankind has created God in their own image. A basic religious fault of our day is man's concept of a limited God, a concept which is consequent upon a limited faith in God. It was said of Jesus, under certain circumstances, that He could do no mighty works because of the people's unbelief (Matt. 13:58).

The Personality as Divine Power.

In the concluding chapter of the Gospel according to Matthew the author represents Jesus, following His death and resurrection, as prefacing the Great Commission to His disciples with a claim to "all power." Says Jesus, "All authority [power, Grk. *exusia* power, authority, weight, especially moral authority, influence] has been given to Me in heaven and on earth" (Matt. 28:18). The statement of the resurrected Christ of Revelation 1:18 corresponds to the foregoing declaration. Here Christ declared, "I have the keys [authority] of death and of Hades." Jesus followed up His claim to all authority with the commission, "Go therefore and make disciples of all the nations" (Matt. 28:19a), after which He gave to them the assurance, "and lo, I am with you always, even to the end of the age" (Matt. 28:20b). The relationship of this claim to "all authority," and the promise of His accompanying presence with the disciples, "even unto the end of the age," to the promise of Acts 1:8, is at once evident. In the latter passage we read: "But you shall receive power, when the Holy Spirit is come upon you, and you shall be My witnesses . . . even to the remotest part of the earth" (Acts 1:8). In Acts 1:8 Luke uses a different word for power than that used by Matthew in 28:18. Here it is the Greek word *dunamis,* which means physical power, force or might, such as powerful deeds and marvelous works.[4]

The second passage is a corollary of the first. The Holy Spirit is what Chadwick calls "the Paraclete, or Other Self of the Christ"[5] indwelling the disciples after their baptism in the Spirit at Pentecost, to the limit of their spiritual capacities. The power of the Holy Spirit is not an impersonal gift of Christ to His disciples. Rather, that power is the power of the divine personality of Christ given in the Holy Spirit,

---

[4]Alexander Souter, *A Pocket Lexicon to the Greek New Testament* (Oxford: The Clarendon Press), p. 69). It is from this word (*dunamis*) that the English language gets its word *dynamite.*

[5]Samuel Chadwick, *The Way to Pentecost* (Berne, Indiana: Light and Hope Publications, 1937), p. 21.

indwelling the hearts and lives of the Christian disciples. Thus we have only as much of the divine power as we have of the divine personality. God does not give His power to His followers. He gives Himself, and His power is in His personality. To preach the gospel of Jesus Christ is to preach the power, the dynamite, of God. To preach, in the true sense of the term, is to witness to the person of Christ. Said Paul, "I am not ashamed of the gospel, for it is the power of God for salvation to everyone who believes" (Rom. 1:16a).

The Adequacy of Divine Power.

The first significance of the baptism in the Spirit was a personal experience of the infinite power of God; the "violent rushing wind" (Acts 2:2). It is a new manifestation and demonstration of the Spirit's power that the present-day spiritually anemic Church needs most, if she is to save herself and fulfill her mission to this generation.

It was in recognition of the need and adequacy of this spiritual power that Paul offered his great prayer for the Christian Church.

> For this reason I bow my knees before the Father . . . that He would grant you . . . to be strengthened with *power* [*dunamei*] through His Spirit in the inner man . . . Now to Him who is able to do exceeding abundantly beyond all that we ask or think, according to the *power* [*dunamin*] that works within us (Eph. 3:14, 16-20).

This great prayer finds its fulfillment in the Church's experience of the baptism in the Spirit. Thus the prayer that we may "be strengthened with power through His Spirit in the inner man," and the benediction, "Now unto Him who is able to do exceeding abundantly beyond all that we ask or think according to the power [the power of the Holy Spirit] that works within us," are inevitable consequences of the baptism in the Holy Spirit.

The recognized inadequacy of man to meet the sins and problems of our day, or any day, will be met only when the adequacy of God is recognized, confessed and appropriated. God's adequacy for the ills of mankind is to be found in the personal power of the Holy Spirit. When the church or the individual turns again to tap that resource, a power will be released for the salvation of a world that is presently threatened with destruction through atomic or hydrogen energy, if not through progressive moral degeneracy.

The Application of Divine Power.

The application of the divine power of the personal indwelling presence of the Holy Spirit in the life of the sanctified Christian believer is multifold.

First, the Spirit's power is the assurance of the Spirit-filled believer's victory over temptation and sin. It was this provisional assurance that the Apostle John had in mind when he wrote, "You are from God, little children, and have overcome them: because greater is He who is in you than he who is in the world" (1 John 4:4). Again the Apostle Paul set forth the assurance of this spiritual victory through the indwelling presence of the Holy Spirit most forcibly and beautifully in the eighth chapter of the letter to the Romans, especially verses 11, 31-39.

Second, the Spirit's power is an effective enablement to the execution of the Christian witness. Said Jesus: "You shall receive power, when the Holy Spirit has come upon you; and you shall be My witnesses both in Jerusalem, and in all Judea and Samaria, and even to the uttermost part of the earth" (Acts 1:8). Again, of the early disciples subsequent to their baptism in the Spirit at Pentecost, Luke wrote, "with great power [*dunamei*] the apostles were giving witness to the resurrection of the Lord Jesus, and abundant grace was upon them all" (Acts 4:33). The indwelling presence of the Holy Spirit is quite as much an enabling to witness by a consistent, righteous, exemplary life, as by oral testimony. Each validates the other.

Third, the efficacy of the Spirit's power for the endurance of persecution is well exemplified by the first Christian martyr, Stephen (Acts 7:59, 60). Repeatedly in the early chapters of the Acts of the Apostles, we read of the spiritual victories of the apostles through the energizing presence of the Holy Spirit, in the experiences of most extreme and severe persecution.

Fourth, the practice of demon expulsion by the Spirit-filled apostles dots the pages of the first-century Christian history. A notable failure of such an attempt in the name of Jesus, but in the absence of the indwelling presence of the

Holy Spirit, is that of the sons of Sceva at Ephesus (Acts 19:14-17).

Fifth, the Spirit's power for healing in the first Christian century church is quite as much in evidence as is demon expulsion. The Acts of the Apostles is replete with such divine healings at the hands of the Spirit-filled followers of Christ (see Acts 3:1-12).

Sixth, and finally, death itself was made to give up its victims at the command of these Spirit-filled servants of God. The restoration of Dorcas to life, at the hands of Peter, is a familiar example (Acts 9:36-42). Paul would seem to be thinking of both the healing of the body, and of the final resurrection of the body, when he uttered those words: "But if the Spirit of Him who raised Jesus from the dead dwells in you, He who raised Christ Jesus from the dead will also give life to your mortal bodies through His Spirit who indwells you" (Rom. 8:11). Baptism in the Spirit means the personal manifestation of God, and the manifestation of God makes available His omnipotence.

CHAPTER XV

The Fullness of the Spirit
(Continued)

"He made no distinction between us and them, cleansing their hearts by faith" (Acts 15:9).

". . . that my offering of the Gentiles might become acceptable, sanctified by the Holy Spirit" (Romans 15:16b).

The Fullness of the Spirit Signifies Divine Purification

And there appeared unto them tongues as of fire distributing themselves, and they rested on each one of them" (Acts 2:3). John the Baptist's prophetic words concerning Christ are here fulfilled:

I baptize you in water for repentance; but He who is coming after me is mightier than I, and I am not even fit to remove His sandals; He Himself will baptize you with the Holy Spirit and fire. And His winnowing fork is in His hand, and He will thoroughly clean His threshing-floor; and He will gather His wheat into the barn, but He will burn up the chaff with unquenchable fire (Matt. 3:11, 12).

There are two things about this spiritual phenomenon which arrest the reader's attention: namely, its *meaning* and its *administration.*

The Meaning of the Tongues of Fire.

The meaning of the phenomenon of the tongues of fire on the day of Pentecost is not far to seek. It must be borne in mind that in the Spirit's effusion at Pentecost, God was manifesting, or revealing, Himself primarily to the believing disciples of Jesus Christ, who on that day "were all together in one place" (Acts 2:16). They had given up their own temporal interests, and had dedicated themselves in faith to the pursuit and execution of the will of God in Christ.

At last their hopes of an earthly kingdom were forever gone (see Acts 1:6, 7). They were now in earnest and desperate pursuit of the inner spiritual kingdom which Christ had promised to them. Before the inner reign of Christ could be fully realized in their lives, there must be an inner purification, a consuming of the inner nature of the sinful self, a renovation of every secret chamber of the soul, that nothing foreign or opposed to the nature of God might remain within. It was God's purpose that His disciples should be so inwardly pure that they might declare their independence of the domain of sin and the Devil, as did Christ when He said, "The ruler of the world [Satan] is coming, and he has nothing in Me" (John 14:30). There was to be no claim foreign to the claim of Christ upon or within the lives of these disciples of Jesus.

For the purpose of this inner purification, God revealed Himself to the waiting disciples under the symbol of "tongues like as of fire." Consistently, throughout the Scriptures, "fire" is employed as a symbol of divine purification. Fire has ever been a symbol of the holiness and justice of God. Thus, God revealed Himself to His servants in ancient times (see Deut. 4:25; Ezek. 1:4; Exod. 3:2; 19:18; Isa. 6:4; Dan. 7:10).

Malachi predicted the coming and the work of Christ under the symbol of fire:

> "Behold I am going to send My messenger, and he will clear the way before Me. And the Lord, whom you seek, will suddenly come to His temple; and the messenger of the covenant, in whom you delight, behold, He is coming," says the Lord of hosts. "But who can endure the day of His coming? And who can stand when He appears? For He is like a refiner's fire and like fuller's soap. And He will sit as a smelter and purifier of silver, and He will purify the sons of Levi and refine them like gold and silver, so that they may present to the Lord offerings in righteousness" (Mal. 3:1-3).

Likewise, in His post-ascension and second-coming appearances, Jesus is represented under the symbol of fire (Rev. 1:12-18). Even the word of God is likened unto fire: "Is not My word like fire? declares the Lord" (Jer. 23:29a).

Finally, God Himself is represented by the author of the letter to the Hebrews under the symbol of fire: "Our God is a consuming fire" (Heb. 12:29). Thus, it was God the Holy Spirit in consuming fire who manifested Himself in "tongues as of fire" to the disciples on the day of Pentecost, purifying, sanctifying, their inner natures through and through (cf. Acts 15:8, 9).

The Administration of the Tongues of Fire.

The administration of the "tongues as of fire" at Pentecost likewise arrests our attention. Although "there came from heaven a noise like a violent rushing wind [that], filled all the house where they were sitting," and although there was the general or mass appearance of fire, this holy fire was distributed among them, or distributed itself among them individually. Thus while the Spirit was initially a sudden general manifestation of God to the company of waiting, believing disciples, as God began to administer His purifying efficacy to those disciples He did so on an individual and personal basis. The Spirit symbolized by "tongues as of fire" rested on each one of them. The following is a pertinent observation on this passage. "St. Luke means that the tongues or flames of fire appeared first in one mass over the assembled Church, and then divided, one flame or tongue sitting upon the head of each disciple."[1] This fire-symbolized unity of God so diversified and individualized itself as to meet on an individual and personal basis the heart condition and need of each of Christ's disciples at the same time. In this manner, God the Holy Spirit always deals with His children in saving or sanctifying efficacy. There may be, and frequently is, a general manifestation of God's presence to His people; but at the same time the dealings of God and the administrations of His grace are always on an individual and personal basis. Of this phenomenon, G. Campbell Morgan has said: "The symbol of sight—'tongues . . . of fire,' a plurality and a unity, the tongues were many; but the fire was One."[2]

At the first great general Christian council held at Jerusalem (Acts 15), Peter speaking in defense of the gospel for

---

[1]Dummelow, *A Commentary on the Holy Bible,* p. 820.

[2]G. Campbell Morgan, *The Acts of the Apostles* (New York: Fleming H. Revell, 1924), p. 24.

the Gentiles, declared that their purification was on the same basis as that of the disciples at Pentecost. Said Peter: "And God, who knows the heart, bore witness to them, giving them the Holy Spirit, just as He also did to us; and He made no distinction between us and them, cleansing their hearts by faith" (Acts 15:8, 9). At this juncture, the testimony of Adam Clarke is significant: "Christ baptizes with the Holy Ghost, for the destruction of sin, the illumination of the mind, and the consolation of the heart."[3]

Finally, the tongues of fire were the manifestation of God's personal purifying presence to the inner impure natures of the disciples, making them inwardly clean in preparation for complete and uncontested possession and dominion by His Spirit. In the midst of the general manifestation of the Spirit's presence, there was an individualization, or personal manifestation, providing for the individual conditions and needs of each disciple. Thus, while this purification, or sanctification, of the disciples' inner natures was primarily negative, it was a necessary provision of God for the positive work which was to immediately follow. This was to be the complete filling and possession of their inner beings by the personal presence of the Holy Spirit, giving them power over sin, the world, and the devil, and energizing them with a dynamic spiritual power for the proclamation of the gospel of Christ to all men throughout the world of their day.

The Fullness of the Spirit Signifies Divine Possession

"And they were all filled with the Holy Spirit" (Acts 2:4a). It was God's evident purpose in the creation of mankind to personally indwell them by His Spirit. The Fall evicted the Spirit of God from their lives. Redemption through Christ provided a means of reconciliation between an offended God and offending humanity. However, reconciliation, important and essential as it is, is not enough to satisfy the heart of God. He longed to indwell the souls of mankind. Before such an unrivaled establishment of God in the soul could be realized, the inner nature of pollution and enmity against God must be cleansed away. For this pur-

---

[3]Adam Clarke, *Clarke's Commentary* (Nashville: Abingdon-Cokesbury Press, n.d.), N.T. 5:683.

pose "Jesus also, that He might sanctify the people through His own blood, suffered outside the gate" (Heb. 13:12). God's purpose in this great cleansing work, provided for the soul of converted man by Christ through the sanctifying Spirit, is set forth by Paul in his first letter to the Thessalonian Christian converts thus: "This is the will of God, your sanctification" (1 Thess. 4:3).

The Fullness of the Spirit Restores Spiritual Union.

The moral and spiritual cleansing of a personal baptism in the Spirit is not an end in itself. Rather, it is a means to a greater end. That greater purpose of God is the personal indwelling of His believing children by His Holy Spirit. This ultimate purpose of God to be realized through the sanctification of His children is meaningfully expressed in the letter to the Hebrews: "For both he who sanctifies and those who are sanctified are all from one Father; for which He is not ashamed to call them brethren" (Heb. 2:11). Such a purpose is likewise expressed by Christ in His High Priestly prayer for His disciples (see John 17:17, 22, 23).

Thus, it becomes clear that this great redemptive purpose of God in Christ was initially realized on the day of Pentecost when the disciples "were all filled with the Holy Spirit," and thus were fully possessed by God.

The Fullness of the Spirit Complements Spiritual Regeneration.

But, the question may be fairly asked, was not the Spirit of God in these disciples from the time of their conversion before their spiritual baptism at Pentecost? That such was the case no careful student of the Word of God can successfully deny. The regenerative work of God in the lives of penitent sinners is a work of the Holy Spirit in the inner nature of man. Indeed, Jesus declared to Nicodemus on this subject: "Truly, truly, I say to you, unless one is born of water and the Spirit, he cannot enter into the kingdom of God. That which is born of the flesh is flesh; and that which is born of the Spirit is spirit" (John 3:5, 6). And Paul declared: "You are not in the flesh but in the Spirit, if indeed the Spirit of God dwells in you. But if anyone does not have the Spirit of Christ, he does not belong to Him" (Rom. 8:9). There is, in fact, no stage or part of the redemptive work that can be divorced from the direct operation of the Spirit of God. Jesus declared that even the work of conviction for sin on the world was to be the work of the Holy Spirit (see John 16:7-11). According to Jesus, there can be no true worship apart from the Spirit of God. "God is Spirit; and those who worship Him must worship in spirit and truth" (John 4:24).

However, the meaning of the effusion of the Spirit at Pentecost, the English Wesleyan scholar, Howard Marshall, strongly argues, was primarily a Spirit baptism upon the believing, regenerated disciples of Jesus in the upper room, rather than on the assembled multitude, as some mistakenly suppose. Marshall states:

> The event was a purely spiritual baptism. There is no mention of any baptism with water at this point. For the event stands in deliberate contrast with Johannine water baptism. It is true that the [3,000] converts later in the day received Christian water baptism as a preliminary to the gift of the Spirit, *but the first outpouring [of the Spirit] was on disciples who already believed in Jesus* [italics added] . . .
>
> Our conclusion is that Luke refers to the Pentecostal experience of the disciples as a filling with the Spirit, and that this means the same as the baptism of [in] the Spirit, the gift of the Spirit, and so on. . . . As a result of the filling with the Spirit the disciples speak in "tongues," that is tongues of languages other than their own . . . The story makes it certain that intelligible human languages are meant, not the unintelligible tongues as are often found in modern glossolalia . . . In other words, the gift of tongues [languages] is used here to proclaim the Gospel . . .[4]

Marshall correctly notes, with J. Kremer, that "Pentecost is not referred to elsewhere in the New Testament. Nevertheless, the same basic experience is presupposed in Pauline theology."[5]

---

[4]Howard Marshall, "The Significance of Pentecost," *The Asbury Seminarian,* Vol. XXXII, April 1977, No. 2 (Wilmore, Kentucky: Asbury Theological Seminary Publishers), pp. 22, 25, 26.

[5]*Ibid.,* p. 30.

Marshall states further:

> It [Pentecost] is the first significant event in the
> story which he [Luke] has to tell in Acts and con-
> stitutes the beginning of the church's mission. The
> *missionary element* is probably the most important
> aspect of the story in Luke's view. The gift of the
> Spirit equips the disciples to witness, Peter's proc-
> lamation of the Gospel occupies the center of the
> account, and the story culminates in the conver-
> sion of some 3,000 hearers of the message.[6]

The Fullness of the Spirit Provides Complete Possession.
It will be noted that it was after His death and resurrection, and in conjunction with the Great Commission,
which was not to be carried out until after Pentecost, that
Jesus "breathed on them, and said to them, 'Receive ye the
Holy Spirit' " (John 20:22). That this was a prophetic act
and word of the Master to be fulfilled on the day of Pentecost
is evident from the prophetic commission of the preceding
and following verses. In fact, the divine outpouring of the
Holy Spirit on the day of Pentecost cannot be separated from
the Great Commission. Jesus said to His disciples, "You shall
receive power, when the Holy Spirit is come upon you; and
you shall be My witnesses . . ." (Acts 1:8a). If the witnessing could not begin until the baptism in the Spirit at Pentecost was a reality in the lives of the disciples, their baptism
in the Spirit could not become a reality in their lives until
the Holy Spirit was outpoured on the day of Pentecost. Likewise, it is in the prophetic sense of the Spirit's fullness that
Christ says: "He abideth with you, and will be in you" (John
14:17b). This utterance is a prediction of that fullness of the
Spirit which they were to experience at their baptism in the
Spirit on the day of Pentecost. Samuel Chadwick says: "The
change from *with* to *in* marks the transition from one dispen-
sation to another."[7] It is indeed the difference between the
personal physical presence of Christ with His disciples and
what His spiritual inner abiding presence through the Holy
Spirit would be as a result of Pentecost. Again Chadwick
remarks:

---

[6]*Ibid.*, p. 31.
[7]Chadwick, *The Way to Pentecost,* p. 44.

There is often some confusion in the interchange of terms, and the elimination of the middle factor. The Son comes in the coming of the Spirit, and abides in the soul in the presence of the Spirit; and in the coming of the Son through the Spirit the Father comes and abides also. 'He will come . . . I will come . . . We will come' all refer to the coming of the Spirit as promised in our Lord's farewell talk with His disciples (John 14:16-23). In their relation to the human soul, the Father and the Son act through, and are represented by, the Holy Spirit. Yet the Spirit is not merged in either the Father or in the Trinity. They are never confused in the unity nor divided in the distinction. Each is Divine and all are one.[8]

The difference between the relationship of the Holy Spirit to the converted and regenerated disciples before Pentecost, and the sanctified disciples after Pentecost, may be better understood by an illustration.

Should a man stand on the shore of the Atlantic Ocean with a five-gallon pail in his hand which had been used as a tar container, and to the inner walls of which a quantity of tar still adhered; he would be unable to *fill* such a pail with the exhaustless water of the Atlantic Ocean. This inability would not be due to a lack of sufficient water, but to the fact that a foreign substance adhered to the walls of the pail, and thus displaced in part the pail's capacity for water. Even though water should be poured into the pail from the ocean until the pail ran over, it still would not be *filled* with water, since the foreign substance would displace in part its capacity for water. A melting of the residue of tar, however, and a thorough cleansing of the pail from this foreign substance, would make it possible to *fill* the pail with water. This analogy is not to be taken in full extension, or in a material sense, as sin is not a material substance, but a spiritual condition.

Likewise a regenerated, but unsanctified, Christian possesses the Holy Spirit of God in his life, but he can never be *filled* with the Holy Spirit of God until the fiery baptism

---

[8]*Ibid.*

in the Holy Spirit has so cleansed and purified his inner nature of the sinful-self, or carnality, as to remove every residue of the foreign nature and thus enable God, by His Holy Spirit, to *fill* his heart and life. In this sense it is proper to say that the sanctified believer is *filled* with the Holy Spirit. As an unsanctified, but regenerated, disciple of Christ, he has the Holy Spirit in his inner life, but he cannot be *filled* with the Holy Spirit until he has experienced the inner cleansing by the Spirit. The believer has indeed all of the Spirit, but not until he is sanctified does the Spirit have all of him. "They were all filled with the Holy Spirit," immediately after, and not before, "there appeared unto them tongues as of fire distributing themselves, and they rested on each one of them."

The Fullness of the Spirit
Signifies Universal Proclamation

"And [they] began to speak with other tongues, as the Spirit was giving them utterance" (Acts 2:4b). The fullness of the Spirit produced a miracle of "other tongues." Any purported miracle must have in it a moral value to validate it. If the moral value validates a purported miracle, then the miracle of "other tongues" at the outpouring of the Spirit on the day of Pentecost was well established.

The Necessity of the Miraculous Proclamation.

The Acts record informs us that there were "Jews living in Jerusalem, devout men from every nation under heaven," gathered for the Pentecostal feast at Jerusalem; people of the Jewish faith throughout the Roman Empire and beyond. And when this noise like "a violent rushing wind" was heard, the multitudes *came together* and *were confounded* "because they were each one hearing them speak in his own language." Thus, they were made to marvel, and they said, "Are not all these who are speaking Galileans? And how is it that we each hear them in our own language to which we were born?" (Acts 2:5-8). Then there follows a list of fifteen different nations represented at Pentecost, into the countries of which Jews of the dispersion had been born, and whose language only these people spoke and understood. These strangers, Hellenistic Jews and Gentile proselytes, exclaimed, "We hear them in our own tongues speaking the mighty deeds of God" (Acts 2:11b).

Whatever may be the interpretation placed upon or the significance of other occurrences of this phenomenon, such as Paul's reference to "tongues" in the first letter to the Corinthians, and the reference to "new tongues" by Mark (Mark 16:17), its occurrence at Cornelius' house at Caesarea under Peter's ministry (Acts 10:46), or its occurrence at Ephesus under Paul's ministry (Acts 19:6)—this initial occurrence is to be understood as the *bona fide* use of the languages of the people present who otherwise would have been incapable of hearing intelligibly the Gospel of Jesus Christ, and by men who themselves were unfamiliar with the languages which they were using. It has been said that "we may see in this event, which seemed to obliterate the barriers of nationality and language, a reversal of the separation and confusion of tongues."[9] This authority further observes that "among modern parallels the most suggestive is the case of St. Vincent Ferrer, who when preaching in Spanish, is said to have been understood by English, Flemish, French, and Italian hearers."[10]

This miracle of the proclamation of the gospel in the different languages of those present at the Jewish Pentecost, and which resulted in the great spiritual awakening that followed the outpouring of the Spirit, seems to anticipate the fulfillment of the Great Commission, as suggested by the universal representation of redeemed humanity, as depicted in the Book of the Revelation (Rev. 5:9-11; 7:9, 10).

The Effects of the Miraculous Proclamation.

Peter, taking advantage of the arrested attention and interest of the assembled multitude, consequent upon this miracle of proclamation in their diverse languages, arose and interpreted the meaning of the phenomena with such effectiveness as to result in the conversion of about 3,000 persons (Acts 2:41).

The miracle of "other tongues, as the Spirit was giving them utterance," was not only the direct means in the hands of God for the confounding and conversion of this multitude

---

9Dummelow, *A Commentary on the Holy Bible,* pp. 820, 821.
10*Ibid.,* p. 821.

on the day of Pentecost, but there was also precipitated that great world-wide missionary movement that was to follow the inauguration of the church on the day of Pentecost. As there were present there at Jerusalem representatives "from every nation under heaven," so this Gospel of Jesus Christ was to be carried to "every nation under heaven," by the Spirit-baptized, Spirit-possessed, and Spirit-directed men and women. The "other tongues" were necessary vehicles for the expression of "the mighty deeds of God," and the result was the conversion of the multitude. This phenomenon was an intelligent and intelligible proclamation of the "mighty deeds of God" to a people who otherwise could not have understood it. It was the work of the Holy Spirit in the lives of the Spirit-filled disciples. It marked the beginning, and it made possible the great missionary evangelistic program to which Christ commissioned His disciples when He said, "Go therefore and make disciples of all nations" (Matt. 28:19); and again, "You shall receive power when the Holy Spirit is come upon you; and you shall be My witnesses . . . even to the remotest part of the earth" (Acts 1:8).

Without the fullness of the Spirit, the church will remain powerless to witness for Christ, either by life or verbal testimony. The fullness of the Spirit provides the power required for world evangelism in this and every generation. Under the baptism of the Spirit, the church will be revived and the world will be evangelized.

CHAPTER XVI

The Abiding Relationship

"Abide in Me, and I in you. As the branch cannot bear fruit of itself, unless it abides in the vine, so neither can you, unless you abide in Me" (John 15:4).

The well-known parable of Christ, The Vine and the Branches, is recorded in the Gospel according to John 15:1-18, which reads thus:

> I am the true vine, and My Father is the vinedresser. Every branch in Me that does not bear fruit, He takes away; and every branch that bears fruit, He prunes it, that it may bear more fruit. You are already clean because of the word which I have spoken to you. Abide in Me, and I in you. As the branch cannot bear fruit of itself, unless it abides in the vine, so neither can you unless you abide in Me. I am the vine, you are the branches; he who abides in Me, and I in him, he bears much fruit; for apart from Me you can do nothing. If anyone does not abide in me, he is thrown away as a branch, and dries up; and they gather them, and cast them into the fire, and they are burned. If you abide in Me, and My words abide in you, ask whatever you wish, and it shall be done for you. By this is My Father glorified, that you bear much fruit, and so prove to be My disciples.

In this parable Christ sets forth the mystical relationship that exists between Himself and those who believe in Him, as also between the heavenly Father and Himself. The theme of this parable may have been suggested to the mind of Christ by remarks made by His disciples concerning a vineyard as they walked together along the way; or possibly it was suggested to His mind by the fruit of the vine which they drank at the Last Supper. However this may be, there are three distinct truths set forth in this parable. They are, *first*, that God is the husbandman of the vineyard; *second*, that Christ is the "true vine" of the Father's vineyard; and *third*, that Christ's true disciples are to be the fruitbearing branches of the vine.

This Parable Suggests a Twofold Relationship

Basically this twofold relationship is between God the Father with Christ the Son, and of God through Christ with those who believe on Him with a living faith for their salvation. Christ said, "I am the true vine, and My Father is the vinedresser [or husbandman]." "I am the vine, you are the branches." In His High Priestly prayer Christ prayed for the spiritual unity of His disciples: "that they may be one, even as We are" (John 17:11b).

As the husbandman, the planter, and the vinedresser of His spiritual vineyard, God the Father is the rightful owner of that vineyard, which here represents the church of believing men and women. There is a twofold sense in which this vineyard belongs to God. *First,* He is the creator of all men, into whom He breathed the breath of life and they became living souls or spiritual personalities (Gen. 2:7). In the *second* instance, this spiritual vineyard belongs to the Father by right of redemption and preservation.

God planted His vine of humanity which He had created in his own image here in this world that it might grow and fructify in His fruitful garden. When through disobedience man fell from favor with God, divine redemption became necessary for him, unless he was to perish forever. Therefore, Christ, the incarnate Son of God—God in human form and flesh—became man's redeemer and reconciler to God. Thus in His human incarnation Christ became the Second Adam, the Adam of redemption. Consequently, through creation and through redemption the vineyard belongs to God the Father.

Again, the divine husbandman carefully cultivates His vineyard. As His most treasured possession, He cultivates and protects His vineyard with a view to its spiritual health and fruitfulness. In the light of His ownership and care for His vineyard, He has a perfect right to expect fruit from it.

In consideration of the uprooting of God's original vineyard, through the Fall, which He had planted in the earth through man's creation, Christ declared Himself to be "the true vine," or the vine of the husbandman's own planting. Christ is the true vine in contradiction to the many false (or wild) vines found in the world of man's religious philosophies. Among these false vines are to be found the great ethnic religious systems such as Hinduism, Buddhism, Zoroastrianism, Shintoism, Taoism and Mohammedanism; and the numerous western religious cults such as Spiritism, Russellism or Jehovah's Witnesses, Mormonism, the Psychic Cults, Transcendental Meditation, Moonism, and many others. Nor are many of the noted humanistic ethical systems of the ages to be exempt from classification as false spiritual vines. Christ is the true vine, in distinction from all these and many other false vines, by reason of the fact that He came forth from the Father and was planted in the earth among men as a man—the one and only God-man. He is, further, the true vine of God's own planting by reason of the fact that He is the living and the life-giving vine (Rev. 1:18; John 10:19). Christ sustains a living relationship with the Father. The Apostle John declared that "In Him was life; and the life was the light of men" (John 1:4).

Again, the branches of Christ's parable are of vital importance to an understanding of the lesson which He sought to teach. To His disciples Christ said, "You are the branches." But Christ's disciples are grafted and not natural branches of the vine. Thus they, through this grafted relationship, bear a vital connection with Christ the true vine, and are wholly dependent upon Him for their spiritual existence and sustenance. This dependency is borne out by an analogy drawn from the California English walnut. The English walnut is not native to California and will not of itself grow and bear fruit in that part of the country. The black walnut, however, is native to California and thus grows and bears its fruit there. Consequently, the California nut-growers plant the black walnut trees, and then when they have reached a certain maturity, they are cut off above the ground and the English walnut branch is grafted into the trunk of the native black walnut, and it draws its vitality and fruitfulness from that native tree and thus produces the desired fruit. Likewise, Christ is the vine of God's own planting, the vine that is native to the spiritual kingdom of God, who was cut off in His crucifixion-death that He might give His life to those who by faith would be grafted into Him. Thus the believing disciples draw their strength, experience their spiritual vitality, have their security, receive their nurture, and bear their fruit by virtue of their relationship to Christ, the true vine into which they have been grafted. Christians are the fruit-bearing branches of the divine vine. They bear their fruit from the life of the vine Christ Jesus that flows into and through them.

The Sad and Awful Fate of the Fruitless Branches

The fate of the fruitless branches is described thus: "Every branch in Me that does not bear fruit, He takes away." "If anyone does not abide in Me, he is thrown away as a branch, and dries up; and they gather them, and cast them into the fire, and they are burned." Adam Clarke represents Jesus as saying: "As the vinedresser will remove every unfruitful branch from the vine, so will my Father remove every unfruitful member from my mystical body."[1]

The character of the fruitless branches is noteworthy. Some are disloyal, as was Judas. Some are unbelieving, as were the Jews who rejected Jesus when He came. Some are unfaithful, as was Peter who forsook Jesus at His trial. Some are pretentious and dishonest, as were Ananias and his wife following Pentecost. Others are iniquitous and disobedient, and have made shipwreck of faith and a good conscience. Clarke states: "Our Lord in the plainest manner intimates that a person may as truly be united to Him [Christ] as the branch is to the vine that produces it, and be afterward cut off and cast into the fire; because he has not brought forth fruit unto the glory of God."[2] No one can cut off a branch from a vine to which it has never been united. It is both absurd and contrary to the letter and the spirit of the metaphor to speak of being *seemingly* but not really united to Christ. Such language is utterly meaningless in the light of the teaching of this parable.

The Father's purpose in the removal of the fruitless branches from His true vine is twofold. In the first place,

---

[1] Adam Clarke, *Clarke's Commentary* (Nashville: Abingdon Press, n.d.), N.T. 1:627.

[2] *Ibid.*

these lifeless branches would mar the appearance of His vineyard and thus misrepresent it before the unbelievers. Their withered leaves and fruitless branches soon reveal them to be devoid of spiritual life. Thus encumbering the true living vine they mar its appearance and seriously misrepresent its character. Second, these fruitless branches adhering to the vine draw strength from it that otherwise would go into improved fruit bearing through vital, healthy branches. Thus the fruitless branches deprive the fruitful branches of their greater vitality and cause them to produce an inferior quality of fruit.

The foregoing character of the fruitless branches both justifies and necessitates their removal for the sake of the fruitfulness of the divine vineyard. The branches no longer have any right or title to Christ or His saving grace. These branches are withered, or dried up, and thus no longer have any value in God's vineyard. When a man ceases to abide in Christ, he is deprived of all the influences of God's grace and Spirit. He loses his heavenly unction, becomes indifferent, and is spiritually cold and dead to every good word and work. Such fruitless branches are gathered with the unbelievers and united to the ungodly whose interests are foreign to God and all righteousness. They abandon themselves to the wicked inclinations of their hearts and the will of Satan. Their final end, if they do not repent and are reengrafted by faith into Christ, is destruction from the presence of God and everlasting exclusion from the company of the righteous. Certainly Christ's words in this parable offer no support for the doctrine of *unconditional eternal security*.

It is noteworthy that these branches are severed and destroyed, not because of what they did that was wrong, but rather because of what they failed to do that was right and obligatory upon them. The clear teaching of this parable is that fruitlessness, or the sin of omission, is sufficient warrant for the loss of the soul's relationship with God—the severance of the grafted branch from the living vine, Christ Jesus.

The Divine Care for the Fruitful Branches

God's loving care for the abiding branches comes to light in this parable. "Every branch that bears fruit, He prunes it, that it may bear more fruit." In 1933 Hitler introduced his infamous purge. That purge has gone down in history as one of the most unwarranted, cruel, dastardly, bloody acts of all time. His purpose in purging the "Brown Shirts" and the Jews was to eliminate those hindrances to the execution of his Nazi program in Germany. He sought to remove the hindrances to the realization of his ideals and objectives for the Nazi regime. This constituted one of the most selfish and brutal acts of all time which wrought unspeakable suffering and injustice to humanity. In contrast, God's purge of the fruitless branches is in the interest of righteousness, that the life of the spiritual organism may be preserved and its purpose in world evangelism may be realized. Every branch that does not bear fruit God takes away, but every branch that bears fruit He takes away from it that which would prevent it from its greater fruitfulness. These fruit-bearing branches are pruned or purged of their selfish interests, their carnal pride, their sinful fears, their incomplete devotion, their distrustfulness, and all those sinful tendencies that give rise to unwholesome and unchristian attitudes and conduct. They are purged from the disposition to strife among themselves, as the disciples who wrangled over who would be greatest in Christ's future kingdom; and from anger and self-vindication, as those disciples who would have called down fire from heaven upon the Samaritans who refused to give lodging to their Master. They are purged that they may bring forth more fruit—in loyalty to God, in effective prayers, in unselfish love and devotion to others, in greater forbearance and self-sacrifice, in effective witness to Christ.

Christ indicates that it is His Word that purges the fruit-bearing branches: "You are already clean because of the word which I have spoken unto you." The author of the letter to the Hebrews said, "The word of God is living and active and sharper than any two-edged sword, and piercing as far as the division of soul and spirit, of both joints and marrow, and able to judge the thoughts and intentions of the heart" (Heb. 4:12). God's Holy Word is the most effective spiritual and moral purgative known to man. That Word cuts away the taproot sin of unbelief, when sin is considered theologically, that gives rise to all other sin in the life of man. It is likewise effective in cutting away of sinful pride, which is the taproot of all sin, from the psychological perspective.

The Abiding Union of the Christian Believer in Christ

The believer's abiding union with Christ is essential to his more abundant life and fruitfulness. "Abide in Me and I in you," said Christ. "If you abide in Me, and My words abide in you, ask whatever you wish, and it shall be done for you." This abiding relationship with Christ is essential to the continuous and unbroken flow of the divine life of Christ, the true vine, into the lives of the believers, the grafted-in branches. An abiding Christian is like an electric light bulb that is connected to the great electric generator. A non-abiding Christian is like an old-fashioned lamp which shines while it has a temporary supply of oil, but which goes out and remains in darkness when the oil supply is exhausted and not replenished.

An abiding union insures fruitfulness in the life of the believer: "He who abides in Me, and I in him, he bears much fruit, for apart from Me you can do nothing." But this abiding union with Christ also insures answered prayer: "If you abide in Me, and My words abide in you, ask whatsoever you wish, and it shall be done for you." Here is the assurance of the supply of the believer's needs, the Holy Spirit's deliverance in temptation, the salvation of those for whom we are concerned, revivals in our churches, a missionary compassion for the evangelization of the unsaved world of mankind, spiritual and physical healing, and adequate resources to carry on the work and service of God. Paul declared, "My God shall supply all your needs according to His riches in glory in Christ Jesus" (Phil. 4:19).

The fruitful life of the abiding believer is God's greatest glory and honor. Said Christ: "By this is My Father glorified, that you bear much fruit and so prove to be My disciples." The effectiveness of God's name and glory in the world will depend in large measure upon the believer's spiritual vitality resultant from his abiding relationship with Jesus Christ, the true vine.

In conclusion, the genuine and effective Christian life consists in spiritual vitality born of a union with the Father through His Son Jesus Christ. A failure to maintain this union inevitably results in the loss of spiritual fruitfulness, and eventually the relationship with God. In turn, this leads to severance from God and the Christian community with the resultant death and doom of the soul, unless restoration to Christ is experienced. On the other hand, the abiding life brings purging and purification of the believer by the Father with the resultant beautification and fructification of God's spiritual vineyard. Such are the teachings of Christ's parable of the vine and the branches.

CHAPTER XVII

The Life Everlasting
or
Christian Immortality

"And this is eternal life, that they may know Thee the only true God, and Jesus Christ whom Thou hast sent" (John 17:3).

Millenniums ago Job voiced the curiosity of the human mind concerning the future life in his immortal words: "If a man dies, will he live again?" (Job 14:14). Throughout the history of the human race, men of all nationalities, religions and philosophies have sought, in one way or another, to find the answer to that question. There are but two exceptions to this attitude of mind toward man's future hope. The one is represented by the ancient Jewish sect of the Sadducees and the other by certain sophisticates of every enlightened age. The first is organizationally dead and the second is intellectually and spiritually dead. The significant lines of Pascal bear testimony to this fact: "The immortality of the soul is a thing so important that only those who have lost all feeling can rest indifferent to it, can be content to know if it is not, or if it is."[1]

On the survival of the soul after physical death, S.E. Frost writes significantly:

> . . . the human mind has never been content to let the matter rest here. Throughout the history of mankind there has persisted a conviction, sometimes divine and at other times very vivid, that death cannot be the end, that the grave is not a victory of a man's foes, that death does not inflict a cosmic sting. In every age there have been

---

[1] Quoted by Frederick D. Kershner in *Horizons of Immortality* (St. Louis, MO: Bethany Press, 1926), p. 12.

millions firm in the belief that what is truest in humanity persists in some form or state after death.[2]

The idea of immortality is one of those fundamental concepts of the human mind that forbids it to rest until it rests in a valid answer to this age-old question raised by Job.

Dietrich Bonhoeffer[3] argues that atheistic unbelief is the ultimate of sin which so completely excludes God from man's life that it embraces in itself all other sins, and thus even suicide or any other act adds nothing to the guilt of such a man outside of God's claims upon his life (see John 16:7-9; Rom. 14:23).

The words of Christ are highly significant at the outset of any consideration of Christian immortality. Said He: "And this is eternal life, that they may know Thee the only true God, and Jesus Christ whom Thou has sent" (John 17:3); and again: "I came that they might have life, and might have it abundantly" (John 10:10b); and yet again: "I give eternal life to them" (John 10:28a; see also John 3:16, 36; 6:54; Rom. 6:23; John 1:1-14; 1 Thess. 5:23).

The sincerely concerned, wealthy young Jewish ruler who came running to Christ voiced his quest in the words, "What shall I do to inherit eternal life?" (Mark 10:17b). The conceited Jewish lawyer, with the purpose to ensnare Jesus in His own words, voiced the question, "Teacher, what shall I do to inherit eternal life?" (Luke 10:25b).

Christian Immortality: What Is It?

Dagobert D. Runes states that the word immortality is derived from the Latin negative prefix *in* (not) plus the Latin root *mortalis* (mortal). Taken together the result is "not mortal," or not subject to death. Runes then proceeds to give the following formal definition of immortality:

The doctrine that the soul or personality of man survives the death of the body. The two principal

---

[2]S. E. Frost, *The Basic Teachings of the Great Philosphers* (Philadelphia: The Blakiston Company, 1942), p. 171.

[3]Dietrich Bonhoeffer, *Ethics*, Eberhard Bethge, ed. (New York: The Macmillan Company, 1965), pp. 166-172.

conceptions of immortality are: (a) *temporal immortality*, the indefinite continuation of the individual mind after death and (b) *eternal*, ascension of the soul to a higher plane of timelessness.[4]

It is our present purpose to treat the idea of immortality *per se* in its Christian meaning. Thus, immortality will be regarded, in accordance with Runes' definition, in part, as that "doctrine that the soul or personality of the man survives the death of the body," and as the "ascension of the soul to a higher plane of timelessness." Again, the idea of immortality here will be restricted to the present and post-existence, or life after death, as opposed to pre-existence, which is not a Christian doctrine. Thus, the soul will be regarded as everlastingly conscious and identical, but not eternal, in the sense of being uncreated.

The Source of Christian Immortality

The problem of the origin of souls or self-conscious personalities is very old and somewhat complex. The traditional Roman Catholic position, and a position held by some Protestant thinkers even today, maintains that all souls are directly created by God at conception. God, according to this position, cooperates in the human act of procreation by furnishing a directly-created soul for the humanly produced body. Thus, in this view, the soul as an entity is divinely-created and added to the body at conception. Paul J. Glenn,[5] a Roman Catholic scholar, makes clear this position. He holds that God directly creates the soul of each child at conception and adds it to the body of the fetus which body is physically produced through conception by the parents.

Glenn's position, called *creationism*, is fraught with many insurmountable difficulties. Of the many, only two of the most important need concern us here.

The first problem, the inheritance of "original sin," or "depravity," is not the least of the difficulties involved in the theory of *creationism*. St. Augustine, in his later years,

---

[4]Dagobert D. Runes, *The Dictionary of Philosophy* (New York: Philosophical Library, 1942), p. 142.

[5]Paul J. Glenn, *An Introduction to Philosophy* (St. Louis, MO: B. Herder Book Company, 1944), pp. 314, 315.

saw the difficulty and concluded that in some manner the soul of the child must proceed from the souls of the parents. Augustine's position is known as *traducianism*. Glenn objects seriously to Augustine's position and attempts to evade the dilemma by substituting a third factor, which he designates "human nature," a kind of scapegoat for inherited depravity.

The second serious problem in the theory of *creationism* is that of involving God in objectionable unethical cooperation. Ethically forbidden cohabitation in extramarital relations is frequently biologically productive. If God is the creator of each soul directly at conception, then it becomes quite clear that He could not retain His moral integrity while cooperating with His creatures in the commission of an immoral act. Since God's moral integrity would be thus violated, the ethical idea of God would necessarily be degraded and the holiness of God would be thereby cancelled. The far-reaching implications of this ethically and theologically embarrassing consideration are not difficult to imagine.

What then is the origin of the soul? There seems to be but one satisfactory answer to the question. That answer is found in the book of Genesis. There it is stated that "God created man in His own image, in the image of God He created him; male and female He created them" (Gen. 1:27). Then further, the writer of Genesis explains, "The Lord God formed man of dust from the ground, and breathed into his nostrils the breath of life; and man became a living being" (Gen. 2:7). Following this account of creation, the author of Genesis appears to strive to make clear God's plan and purpose in the human procreative process.

> And God blessed them; and said to them, "Be fruitful and multiply, and fill the earth, and subdue it; and rule over the fish of the sea and over the birds of the sky, and over every living thing that moves on the earth" (Gen. 1:28; cf. Ps. 8:3-8).

Obviously, when God created man He endowed him with the higher spiritual principle of immortal conscious personality, and then committed to him the tremendous responsibility, but also the challenging and glorious privilege of procreating himself, body and soul, or personality, as a unitary being, functionally, though chemically compounded. Man was quite evidently a divinely effected synthesis of *dust* and the *breath* of God. God "breathed into his nostrils the breath of life; and man became a *living being.*" It is not to be overlooked that this conclusion implies the necessity of the "bodily form" for the identity of the person. Paul's argument is clear and convincing in favor of the necessity of a bodily resurrection for *personal identity,* as also for divine victory over physical death (see 1 Cor. 15). Hence it appears to be both scriptural and logical to conclude that at conception there emerges a new entity from the synthesis of the parents, and that each new emergent is an everlasting self-conscious spiritual personality. Accordingly, man is endowed with the power of procreating the soul or personality, as well as the body of the child, and thus the unsolvable problems inhering in the theory of *creationism* are eliminated and man is dignified by God-given self-creative powers. His responsibility for the right use of those powers also becomes very great. In the light of these considerations, the only logically consistent position seems to be that of *traducianism,* as advocated by St. Augustine, notwithstanding the fact that Augustine failed to make clear the "how" of this unitary procreation of man. Thus the first spiritual unitary personality had its origin in the creative act of God. But all subsequent personalities have had their origins in man's divinely-delegated procreative powers, as unitary persons, functionally.

Christian Immortality Distinguished From Other Concepts of Futurity

First the concept of Christian *immortality*, in the restricted sense, must be clearly differentiated from the idea of *eternal. Immortality* looks to a blissful, endless future existence of conscious personalities in relation to and contingent upon God. Eternal conveys the idea of timelessness, both in the past and in the future. Eternal, as applied to immortal conscious personalities, would imply that such personalities were uncreated. If they were uncreated, they would not be contingent upon God. If they were not contingent upon God, they would be self-existent, and if they were self-existent, they would be divine, and divinity does not belong to human persons.

Second, the Christian concept of immortality must be clearly differentiated from the Oriental view of *pre-existence, transmigration of souls,* and the doctrine of *Karma,* all three of which doctrines are inseparably linked together. Pre-existence of souls has taken different forms in various schools of thought. The best known and most representative doctrines of pre-existence are those of Plato and the Hindus of India. To these two views it may be of interest to add the Mormon view, which differs from the foregoing only in certain respects.

A third idea that must be clearly distinguished from the Christian concept of immortality, as the idea is considered here, is that of *temporary life after death.* This view would be, in the very nature of the case, limited immortality rather than Christian immortality. It is a view that was held, concerning the souls of both the gods and men, by certain of the Greek and Roman thinkers, and it is a view held by many primitive and other pagan peoples in the world today.

Again, the Christian doctrine of immortality must be clearly differentiated from *conditional immortality,* as taught by the religious philosopher William Earnest Hocking of Harvard University, a sort of "take it or leave it at will" doctrine. And it must be disassociated from the doctrine of *annihilationism,* usually applied to the complete extinction of the wicked at death, or as held by some, at the final judgment. But by some others, especially certain materialists such as Bertrand Russell, it has been applied to *all* future existence. The Russellites and the Seventh-Day Adventists have been strong advocates of the former view, i.e., for the wicked.

Finally, while it is not our purpose here to treat extensively the Old Testament views of immortality, those views do indeed lie back of the Christian doctrine as found in the New Testament. The early Hebrews and later Jews of the Old Testament appear to have progressively grasped the doctrine of immortality—often very faintly understood, but at other times with remarkable insight they anticipated the Christian doctrine. Except for a few notable insights, such as Job, Isaiah, and Daniel, this doctrine appears to have reached its clearest understanding by the Jews during the Inter-Testamental period, just prior to the Christian era.

The Christian Doctrine of Immortality "Per Se"

The orthodox Christian doctrine of immortality stands alone and unique among the many other ideas of the soul's destiny in its teaching concerning the future of the redeemed. There appear to be three significant advances in Christian thought over the Jewish concept of a future life: (1) the emphasis upon individual immortality becomes clearer, though individual relation to the group or nation is also important, (2) the idea of the resurrection becomes more evident, and (3) the nature of the future life becomes more distinct and explicit.

First, Jesus taught the *Kingdom of Heaven* as a community of the redeemed on earth, but so constituted as to be capable of everlasting continuance. Although the individual is a member of the Spiritual Kingdom, he stands also in direct personal relation with God. Indeed, Christ perfected the idea of the individual and brought it forth into a clearer light than at any previous time. Here there emerges the provision of both an immortal spiritual individual and an immortal spiritual community of the redeemed.

Second, while, Job, Ezekiel, Daniel and Isaiah all caught faint glimpses of immortality through a bodily resurrection, it remained for Christ and Paul to explicate this great doctrine more clearly.

Logically, a future life of everlasting bliss could be realized only through the reconciliation of man with God. Since God only, and not the human personality, is infinite, it follows that for immortality, as herein defined, the finite human person is contingent upon the infinite personality of God. The experience of sin had made such a relationship impossible of attainment for man, apart from divine intervention. A Mediator was required for the reconciliation of guilty and alienated man with the pure and holy being of God. Such a Mediator must be, in the very nature of the case, both divine and human. Hence the necessity of the incarnation of God in man, the God-Man, Christ Jesus. The incarnation and atoning death of Jesus Christ would have been incomplete for redemptive purposes without the resurrection and ascension. The assumption of human nature by divinity, the substitutionary death of Christ, and His bodily resurrection and ascension, bridged the great gulf between man's alienated soul and God; and thus Christ afforded a way for alienated man to return to an everlasting blissful relationship with God. Christ said, "I am the way, and the truth, and the life; no one comes to the Father, but through Me" (John 14:6). Again Christ said, "I am the resurrection, and the life; he who believes in Me shall live even if he dies, and everyone who lives and believes on Me shall never die" (John 11:25, 26). Paul makes this doctrine of the "resurrection unto life" explicit in 1 Corinthians 15. It was also the very heart of the message of the apostolic Christians, as that message is recorded in the Acts of the Apostles. In Christ was furnished the means for the realization of the individual and personal immortality toward which the mind of man had ever persistently striven, but to which it had never been able to attain unaided by divine revelation. The ascended Christ's words as recorded in the Revelation are significant at this juncture. "I am the first and the last, and the living one; and I was dead, and behold, I am alive forevermore, and I have the keys of death and of Hades" (Rev. 1:17, 18). Christ's authority over death and the grave is the assurance of believing man's immortality.

Third, while there remains much unrevealed concerning the nature of immortality in the Christian teaching, it becomes evident that this future life is unending, that it is entirely free from the experience of sin with its woeful consequences, that it is characterized by personal identity and consciousness, that a *spiritual bodily form* is provided for the personal identity of the immortal spirit, and that endless growth in God's grace and infinite progression will continue. This is made clear in Paul's first letter to the Corinthians, chapter 15. It is further evident, from the teachings of the apostles especially, that the finite redeemed and immortal soul will experience a continual progressive development toward the infinite character of God throughout the aeons (see Heb. 12:22-24). On this question Wesley says: "Yet he still grows in grace and in the knowledge of Christ, and in the love and image of God, and will do so, not only till death but probably to all eternity."[6]

Although the idea of immortality may not be empirically demonstrable, it may be and has been courageously believed by millions of people since the days of Christ.

---

[6]John Wesley, *A Plain Account of Christian Perfection* (Louisville, KY: Pentecostal Publishing Co., n.d.), pp. 24, 25.

CHAPTER XVIII

The Life Everlasting
or
Christian Immortality (Contd.)

"Thou gavest Him authority over all mankind, that to all whom Thou hast given Him, He may give eternal life" (John 17:2).

"I am the first and the last, and the living One; and I was dead, and behold, I am alive forevermore, and I have the keys of death and of Hades" (Rev. 1:17b-18).

The Necessary Grounds for Christian Immortality

The necessary grounds for a satisfactory concept of immortality may be considered in a sixfold manner.

First, the everlasting freedom of personality is requisite to personal immortality. Since only spiritual persons are morally free, and since moral freedom is requisite to spiritual personality, then it follows that if spiritual personality is to experience immortality, it must remain everlastingly free. To deprive a person of moral freedom would mean the cancellation of an essential note of human personality which would reduce man to a robot, and Christ redeems persons, not robots.

Second, rational consciousness must ever characterize the immortal person. Since rationality is an essential characteristic of spiritual persons, differentiating them from all lower forms of life, it follows that if personal immortality is to be experienced, rationality must ever characterize the person. This is that "something" closely akin to God. Says Paul concerning the new man of redemption: he "is being renewed to a true knowledge according to the image of the One who created him" (Col. 3:10).

A *third* necessary ground for immortality is moral responsibility. Moral responsibility is the direct consequent of personal freedom and rationality. Therefore, while personality remains rational and free, it will be morally responsible.

Freedom without responsibility is always dangerous, and will eventually be self-destructive, as also destructive of the best interest of others. Responsibility places the necessary limitations on freedom.

The *fourth* necessary ground for personal immortality is the indestructibility of the soul. Plato argued the indestructibility of the soul on the ground of its simplicity as opposed to the compound. If it has no parts, said Plato. then it cannot be dissolved. Although Plato's argument has been challenged, it will be evident that if the soul is to be immortal, it must be indestructible. Perhaps the greater weight of evidence for the indestructibility of the soul rests in the fact that spiritual personalities are ends in themselves, rather than means to ends. Therefore, as ultimates in God's plan, they are in the very nature of the case indestructible. (Could personalities—individuals—possibly be the true atoms of the universe?)

A *fifth* ground of personal immortality is improvability. Personality is spiritual. Spirit is always active. Activity for the redeemed bespeaks purposeful progress, for a rational, free, and moral person could not remain active without purposeful progression. Cessation of activity would result in spiritual annihilation, and annihilation is not a tenable doctrine. Morality requires purposeful or worthy ends, and therefore the activity must be directed toward a worthy end. That end is the further development of immortal personality in Christ. Paul seems to have grasped this idea at the close of his master-work on love. Said he, "But now abide faith, hope, love, these three; but the greatest of these is love" (1 Cor. 13:13). One has observed that by faith comes anticipation; by hope, apprehension; and by love, appreciation, or enjoyment. Thus considered, these are the three virtues necessary to the unending progressive enrichment of the immortal person in Christ.

A *sixth* necessary ground for immortality is the existence of a moral sphere. If a moral sphere is presently necessary for the self-realization and continuance of moral personality, then in order for the continuance of moral responsibility, in the endless future, the universe must of necessity afford an infinite moral arena. Such a moral universe inhabited by free rational moral persons, in relation to and dependent upon God, cannot be logically a realm of closed moral probation. The absence of evil and temptation does not imply the absence of man's moral freedom. If such were the case, then there could have been no original sin, in the sense of a *first* unethical act. Thus Keyser has said: "Sin is an eternal possibility, but never an eternal necessity."[1] Should it be objected that such a position would allow for a "second chance Fall" of redeemed man after death, it should be noted that the following factors would preclude such an eventuality. (1) All actual sin and temptation, in the sense of enticement by a tempter, will be absent; (2) redeemed man will live in the light of the total effects of the Fall, and of God's redeeming love that provided his deliverance from sin and its consequences through reconciliation to God in Christ; (3) his love and devotion to God will be not only a personal, historical decision, but a continuous choice of love, devotion, and service to God.

The foregoing may be considered somewhat analogous to the successful continuous marriage relation. At a point in history the man and woman make their mutual choice of each other, seal that choice by matrimony, and then throughout life continue to choose one another momentarily. Divorce is always possible, and while much as it is deplored, few would wish it to be legally impossible. Certainly the marriage relation is more meaningful by reason of the continuous mutual choices of the partners throughout life, growing in mutual appreciation and enrichment with the fuller and deeper knowledge and understanding of each other, than were they compelled legally or otherwise to remain together.

Likewise, it would seem reasonable that redeemed man's continuous loving choice of God, both here and hereafter, would be more meaningful to both God and man than if man were deprived of his moral freedom and thus reduced to a redeemed robot. Nor does there appear to be any valid support in the Scriptures for the age-old teaching that redeemed

---

[1]L. S. Keyser, *A System of General Ethics* (Burlington, IA: The Lutheran Literary Board, 1934), p. 138.

man will be deprived of moral choice in the hereafter. Indeed, emphasis upon death as the closed door of reprobation has been highly effective in decision-getting in evangelistic preaching. Such emphasis, however, does not of necessity make the teaching reasonable or scripturally valid.

The Validity of Christian Immortality

Certain fundamental reasons for the necessity of immortality to satisfy the human mind are noteworthy.

First, nothing short of immortality, with its implications for the present and future life, will satisfy the demands of a person's moral nature for a sense of justice not realized in the present life.

Second, immortality is required for the fuller realization of the development of personality not possible of attainment in the present life. The awakening of a person's mind to the vastness and richness of an infinite universe within the brief span of a lifetime cannot logically terminate with a sudden cessation of personal existence. Such a consideration would be disillusioning and destructive of the value and worthfulness of the present life.

In the *third* instance, it is evident that immortality is necessary to the very nature of the redeemed personality. The personalities of God and men created in His image are the only ultimate realities in the universe. They are the only entities that exist of and for their own ends. All else is contingent upon personalities and exists for those personalities. In other words, all else besides personality possesses only *instrumental value.* Personality has *intrinsic* value. Finally, to destroy all personalities, including God, would mean cessation of all existence. The fallacy of such an argument is self-evident.

Fourth, the reason that immortality is essential to the nature of personality grows out of a consideration of the creativity of human personality. What man creates in the realm of social and moral values through constructive thinking and activity enriches life, and in a sense, the universe itself. As the universe created by God is contingent for its existence upon the Creator, so are the values created by men contingent upon their creators. Thus, the cessation of existence would be destructive of all values inhering in the

creative personalities. Such a disposal of values would not
be worthy of the character of God.

A *fifth* reason the nature of personality does not admit
of annihilation is that it is spiritual, it cannot become inert
and thus cease to exist. Hence, the nature of personality as
ultimate, creative, and active, logically establishes the
necessity of its immortality.

Sixth, the immortality of human personality stands on
the necessity of the fulfillment of the purpose of creation.
To say that man was created good is to say that God had
a good end in view for him. Otherwise, there would be the
dilemma of a morally good, spiritual personality existing for
no good purpose in the universe. Furthermore, such a purpose as would be worthy of the free moral personality of man
could not be logically realized within time. Only the contemplation of timelessness could possibly satisfy such an intellectual and spiritual demand.

Seventh, the validity of immortality is attested by the
demand for the fulfillment of the purpose of redemption.
When the cost and the intricacy of the divine plan of redemption are contemplated, the mind revolts at the thought of
an ultimate cessation of the existence of spiritual personalities redeemed at such great cost and care.

Eighth, and finally, the immortality of man is necessary
to the satisfaction of the divine desire for personal companionship. Love is the very essence of God. But love demands
an object upon which to bestow itself, an object which must
be capable of response to its overtures. Impersonal creation
is incapable of thus responding. Therefore, God requires personal beings for the full satisfaction of His own nature. Paul
speaks of "the riches of the glory of *His* [God's] *inheritance*
in the saints" (Eph. 1:18). Anything short of such a conception of God would resolve itself into something comparable
to Aristotle's idea of God as the "unmoved mover." A personal, loving God could have no pleasure in a lonely self-
existence. Nor could He have pleasure in the temporary
enjoyment of the fellowship of His redeemed creatures only
to snuff out their existence eventually. If God is personal,
His nature demands the everlasting personal companionship
of human personalities whom He has created and lovingly

redeemed, and who have freely chosen Him for their everlasting companionship.

The Source of Christian Immortality

Eternal life, or immortality, was resident in man before the Fall through God's indwelling Spirit, but it was lost through the greatest of all world tragedies—the Fall. The Genesis account informs us that "the Lord God . . . breathed into his nostrils the breath of life; and man became a living person" (Gen. 2:7). When man disobeyed God and separated himself from Him, he lost this divinely-endowed immortality of the soul. God then set a boundary upon him by removing him from the Garden where he had access to the tree of life, lest he should eat of the tree and live forever in his sins (Gen. 3:22).

Jesus Christ, as God incarnate, is now the only source of eternal life open to man. Paul declared that *God "alone possesses immortality* and dwells in unapproachable light." J. B. Phillips translates this passage thus: "God . . . the only *source of immortality*" (1 Tim. 6:16; cf. Rom. 6:23). Jesus Christ is man's only access to the divine immortality, or eternal life. Paul states that "the free gift of God is eternal life in Christ Jesus our Lord" (Rom. 6:23b).

Wesley states that:

> . . . God hath given us, not only a title to, but the real beginning of, eternal life: And this life is purchased by, and treasured up in, his Son; who hath all the springs and fullness of it in himself, to communicate to his body, the Church. This eternal life then commences when it pleases the Father to reveal his Son in our hearts; when we first know Christ, being enabled to 'call him Lord by the Holy Ghost.' . . . Then it is that heaven is opened in the soul, that the proper heavenly state commences . . . our knowledge and our love of him increases, by the same degrees, and in the same proportion, the kingdom of an inward heaven must necessarily increase also; while we 'grow up in all things into Him who is our Head.'[2]

---

[2]John Wesley, *The Works of John Wesley* (Grand Rapids: Baker Book House), 6:430.

On the necessity of the impartation of the divine life, as opposed to mere imputation, for the realization of the everlasting life or immortality of the believer, Wesley is very specific and emphatic. He declares:

> . . . none shall live with God, but he that now lives to God; none shall enjoy the glory of God in heaven, but he that bears the image of God on earth; none that is not saved from sin here can be saved from hell hereafter; none can see the kingdom of God above, unless the kingdom of God be in him below. Whosoever will reign with Christ in heaven must have Christ reigning in him on earth . . .[3]

The Meaning of Christian Immortality

Eternal life is primarily qualitative, though it is also consequently quantitative. Geddes MacGregor[4] observes that there are three words used in the Greek New Testament to express the various kinds of life. The first is *bios*, which refers to the life span, the temporary vitalizing principle of a natural organism, and from which we get our word biology. The second word is *psyche,* which indicates the animating principle, and from which we get our word psychology. Third, there is the word *zoe,* which signifies a higher quality of life, and is the principal word used for immortality in the New Testament, especially in John's writings. In the New Testament this *zoe,* or *eternal life,* is declared to be the result of one's having been born again (John 3:3). It is the consequent of putting on Christ in Galatians 3:25; it is the result of being quickened together with Christ in Ephesians 2:5; it is the consequent of being in Christ in 2 Corinthians 5:17; it results from *putting on the new man* in Ephesians 4:24; and of being a new creature in Christ in Galatians 6:15. It is significant that *zoe* is generally used with the definite article in the Greek New Testament, and thus indicates that the readers must have been quite familiar with the concept and what it signified.

---

[3]Burtner, Robert W., and Robert E. Chiles, *A Compend of Wesley's Theology* (Nashville: Abingdon Press, 1957), p. 278.

[4]Geddes MacGregor, *Introduction to Religious Philosophy* (Boston: Houghton Mifflin, 1959), p. 192.

This *zoe,* or *eternal life,* in the New Testament is the supreme blessing of God mediated to men by Jesus Christ. It is the *very quality* of God's life given to believing man by Jesus Christ. Wesley[5] regards the "spirit" in 1 Thessalonians 5:23 as something adventitious, or added to man's natural constituent parts" of body and soul, rather than indicating that man is a trichotomy. The Old Testament is concerned primarily with life as "length of days on earth"—such as "three score years and ten." The New Testament and Christianity are concerned primarily with the quality of the life that lasts, rather than the span of years during which one may exist through animation by the life provided by nature. Christ said that He came that men might have life, and "might have it abundantly" (John 10:10). The life of Christ is an infinite, divine energy which transcends all forms of empirical or sensible manifestations. It is God's life in Christ imparted to the true believer. "I give eternal life to them," said Jesus, "and they shall never perish" (John 10:28).

Quantitative life could never be adequate for man's fullest self-realization. George Paget Thompson, Nobel Prize winning scientist, suggests that natural life may be extended, or old age may eventually be postponed indefinitely through improved medical science. Should this scientific achievement be realized, the following conditions would result. First, all death would be either accidental or voluntary. Second, life insurance would have to be converted to immortality insurance. Third, sickness or disability might be prolonged indefinitely. Fourth, if man lived 500 years, there would be no reason to believe that he would be any nearer to the realization of his life's goals at 499 years than he is now at seventy-nine or eighty years of age. Fifth, on the other hand, the longer span might give some persons more time to make a greater shipwreck of life, and incidentally, it would considerably increase the tax burden to provide social security for man from the present retirement age of sixty-two or sixty-five years to the 500-year mark.

---

[5]John Wesley, *Explanatory Notes Upon the New Testament* (London: The Epworth Press, rep. 1954), p. 763, n. 23.

MacGregor[6] observes that there are many noted witnesses to the value and superiority of qualitative over quantitative life. Benjamin Franklin said in *Poor Richard.*, "Wish not so much to live long as to live well." Ralph Waldo Emerson said, "It is the depth at which we live and not at all the surface extension that imports" (*Society and Solitude,* "Works and Days"). Crabbe stated: "Life is not to be measured by the time we live" (*The Village,* Book II). Sallust, the Roman historian, said, "No parent could wish for his children that they might live forever, but rather that their lives might be good and honorable" (*Jurgurtha,* Chap. 85, Sec. 50). Seneca said, "The wise man will live as long as he ought, and not as long as he can, for he is always thinking about the quality, not the quantity of his life" (*Epist. ad Lucilium,* 70, 4).

The Effects of Christian Immortality

Eternal life has exceedingly large and significant effects on the present life of man. First, it awakens the natural life (*bios*) and the innate potential of persons and causes them to germinate and grow, just as the warmth of the sun stimulates germination in the seed and causes it to spring into new life and fruition. Second, it unites the eternal life of God in Christ (*Zoe*) with the natural life of man (*bios*) in the conversion experience, and thus lifts man to a higher level of life and living here and now, but which will continue forever.

As an illustration of the foregoing principle, one might consider a box of seed placed in the dark basement where there are objects painted with luminous paint in each of the four corners of the room. With the box in the center of the room, as the seed sprouted and grew, the plants would bend in four different directions, depending on their proximity to the luminous objects which would pick up and reflect such light as existed in the apparent darkness. Should the window blind be slit to let in a beaming ray of sunlight, the plants would all then turn toward the sunlight. Just so, there are many natural objects in the world that reflect the sunlight of God's natural revelation (see Ps. 19), and that appeal to

---

[6]MacGregor, *Introduction to Religious Philosophy,* p. 192 ff.

man's natural aspirations and drives; but when Christ shines forth on men, He is the true light of God that brings to them spiritual illumination and life everlasting (John 1:9), unless they turn willfully away from Him into outer darkness. If they do so, they will die in their natural sinful state, devoid of this essential quality of eternal life, the life of God in Christ, though they will continue to exist in endless progressive degeneracy.

Eternal life has the effect for the future of an unbroken continuity of the presently experienced divine life. Jesus said, on the occasion of the raising of Lazarus, "Everyone who lives and believes in Me shall never die" (John 11:26b).

Finally, there will be the continued development of the redeemed personality as it moves forever toward the infinite divine perfection, even in the future life (cf. Matt. 5:48). The author of the letter to the Hebrews says concerning the redeemed in the life to come: "You have come . . . to the spirits of righteous men made perfect" (Heb. 12:22a-23b).

Chapter XIX

The Wisdom and Rewards of Soul-Winning

"This man receives sinners and eats with them"
(Luke 15:2b).

*"The fruit of the righteous is a tree of life, and he
who is wise wins souls"* (Prov. 11:30).

In order to get the setting for this message, the reader
is requested to read the fifteenth chapter of Luke in its
entirety.

The noted Presbyterian soul-winner and church builder,
and one-time president of McCormick Theological Seminary
in Chicago, John Timothy Stone, while addressing a ministerial association of which the writer was a member, presented the following illustration on the issue of soul-winning.
Said Dr. Stone: "Hypothetically I hold in my hand two
objects. One is a beautiful, ornate, symmetrical, and attractive agate, which every boy in town would earnestly desire
to possess. Beside it is an object rough and coarse in appearance, unsymmetrical and unattractive, just a worthless acorn
admired and desired by none, of value only as pig feed."
"However," continued Dr. Stone, "should those two objects
be buried together in fertile soil where the rain would moisten
and the sun would warm the earth, producing conditions
favorable to germination, the acorn would soon sprout, grow,
and eventually develop into a great spreading oak of beauty
and value. The agate, on the other hand, would remain forever
unresponsive to the atmospheric challenges. The difference
in these two objects," said Stone, "is the fact that the acorn
is possessed of the germ of life, and life is insurgent and can
ever reproduce itself, while the agate is inanimate and can
never reproduce itself; it can never be other than what it is—
just a beautiful, glassy, cold agate. It will deteriorate, but
it will never reproduce itself." The application of Stone's
parable needs little elaboration. The church, regardless of
culture, beauty of form, perfection of ritual, architectural

splendor or material prosperity, that does not have in it the germ of spiritual life, will die with the generation that produced it. The church possessed of the Spirit of God, though lacking any or all of these admirable graces and characteristics, will reproduce itself spiritually and there will be another generation of Christians.

In the fifteenth chapter of the Gospel according to Luke, Jesus presents four of His great parables, each of which has a direct bearing on the winning of lost men to God. They are the parable of the *lost sheep*, the parable of the *lost coin*, the parable of the *prodigal son,* and the parable of the *elder son*. It is the writer's purpose to examine the teachings of these parables, together with a view to ascertaining the Master's art of soul-winning, that we may know better how to win men to Christ.

Note the setting for the Master's parables, as suggested by the opening words of the chapter. "Now all the tax-gatherers and the sinners were coming near to Him to listen to Him. And both the Pharisees and the scribes began to grumble, saying, 'This man receives sinners and eats with them' " (Luke 15:1, 2). Thus it becomes evident that Christ had two audiences before Him: *first,* the tax-gatherers and sinners ("publicans and sinners") who were attracted to Him by His affectionate personality and His gracious invitation; *second,* "the Pharisees and scribes" (the religionists of the Jewish church of Christ's day), who, because of the absence of spiritual life within themselves were present to criticize Christ for evangelizing and admitting into His fellowship the despised tax-gatherers and sinners. The message of the parables that follows is for the benefit of both audiences. The first three parables are primarily, but not exclusively, for the encouragement of the tax-gatherers and sinners, while the last is a severe rebuke to the spiritual deadness of the religionists.

These Parables Teach Four Requisites to Soul-Winning

Effective soul-winning requires a definite recognition of the fact that persons without Christ are spiritually lost. Christ emphasizes the lostness of persons in each of the four parables.

> What man among you Pharisees and scribes if he has a hundred sheep and *has lost one of them,* does not . . . go after the one which *is lost,* until he finds it? . . . Or what woman, if she has ten silver coins and *loses one coin* . . . For *this son of mine was dead,* and has come to life again; *he was lost* . . . this brother of yours *was dead* and has begun to live, and *was lost* and has been found.

Even the elder son's lost condition (spiritual destitution), while remaining in his father's house and service, is implied in his own complaint: "Look! For so many years I have been serving you, and I have never neglected a command of yours; and yet you have never given me a kid [a young goat], that I might be merry with my friends." The father's reply, "My child, you have always been with me, and all that is mine is yours," makes clear the elder son's failure to appropriate his father's blessings while remaining in his father's house. He was in fact *a servant rather than a son.*

The manner in which each was *lost* in the four parables is interesting and instructive. The sheep was *lost* through careless straying from the safety of the flock and fold. The heedless following of natural inclinations for provender until the flock and shepherd had been lost to sight suddenly brought the wandering sheep to a sense of its *lostness,* with the resultant panic of fear and aloneness that drove it madly into greater danger and helplessness. Let it be noted that this sheep that was *lost,* was but one of a hundred. That there are those who *stray* from the spiritual fold, observation and experience eloquently testify. Their state of helplessness and hopelessness is quite as pitiable as that of the lost sheep, but their recovery is always a possibility, and it places a definite obligation upon the church.

On the other hand, the coin was lost through the carelessness of the owner. It possessed no volition of its own. It was quite irresponsible. The owner bore full responsibility for its misplacement. This type of loss occurs more frequently than that of sheep; one out of ten coins was lost, whereas one out of a hundred sheep went astray. The carelessness of the church in relation to the weak Christians or the ignorant unevangelized may occasion greater spiritual losses than the carelessness of those who stray from God.

For this loss the church is directly responsible and can find no self-justification.

The parable of the prodigal son introduces an entirely different type of spiritual loss. Here personal volition asserts itself. This younger son addressing his father demanded: "Father, give me the share of the estate that falls to me . . . And not many days later, the younger son gathered everything together and went on a journey into a distant country, and there he squandered his estate with loose living." He sought freedom from paternal restraint and liberty for unbridled selfish expression and realization, and deliberately departed from his father's care and correction. It would appear that most of those who are lost follow this deliberate course of sin to ruin. This lad was one of his father's two sons. All culpable sin must in the final analysis involve the exercise of personal volition against God.

The fourth parable involves the loss of the elder son who, though remaining in his father's house, failed to appropriate his father's provisions. He, like so many in the church, who, though faithful in attendance in the regular services of the church, grow faithless and deprive themselves of the blessings of the Father. There are many in the church of every generation who become self-righteous and spiritually dead, and never have so much as "a kid" [a young goat] to say nothing of a "fatted calf," that they might make merry with their friends. Little wonder that this spiritually-starved, self-righteous fellow became *suspicious, angry, stubborn, resentful,* and *disdainful* in his embittered spirit. He was quite as *lost* as the others, and much more difficult to recover than they. In fact, the eldest son is the only one whose recovery is not recorded by Jesus. As a representative of the Pharisees and scribes, it may be questioned whether he was ever restored to the Father.

The spiritual state and responsibility of this *elder son,* as representative of the Jewish nation of his day, is aptly set forth in the following lines of a poem under the caption, "Twas a Sheep."

> *Twas a sheep, not a lamb, that strayed away*
> *In the parable Jesus told:*
> *A grown-up sheep that had gone astray*
> *From the ninety and nine in the fold.*

Out in the meadows, out in the cold,
  Twas a sheep the Good Shepherd sought;
Back to the flock and into the fold,
  Twas a sheep the Good Shepherd brought.

Why, for the sheep, should we earnestly long
  And so earnestly hope and pray,
Because there is danger, if they go wrong,
  They will lead the young lambs astray.

For the lambs follow the sheep, you know,
  Wherever the sheep may stray:
If the sheep go wrong, it will not be long
  Till the lambs are as wrong as they.

So, with the sheep, we earnestly plead
  For the safety of the lambs;
If the lambs are lost, what a terrible cost
  Some sheep may have to pay.[1]

Further, while the sheep, the coin, and the two sons were lost, and would perish if they were not recovered, they nevertheless bore such marks of identification with their former states that it was possible for the searchers to recognize and recover them. The lost sheep was still a sheep and could be identified by its shepherd; the coin, though corroded and worn, still bore the original image, and thus enabled the woman to recognize it; and the prodigal son, though *lost*, and spiritually *dead*, still bore the image of the father, which might be restored. Likewise, the elder brother is designated *a son* by the father. There is a vast difference between "a son by creation" and "a son by redemption," however. All are sons of God by creation, but only those having appropriated the provisions of Christ's redeeming atonement are sons by redemption. God's image in sinful man may be ever so seriously marred, but in no man is it completely obliterated.

These parables clearly teach that there can be no true effective evangelistic effort until there is a frank, clear recognition of the fact that men are *lost* and will perish in their sins without the saving mercies of God in Christ.

---

[1]Florence Fitzpatrick, publisher unknown.

*Effective soul-winning requires a temporary disregard
for the things at hand.* "What man among you, if he has a
hundred sheep and has lost one of them, does not leave the
ninety-nine . . . and go after the one which is lost."

The shepherd might well have contented himself with
the ninety-nine remaining sheep, and even excused himself
from going in search of the lost one, by reason of his obligation to the flock left in safety. Whenever present personal
interests take priority over evangelism, the *lost* will go
unsought. Even the father's concern for the *lost* son is such
as to take priority over personal interests: "while he was still
a long way off, his father saw him, and felt compassion for
him, and ran and embraced him, and kissed him." Jesus
placed priority on personal relationship with God when He
exhorted His followers to "seek first His kingdom, and His
righteousness" (Matt. 6:33a), rather than food and clothing
and things material, such as those to which the Gentiles gave
priority.

A parishioner once came to the writer on one of his pas-
torates, and with tears in her eyes and a sob in her voice she
said: "Last night, as I was en route from my home to the
grocery store for provisions, I passed the home of a neighbor
lady who lived alone. I observed while passing that she sat
in her living room with her head buried in her hands, as
though in deep trouble or distress. God spoke to me, telling
me to visit Nellie and point her to Jesus Christ for help. I
knew she was not a Christian and that I had both a responsibility and a challenge to lead her to the Saviour. However,
I silenced the voice of God to my soul with the argument
that I must secure groceries before the store closed that my
family might have the necessary food, and that I would go
to see Nellie in the morning. This morning," she said, "when
I scanned the headlines of the paper, I was shocked to discover that Nellie had committed suicide last night." My
parishioner had refused to leave the ninety and nine safe in
the fold to seek the one that was *lost.* And the *lost* one
perished!

The evangelist Philip, at the prompting of the Spirit, left
a flourishing spiritual awakening in Samaria to search for
and lead a lone, searching, Ethiopian nobleman to Christ on
the desert way to Gaza. Christ's example in this respect is

sufficient to show Christians the way. Says Paul: "For you know the grace of our Lord Jesus Christ, that though He [Christ] was rich, yet for your sake He became poor, that you through His poverty might become rich" (2 Cor. 8:9).

Effective soul-winning requires diligent search for the lost. The shepherd is represented in the parable as going "after the one which is lost, until he finds it." And the woman who had lost the coin is said to "light a lamp and sweep the house and search carefully until she finds it." Even the father, longingly and anxiously awaiting his wayward son's return, at a great distance saw him "and felt compassion for him, and ran and embraced him, and kissed him." Nor was the father's concern for the salvation of his elder son any less, for we read: "his father came out and began entreating him."

The self-sacrifice, diligence, sympathetic interest, and tact with which Philip applied himself to the task of winning the Ethiopian nobleman to Christ on the Gaza way is a notable example for every Christian worker to follow (Acts 8:29-40). Philip made haste, at the Spirit's bidding, to identify himself with the man: "And the Spirit said to Philip, 'Go up and join this chariot.'" Next the evangelist ascertained the man's interest, for he heard him read the prophet Esaias, and said, "Do you understand what you are reading?" Then, at the right moment, "Philip opened his mouth, and beginning from this Scripture he preached Jesus to him." Nor was the evangelist satisfied until he felt certain of his convert's saving relationship with the Lord. Upon the nobleman's request for water baptism Philip replied: "If you believe with all your heart, you may": to which the convert heartily responded: "I believe that Jesus Christ is the Son of God." Satisfied with the man's saving faith, Philip baptized him and then, his mission completed, "he went on his way rejoicing" (Acts 8:26-49).

Personal work, or evangelistic effort for the salvation of the *lost,* is frequently little more than a passing sentiment with many Christians today. Not a few Christian workers are too easily discouraged in their quest for the recovery of *lost* men. It was not until repeated efforts with discouraging lapses had been experienced that Jerry McCauley, who became the great apostle of Water Street Mission in New York City, was finally established in Christ. When no circumstance or hindrance is allowed to deter the Christian worker from finding the object of his quest, men will be won to God.

Effective soul-winning requires spiritual burden-bearing. Of the shepherd's quest for His lost sheep, Christ said, "And when he has found it, he lays it on his shoulders, rejoicing." And the woman who lost the coin is said to "light a lamp and sweep the house and search carefully until she finds it." Even the father's loving vigil for His lost son was a spiritual burden.

The Good Samaritan's restoration of the robbed, beaten, and helpless man by the wayside (Luke 10:30-37) is instructive to the soul-winner. Having been moved with compassion to go to the unfortunate man and minister to his wounds, "he put him on his own beast and brought him to an inn, and took care of him" (Luke 10:34b). Thus the Samaritan lifted the wounded man to his beast of burden and allowed him to ride to a place of safety and care, while the owner sacrificed his comfort and walked. He was even moved to pay for the man's care at the inn. Soul-winning is costly in time, energy, effort, and sometimes even money.

There are many *lost* persons who will never get back to God unless some faithful soul-winner bears the burden of their salvation in fasting and soul-travailing prayer. The prophet's words are as true today as when they were first spoken: "As soon as Zion travailed, she also brought forth her sons" (Isa. 66:8b).

It is worthy of note that illumination and renovation characterized the woman's search for the *lost* coin: "what woman . . . does not light a lamp and sweep the house" in her diligent effort to find the lost coin. Likewise spiritual illumination and moral renovation will always accompany sincere soul-seeking.

Trench understands the woman in this parable to represent the Church.[2] Thus, the Church is God's agency in seeking the lost. Though the sheep and the younger son were lost outside of their fold and home, this coin was lost in the woman's own house—*within the church.* May there not be

---

[2]Richard Chenevir Trench, *Notes on the Parables of Our Lord* (Philadelphia: William Sychelmoore, n.d), p. 294.

a subtle hint here that the religionists, the scribes and Pharisees, who gathered to oppose the salvation of the publicans and sinners, are themselves lost within their own Jewish religious communion?

It is especially noteworthy that, though doubtless long lost and corroded, the coin retained sufficient of its original image to be identified when found. Likewise, the lost person, no matter how long lost and far distant from God, is never so depraved as to have completely lost the divine image in which mankind was originally created. Though marred and sullied by the Fall and sinful departure from God, there ever remains the stamp of the divine image—mankind's personhood—what Trench calls the "traces of the mint from which it proceeded."[3]

Concerning the candle, Trench remarks:

> The *candle* is the Word of God; which candle the Church holds forth, as it has and exercises a ministry of this Word. It is by the light of this Word that sinners are found, that they find themselves, that the Church finds them.[4]

Indeed, in the process of searching for the lost coin, there would be of necessity much rearranging of the furnishings and no little amount of dust raised. As Trench remarks:

> The charge against the Gospel is still the same, that it turns the world upside down (Acts 17:6). . . . She meanwhile who bears the candle of the Lord, amid all this uproar and clamor is diligently looking for and finding her own again.[5]

While the sheep strayed away and was lost by its own wandering, the coin was lost by the woman's own carelessness, even so many are lost by the lack of concern on the part of the Church.

The results suggested by this parable are most encouraging. The woman got her house cleaning done in the search for the lost coin, and when found, a time of great rejoicing

---

[3]*Ibid.*, p. 295.
[4]*Ibid.*
[5]*Ibid.*, p. 296.

followed. Likewise, a soul-saving revival invariably results in the spiritual illumination and purification of the Church with consequent spiritual rejoicing.

There Are Certain Rewards of Soul-Winning

Soul-winning saves lost men from spiritual death unto Christ and eternal life. The success of the shepherd's quest for the lost sheep is marked by the words, "he has found it," and likewise, the woman's successful quest for the lost coin is identified in Christ's words, "she finds it." The father twice exclaims concerning the recovery of his prodigal son "this son of mine was dead, and has come to life again; he was *lost*, and has been found . . . This brother of yours was dead and has begun to live, and was *lost*, and has been *found*."

If men are not really *lost* in sin, then they are not really found and saved by Christ. If they are not really dead in sin, then they are not really made alive in Christ. If true spiritual lostness and death characterize the sinner, then the greatest thing in the world that any man can do is to find such a spiritually dead and *lost* person and bring that person to Christ the Saviour who willingly gives everlasting life to all who come to Him. In sin men are *lost*; in Christ they are *found*. In sin men are spiritually *dead*; in Christ they *are made alive* again. Paul wrote to the Ephesians: ". . . you were dead in your trespasses and sins" (Eph. 2:1). "For the wages of sin is death, but the free gift of God is eternal life in Christ Jesus our Lord" (Rom. 6:23). What a glorious privilege and reward is afforded the soul-winner in bringing *lost* and spiritually dead men to the Saviour, Jesus Christ, who is the source of everlasting life!

James is specific and emphatic in his citation of the soul-winner's reward when he says: "let him know that he who turns a sinner from the error of his way will save his soul from death, and will cover a multitude of sins" (James 5:20).

A missionary en route to Africa walked out one morning on the deck of the ship on which he was sailing, and there he observed a despondent sailor boy standing alone by the rail, looking forlornly out across the dark waters. The missionary engaged the boy in conversation and learned that he had in his pocket a revolver with which he intended to take his own life that morning. Discouraged and downcast, the boy had thought life not worth living. The missionary pointed the sailor to Christ and prayed for him there on the ship's deck. The boy took hope anew, found salvation in Christ, threw the weapon of his intended suicide into the ocean, and turned about to face a new meaningful life in Christ. The missionary soul-winner saved a soul from death there on the deck of the ship that day.

The author on a certain occasion while searching for souls for Christ, found himself among the squalor and shambles of the city in which he was pastoring. A knock at the door of a dwelling unfit for human habitation revealed a family of three: an ill and unkempt mother, a young daughter, and a father whose beastly disposition ultimately sent him to the penitentiary. Kind words of invitation to church and an earnest prayer resulted in the family's attendance at the services of the church, where soon the mother and daughter were beautifully converted to Christ. The mother ever after remained a faithful Christian and a respected and useful member of the church. The daughter eventually went away to college where she developed into a beautiful, talented young lady, married an accomplished and promising young ministerial student, and together they devoted their lives to the service of Christ. What greater reward could a soul-winner desire?

Tradition holds that the Ethiopian nobleman, converted under the personal ministry of Philip en route to Gaza, carried the gospel to his people in the great kingdom of Ethiopia, where the Coptic Christian Church continues to the present day with a total of some ten million members. If this tradition is correct, then Philip's reward was beyond his comprehension.

Soul-winning is productive of spiritual rejoicing and liberality. The shepherd, unable to contain his joy at the recovery of the lost sheep, "calls together his friends and his neighbors, saying to them, 'Rejoice with me, for I have found my sheep which was lost!' " And the woman, whose regard for money was such as to set her in diligent search for a lost coin worth approximately fifteen cents in our money, suddenly became extremely liberal when she found it, and called "her friends and neighbors" to a festivity, saying, "Rejoice with me, for I have found the coin which I had lost!"

While not so stated specifically, it appears quite evident in both instances, from the calling of the friends and neighbors together for an occasion of rejoicing over the recovery of the lost property, that such occasions entailed considerable expenditure for entertainment on the part of the happy finders. Likewise, upon the occasion of the prodigal's return, the joyful and grateful father suddenly became recklessly liberal and commanded his servants to "bring out the best robe and put it on him, and put a ring on his hand and sandals on his feet; and bring the fattened calf, kill it, and let us eat and be merry." On the other hand, the elder brother, representing the spiritless religionists of his day (the Pharisees and the scribes), having heard the orchestral music of the feast, complained bitterly of the father's extravagance over the pitiable prodigal's return. It is noteworthy that this spiritually-starved and shriveled-souled elder son knew nothing of spiritual liberality or rejoicing, as indicated by his own admission:

> Look! For so many years I have been serving you
> ... and yet you have never given me a kid [a young
> goat], that I might be merry with my friends: but
> when this son of yours came, who has devoured
> your wealth with harlots, you killed the fattened
> calf for him.

The father's reply clearly indicates that his elder son's spiritual paucity was due to his failure to appropriate his father's blessings: "My child, you have always been with me, and all that is mine is yours."

The foregoing incident calls to mind the disciple's indignation on the occasion of the grateful woman's anointing of Jesus with the precious alabaster ointment in the house of Simon the leper (Mark 14:3-9). One cannot but suspect that Judas Iscariot's starved and perverted soul was the moving spirit in this complaint against the woman's grateful extravagance, in the light of the fact that immediately following this incident the record depicts Judas' betrayal of Christ to the chief priests for thirty pieces of silver (Mark 4:10, 11). A spiritually-dead Christian or church is the greatest hindrance to vital evangelism with its resultant spiritual victories in liberated, restored, and animated souls. As the recovery of the *lost* sheep, the finding of the *lost* coin, the return of the *lost* prodigal and the resurrection from the dead of Lazarus (John 11) all resulted in feasts of rejoicing, so the restoration of a *lost* person to Christ will inevitably produce spiritual festivity in the hearts of true Christians and the Church. Complaints against such "spiritual liberality" can only come from spiritually dead, shriveled, and embittered souls who know nothing of the joy of Christ's saving grace.

Let it be noted that the rejoicing follows rather than precedes the success of soul-winning. Said the Psalmist: "Those who sow in tears shall reap with joyful shouting. He who goes to and fro weeping, carrying his bag of seed, shall indeed come again with a shout of joy, bringing his sheaves with him" (Ps. 126:5, 6). Daniel envisioned the rewards of soul-winning when he wrote: "And those who have insight will shine brightly like the brightness of the expanse of heaven, and those who lead the many to righteousness, like the stars forever and ever" (Dan. 12:3).

Soul-Winning Glorifies God

That the winning of lost men to God through Christ is God's chief purpose and greatest glory appears evident from Christ's words: "I tell you that in the same way, there will be more joy in heaven over one sinner who repents, than over ninety-nine righteous persons who need no repentance." And again: "In the same way, I tell you, there is joy in the presence of the angels of God over one sinner who repents."

Perhaps the most familiar passage in the Bible testifies that God's supreme redemptive purpose is the salvation of *lost* men. "For God so loved the world, that He gave His only begotten Son, that whosoever believes in Him should not perish, but have eternal life. For God did not send the Son into the world to judge the world; but that the world should be saved through Him" (John 3:16, 17).

Paul declares in 2 Corinthians 5:18-20 that "God was in Christ reconciling the world to Himself," and that God has "committed to us the word of reconciliation," and "gave us the ministry of reconciliation," and "we are," therefore, "ambassadors for Christ" to beseech men in Christ's stead to be reconciled to God.

Almost the last words of the Bible represent the salvation of *lost* men as God's supreme purpose and glory: "And the Spirit and the bride say, 'Come.' And let the one who is thirsty come; let the one who wishes take the water of life without cost" (Rev. 22:17).

Finally, Paul declares that "Christ Jesus came into the world to save sinners" (1 Tim. 1:15b). And the author of the letter to the Hebrews declares that it was "for the joy set before Him [the redemption and reconciliation of *lost* men to God] that he endured the cross, despising the shame, and has sat down at the right hand of the throne of God" (Heb. 12:2b). This joy of Christ is the salvation of *lost* men and women.

Was a greater compliment ever paid Jesus Christ than those words spoken by His bitterest enemies, the Pharisees and scribes, the ardent legalistic religionists of the day, when in derision they sneered, "this man receives sinners and eats with them." The Christian believer who brings *lost* men to Christ's spiritual feast is saving souls from death to life and is doing God's service, which carries with it its own spiritual compensation. "This man [Christ] receives sinners and eats [fellowships] with them."

To His first-century disciples Christ said: "you shall be My witnesses"; and again: "You shall receive power when the Holy Spirit has come upon you and you shall be My witnesses . . . even to the remotest part of the earth" (Acts 1:8). Again Jesus said to His followers: "The harvest is plentiful, but the workers are few; Therefore beseech the Lord of the harvest to send out workers into His harvest" (Matt. 9:37, 38).

No generation ever presented a greater challenge to the Christian church than the present. A morally and spiritually bankrupt world lies prostrate at the door of the church today. The spectacle of the unfortunate cripple who had been from birth daily framed in the archway of the ornate Gate Beautiful which led to the Jewish temple is a graphic portrayal of much of modern Christendom in its relation to an unevangelized world. The Jewish formalistic worshipers, who passed to and fro daily under the archway of the Gate Beautiful, could assist the unfortunate beggar with nothing more than the material pittance of alms which they dropped in his outstretched hand. Spiritual life they had not, and consequently they could not dispense it. On the other hand, Peter and John, having no material possessions, beheld the unfortunate man, and motivated and energized by divine love, confidently extended a hand and declared: "I do not possess silver and gold, but what I do have I give to you: In the name of Jesus Christ the Nazarene—walk!" (Acts 3:6).

The story is told of an incident which occurred when Thomas Aquinas, the great thirteenth-century Roman Catholic theologian and philosopher, was visiting the Pope at Rome. As the Pope bade St. Thomas view the stacks of money in the church's treasury he said exultantly: "No longer, St. Thomas, can the church say with Peter and John of old, 'Silver and gold have I none,' to which St. Thomas replied, "Nor can the church any longer say with Peter and John to the crippled beggar, 'In the name of Jesus Christ of Nazareth arise and walk.' " Material wealth does not produce spiritual compassion!

Will we experience spiritual renewal in the church in our time and go forth with a dynamic witness for Christ on the greatest mission of evangelism the modern world has ever witnessed?

Chapter XX

The Church Must Evangelize Each Generation

"The harvest is plentiful, but the workers are few"
(Matt. 9:37).

Matthew graphically depicts the threefold basis for world evangelism when he records concerning Jesus' own holistic ministry that,

> . . . Jesus was going about all the cities and the villages, teaching in their synagogues, and proclaiming the gospel of the kingdom, and healing every kind of disease and every kind of sickness. And seeing the multitudes, He felt compassion for them, because they were distressed and downcast like sheep without a shepherd. Then He said to His disciples, "The harvest is plentiful, but the workers are few. Therefore beseech the Lord of the harvest to send out workers into His harvest." And having summoned His twelve disciples, He gave them authority over unclean spirits, to cast them out, and to heal every kind of disease and every kind of sickness (Matt. 9:35-10:1).

A definition of Christian evangelism implies four things: first, a sender or commissioner; second, a messenger, or one who is sent; third, a message, or that which is sent; and fourth, recipients, or those to whom the message is sent. The Lord God of Heaven, the King and highest authority of the universe, sends His glorious message of universal salvation by His messengers—the redeemed men and women—to those who are foreigners and strangers to the grace and mercy of a loving and compassionate Heavenly Father, and who still grope in darkness and the shadow of death. Jesus declared to His disciples, just before He returned to heaven, "You shall receive power when the Holy Spirit has come upon you; and you shall be My witnesses both in Jerusalem, and in all

Judea and Samaria, and even to the remotest part of the earth" (Acts 1:8).

The writer attempts to draw no sharp line of demarcation between Occidentals and Orientals; the day of that distinction is past. The man or woman who is saved and possessed of the burning compassionate love of the Son of God and a desire for the salvation of his fellow beings will be a witness anywhere. If he lives in America, he will be a witness to Americans. If he dwells in the British Empire, he will be a witness to the subjects of that Empire. If he goes to the heart of the jungles of South America, Africa, India, China, or to the Islands of the Sea, he will go witnessing to the saving power of Jesus Christ. The person or the church that is evangelistic where he or it is will be a witness anywhere; and the person or the church that is not evangelistic where he or it is, would not be a witness anywhere. The evangelistic spirit should not be confined or limited by national differences, racial prejudices, the color of the skin, the accent of the tongue, or geographical boundaries. It is said of those early followers of Jesus, "they went out and preached everywhere . . ." (Mark 16:20; cf. Acts 8:4). Philip climbed into the chariot with the Ethiopian treasurer and from the book which the Ethiopian was reading, he preached to him Christ. Paul left the shores of Asia Minor, and set sail for Europe that he might preach the gospel where he had seen a man of Macedonia in a vision calling, "Come over to Macedonia and help us" (Acts 16:9).

The Church Must Evangelize Each Generation Because Christ Made Provision for the Salvation of All Mankind

"For God so loved the world, that He gave His only begotten Son, that whoever believes in Him should not perish, but have eternal life" (John 3:16). Again we read, "And He Himself is the propitiation for our sins; and not for ours only, but also for those of the whole world" (1 John 2:2). When Jesus Christ cried out with His last breath on Calvary's cruel cross, "It is finished!" (John 19:39), He meant that He had provisionally redeemed the whole universe, that salvation had been provided for the last man to the end of time. The atoning work of the Son of God is just as extensive as the fall of man, even to the lowest and most degraded person or tribe of pagan people on earth. The devil did nothing in his deadly work at the Fall, for the undoing of which Christ has not made provision in His atonement. We have not yet seen the complete restoration of all creation, but it will be accomplished eventually—willfully disobedient mankind excepted. Anything less would be an incomplete victory for the Son of God; anything less would fall short of the purpose for which Christ came into the world, for said John, "The Son of God appeared for this purpose, that He might destroy the works of the devil" (1 John 3:8).

If it then be true that salvation and liberation from the power and prison house of sin and death has been provided in Christ for all men, and until now a great percentage of mankind remains enslaved to Satan because they have not been told of their freedom, is it not the duty of the Christian church to hasten to them with the declaration of their liberty in Christ?

The Church Must Evangelize Each Generation Because Christ Is the Great Evangelizing Example of the Church for All Time

First, He was evangelistic in His self-denial. Of Him, the great Apostle declared, "For you know the grace of our Lord Jesus Christ, that though He was rich, yet for your sake He became poor, that you through His poverty might become rich" (2 Cor. 8:9). When certain individuals came inquiring about the dwelling place of our Lord, He replied, "The foxes have holes, and the birds of the air have nests; but the Son of Man has nowhere to lay His head" (Matt. 8:20).

Second, Jesus was the great evangelizing example of the Church in His proclamation of Divine Truth. He preached to the haughty self-righteous Jews of the sacred city. He preached to the rabble of Palestine. He preached to the skeptical of His home community. He preached to the demented among the tombs of the Gadarenes. He preached to the disgraced woman taken in adultery. He preached to the immoral Samaritan woman at the well of Jacob. He preached to the crowds, and He preached to the few. His message was ever the same: "For the Son of Man has come to seek and to save that which was lost" (Luke 19:10). If Jesus, whose name Christians bear, and whose life they would emulate, exemplified the evangelistic spirit, how can the Christian church refuse to follow Him in His soul-saving ministry?

The Church Must Evangelize Each Generation Because the Work of Evangelism Was the Last Positive Command of the Son of God to His Disciples Before He Ascended From this Earth to His Father in Heaven

Said Jesus: "Go therefore and make disciples of all the nations, baptizing them in the name of the Father and the Son and the Holy Spirit . . . lo, I am with you alway, even to the end of the age" (Matt. 28:19, 20).

Last commands are usually so made because of their importance. The employer, not infrequently, states or restates his most important instructions to his employees before leaving for a prolonged absence. The dying man calls his attorney and makes his last and unalterable will. This may be but a command concerning the distribution of his earthly possessions. Jesus Christ, before His departure, left to His followers as His last and most important mandate what is known as the Great Commission, "Go therefore and make disciples of all the nations . . . and lo, I am with you alway" (Matt. 28:19, 20a).

Further, Jesus made obedience to His mandate the test of love for Himself. "If you love Me, you will keep My commandments" (John 14:15). We are naturally made to ask, Does the extent of obedience to this great and last mandate of the Master to His followers indicate a great degree of love for the Master?

The Church Must Evangelize Each Generation Because It Has A Great Debt To Pay— A Debt Which Cannot Be Otherwise Paid

With the atonement of Jesus Christ a reality in his life experience, with the prospect of heaven before him, and the vision of a world lost in sin about him, the heart of the great

Apostle Paul was impelled to exclaim, "I am under obligation both to Greeks and to barbarians, both to the wise and to the foolish" (Rom. 1:14). Christians today are nonetheless indebted to both God and their fellowmen. Would that Christians today were possessed of the spirit of Paul when he cried, "Thus, for my part, I am eager to preach the gospel to you also who are in Rome. For I am not ashamed of the gospel, for it is the power of God for salvation to everyone who believes, to the Jew first and also to the Greek" (Rom. 1:15, 16).

The Church is indebted, first, to God for the cost-price of its salvation. Men were sold unto sin; taken captive by the devil at his own will and by their consent. The price of salvation is beyond man's ability to pay. Peter declared: "Knowing that you were not redeemed with perishable things like silver or gold from your futile way of life inherited from your forefathers, but with precious blood, as of a lamb unblemished and spotless, the blood of Christ" (1 Peter 1:18, 19). Should men give all of their possessions, and should they work all of their lives for God, they could not so much as pay the interest on the debt of their salvation.

Further, we are indebted to the gospel itself for everything of value in this life. There are multitudes of people in America today who are but miserable parasites on Christian society. For every particle of good that exists in the people of this land today, and for everything good that they possess, they are indebted to the Gospel of Jesus Christ. Go to the pagan lands where the Gospel of Jesus Christ has not penetrated the dense darkness and you will find, instead of hospitals for the sick, homes for the orphans and infirm, schools for the education of the children, and love and affection in the home; the sick are left unattended or to worse fate at the hands of the native medicine men, the aged and the orphans are neglected and uncared for, the multitudes are in gross ignorance, and often the houses are hells instead of homes. Had not the Gospel of Jesus Christ been preached to our ancestors, it is not unlikely that the people of our own fair land would be roaming about as near-nude savages, sitting about a cannibalistic feast, or worshipping demons with the sacrifice of their children. History reveals the fact that such were the ancestors of many Americans before the gospel enlightened them. Nor have we any good reason to believe that we, their posterity, would be any better off than they were had not the gospel been preached to them and to us. Truly everything of value that we possess and enjoy in this life and land we owe, either directly or indirectly, to the Gospel of Jesus Christ.

Any Christian man or woman who has a spark of gratitude to God for the gospel and its blessings cannot but feel a burden of debt to the rest of the world that has not heard this Gospel of the Son of God. The church is indebted to the unevangelized, because it possesses that which would liberate them from sin's bondage and give them a new hope if they but had it. The Church is debtor to God, to the gospel, and to the unevangelized world which lies in pagan darkness. Therefore, the Church must attempt to pay its debt by preaching the glorious Gospel of Christ to the non-Christian world.

The Church Must Evangelize Each Generation Because Self-Propagation is the Law of Life and Growth In the Spiritual Realm, As In Nature

The wise man declared, "Where there is no vision, the people perish" (Prov. 29:18a, KJV). The absence of a vision of "the fields white unto harvest" has caused the people of God in many churches to become selfish, self-centered, and to dry up at the very fountainhead of spiritual life—to become "twice dead and plucked up by the roots." The deadness and fruitlessness of so many Christians can be traced directly to the absence of a vision for the salvation of lost men. No such thing as a spiritually-dead evangelistic church exists. That would be a contradiction in terms. The evangelistic enterprise requires action, and dead things do not act. Nor is there any such thing as a living non-evangelistic church. That, likewise, would be a contradiction in terms.

Not only will the church that is non-evangelistic perish, but those for whose evangelization that church is responsible will also perish. "Where there is no vision, the people perish." This applies to the Church—the Lord's people by redemption—and the world—the Lord's people by creation, and for whose salvation Christ made provision in His atonement. If the Church is to live, she must proclaim the gospel to the lost world (John 7:38).

The Church Must Evangelize Each Generation Because God Has Chosen Redeemed Men to Preach The Gospel, And The Church Is The Company of Redeemed Men on Earth

Doubtless, the angels of heaven would gladly come to earth to preach the Gospel of Jesus Christ to the lost if they could, but they cannot. There are at least two reasons why angels could not preach to fallen mankind. *First,* God has chosen persons to preach, and not angels. *Second,* a witness is one who must have firsthand knowledge of that to which he gives testimony. A gospel witness must have experienced salvation. Angels that have never fallen have not known the power of sin, and, consequently, have never experienced redemption through the atonement of Christ. Therefore, they do not qualify as witnesses.

There is Biblical evidence that the lost in eternity would proclaim warnings, at least, to the impenitent of earth were they privileged to do so. But they, like the angels, are both prohibited from returning to the earth, and disqualified to witness through a lack of knowledge of salvation (cf. Luke 16:26-31).

Even the redeemed in heaven are prohibited from returning to earth to preach the gospel. "If they do not listen to Moses and the Prophets, neither will they be persuaded if someone rises from the dead" (Luke 16:31), said Father Abraham to the lost man in hell. Therefore, the work of evangelizing the world is left to the Christian Church Militant. If the Church does not do it, it will not be done. It has been said that the only feet that God has on earth with which to carry the Gospel of His Son to the unsaved of earth are the feet of Christians; that the only hands that God has on earth with which to minister to the needs of mankind are the hands of the Christians; and that the only tongue that God has with which to proclaim the glorious Gospel of His Son to the lost of earth is the tongue of the Christian. If the Christian church folds her hands, plants her feet, and locks her jaws, the gospel will not be preached and people will be lost. The Christian church must evangelize because God is depending on her for the evangelization of the world.

Finally, The Church Must Evangelize Each Generation That God May Have A Redeemed Representation As A Witness to His Saving Power From Among Every People And Generation on Earth

It is the Lord's plan that no one shall appear in the judgment with a justifiable reason for being lost. Therefore, He has provided that the gospel shall be so preached that there will be witnesses from every tribe and nation. John the Revelator declared, as he previewed eternity and envisioned the redeemed host: "And they sang a new song, saying, 'Worthy art Thou to take the book, and to break its seals; for Thou wast slain, and didst purchase for God with Thy blood men from every tribe and tongue and people and nation' " (Rev. 5:9). If all are to hear the gospel, and if some are to be saved from among all people, then the Christian church must preach the gospel to the ends of the earth in each succeeding generation. The church of today must evangelize the generation of today, or this generation will be forever lost in eternity tomorrow. Tomorrow's church cannot evangelize today's generation, for the generation of today will be gone tomorrow. Yesterday's church did not, and could not evangelize the generation of today, for yesterday's Church is in heaven today. Therefore, either the church of today will evangelize the non-Christian generation of today, or this generation will be forever lost in eternity, and the church of today will bear the responsibility for that loss at the judgment of God. The only way in which the Christian church can continue to enjoy the favor and blessing of the living Lord is by living in obedience to His last great mandate, "Go therefore and make disciples of all the nations, baptizing them in the name of the Father and the Son and the Holy Spirit; teaching them to observe all that I commanded you, and lo, I am with you alway, even to the end of the age" (Matt. 28:19, 20). No claim can be laid to Christ's accompanying presence to the end of the age except as obedience is rendered to His command. The church must either evangelize, or she will lose the presence of Christ from her experience.

G. Campbell Morgan says on those last words of Jesus' command:

> The realization of the promise of His abiding presence is entirely dependent upon the Church's willingness to fulfill her responsibility. She has no right to apply this gracious word to herself save as she fulfills the conditions imposed. If we have no passion in our hearts for the discipling of the nations, we have no warrant for believing that He remains in fellowship with us.[1]

Therefore, let us rise up and go forth in obedience to His command and preach the gospel to all people to the ends of the earth in this our generation.

---

[1]G. Campbell Morgan, *The Missionary Manifesto* (New York: Fleming H. Revell Co., 1909), p. 56.

Other Works by Charles W. Carter

Transformed Africans, or The Conversion of An African Village. Syracuse, N.Y.: The Wesleyan Methodist Publishing Association, 1938.

A Half Century of American Wesleyan Methodist Missions in West Africa. Syracuse, N.Y.: The Wesleyan Methodist Publishing Association, 1940.

The Bible Gift of Tongues. Syracuse, N.Y.: The Wesleyan Methodist Publishing Association, 1951.

Road to Revival. Butler, Indiana: The Higley Publishing Company, 1959.

The Acts of the Apostles: A Zondervan Commentary (Co-authored with Ralph Earle, 1959. Revised and published by Zondervan Company, 1973. Grand Rapids, MI: Zondervan Publishing House. Republished by Schmul Publishers, Salem, Ohio, 1983.

Christian Songs in Temne (Co-author and Editor with George G. Hemminger). Springfield, MO: General Council-Assemblies of God, 1948.

The Wesleyan Bible Commentary (7 Vols.). General Editor and author of Acts, First Corinthians, Ephesians, Hebrews and Job. Grand Rapids; MI: Eerdmans and Bakers, first published 1964-69. Republished by Hendrickson Publishing Company, Peabody, MA, 1986.

The Person and Ministry of the Holy Spirit: A Wesleyan Perspective. Grand Rapids, MI: Baker Book House, 1974. Revised 1977. Published by Schmul Publishing Company, Salem, Ohio, 1983.

A Contemporary Wesleyan Theology (2 Vols.) General Editor and Contributor. Grand Rapids, MI: Zondervan Publishing House, 1983.

Ethics: From Pagan to Christian. (In Chinese) Author and Editor. Taichung, Taiwan: Published by the Oriental Missionary Society, Int., 1971.

Zondervan Pictorial Encyclopedia of the Bible (5 Vols.). Contributor of five articles. Merrill Tenney, Gen. Ed. Grand Rapids, MI: Zondervan Publishing House 1975.

The Beacon Dictionary of Theology. Contributor of fifteen articles. Richard S. Taylor, Gen. Ed. Kansas City, MO: Beacon Hill Press, 1983.

The Wesleyan Theological Journal. Gen. Ed. and contributor 1965-72. Published by The Wesleyan Theological Society.

Higley International Sunday School Commentaries. Gen. Ed. 1960-61. Butler, IN: Higley Publishing Company.

Higley Evangelical Sunday School Commentaries. Gen. Ed. 1960-61. Butler, IN: Higley Publishing Company.

The Holy Spirit in the Early Church (In Chinese). Taipei, Taiwan: Published by the Church of the Nazarene Mission, 1975.

Missionaries Extraordinary; The Life and Labors of Charles and Elizabeth Carter. Published by the author, 1982.